Guruji

Life and Spiritualism

CHHABILENDRA ROUL

RUPA

Published by
Rupa Publications India Pvt. Ltd 2023
7/16, Ansari Road, Daryaganj
New Delhi 110002

Sales centres:

Bengaluru Chennai
Hyderabad Jaipur Kathmandu
Kolkata Mumbai Prayagraj

Revised edition 2024

P-ISBN: 978-93-6156-816-9
E-ISBN: 978-93-6156-244-0

10 9 8 7 6 5 4 3 2 1

Guruji

Dr Chhabilendra Roul, a former officer of the Indian Administrative Service, was a secretary to the Government of India. He is an alumnus of Ravenshaw College (Cuttack, Odisha), Delhi School of Economics (University of Delhi) and School of Public Policy (University of Birmingham). He got his postgraduate degree in economics from the University of Delhi and holds an MBA degree from the University of Birmingham.

Dr Roul began his professional career as a lecturer in economics at Shri Ram College of Commerce, University of Delhi. Subsequently, in a span of more than 35 years in the civil services, he has served both in the state and central governments dealing with multifarious subjects crucial to public economic management and welfare. Under his leadership, the team at the Department of Governance Reforms, Punjab, was awarded the Prime Minister's Excellence Award in Public Administration for the year 2012–13 for outstanding work in functional governance reforms.

Dr Roul has authored two books: *Bitter to Better Harvest: Post Green Revolution Agricultural and Marketing Strategy for India* (2001) and *The International Jute Commodity System* (2009). He has published several research articles in reputed national and international journals. For his seminal contribution to the civil services and research, he has been inducted as a senior visiting fellow by the Institute of Economic Growth, Delhi, adjunct professor at Odisha University of Agriculture and Technology and visiting professor (management) at Amity University, Noida.

'Mr Roul has woven a fascinating account of the life and philosophy of Guruji. The beauty of his narrative is that he never imposes a particular deterministic persona of the great spiritual leader. It is up to the discernible readers to accept or reject him as a spiritual leader of particular elevation or consider him as a fine human being or both.'

—Satyananda Mishra
IAS (Retd), Former Secretary, Government of India, and
Former Chief Information Commissioner, Government of India

'Mr Roul has indeed written a very balanced account, befitting one trained in modern ways of thinking. His account is neither eulogistic nor critical; it is objective as scholarship should be.'

—Dr S.C. Sharma
Chairman, National Medical Commission of India, and
Former Head, ENT Department, AIIMS, New Delhi

'The present book renders a systematic approach of the life and spiritual precepts that constitute the essence of Guruji, delving into his sayings, aphorisms, personal observations by the author and renderings by the people who came to be associated with Guruji. It is up to the readers to go through such accounts and draw their own conclusion. Mr Roul (Rahul for Guruji), has done an excellent job in portraying Guruji, who was ascribed godliness by his ardent followers, in proper perspective.'

—Raghu Rai
Award Winning Photographer, New Delhi

'Roul has written a fascinating book on Guruji. We all saw Guruji as an ordinary human, and yet we knew and always felt that there was a realized soul inside his corporeal frame. Roul had the unique opportunity of being in what could be called the "inner circle" of Guruji's followers. He saw him from very close quarters and, therefore, whatever he has written is authentic.'

—Prakash Singh
IPS (Retd), Former DG (BSF), Former DG (UP), and
Former DG (Assam)

Contents

Part V
The Philosophies

Preface

Humanity does not come across highly spiritual sages, avatars or *puran gurus* (true gurus) quite often. Even if there is one, very few people recognize him/her as an enlightened soul. As Nitin Joshi, a devotee of Guruji, says,

> If you could penetrate the worldly façade he presents, if your gaze can see beyond it to Him, then you shall be blessed with an all-encompassing shelter... Guruji's mannerism and speech are such that they make us believe that He is just like us (they are part of the façade) until the gravity of what He says sinks in. It takes a while for that understanding to develop.

Such recognition of a true guru comes with your karmic earnings and spiritually intelligent perception. When an elevated soul mingles with you and lives the life of a normal human being, it is far more difficult to recognize the higher and finer spiritual attributes of such a soul. Moreover, one becomes a true spiritual seeker when graced by the true guru or almighty, then only one can recognize or find such a puran guru.

Guruji, while living in flesh and blood, never gave any indication of his highly elevated spiritual standing. However, there were plenty of subtle hints and numerous events which provide ample insight into his divinity and spiritual philosophy. His aphorisms, being terse but short utterances, show deep philosophical principles that are neither entirely new nor break away from the spiritual tradition of this great land but are rather a reiteration of core philosophical principles. Simultaneously, he had abjured the obscurantist and out-of-date socio-cultural-religious practices, ordinarily and wrongly touted as core principles of the spiritual and philosophical essence of such a tradition.

These days, one may find several *satsangs* by the *sangat* blessed by Guruji during his physical days, and others after he left his physical body. The satsangs are a genuine outpour of love, regard and gratitude for the revered Guruji. However, the major focus is, directly and indirectly, on the material pursuits and personal gains of the devotees. The gains include, inter alia, satisfaction of the psychosocial needs of individuals—the desire or yearning for mental peace from the emotional and worldly turmoil.

Unfortunately, the spiritual connotations and underlying essence of all these blessings have never been highlighted or contextualized. There are many significant cues that provide the spiritual core—the essence that is Guruji, personified as a divine soul and a master with significant divine and human qualities. As a puran guru, he is the embodiment of love and compassion for each and every person. He is known for his austerity, sacrifices, non-attachment, the highest order of humility, and control over his senses and mind. Guruji, has all the characteristics of a *mahayogi* such as the supernatural powers of clairvoyance, control over the five elements of nature and miraculous healing powers. On another plane, he was a good human being full of wit and amusing jokes, who looked after the needs of his devotees, both materialistic as well as spiritual, being a friend, philosopher and guide. Guruji was not limited to the narrow confines of his family, native village or a particular community. He was rather a universal guru whose philosophy and practice highlighted universal spirituality and divinity.

The human tendency of deification of extraordinary human beings bypasses the idea, being a part of the great spiritual tradition of this land, that there is immense potential in each individual to exploit the power of the human mind to reach higher levels of attainment. Deification creates a barrier, a psychological wall or chasm, between the individual follower and the master. The general refrain is that, 'He/She is God(dess)—that level where we ordinary humans cannot reach, and it is futile to make an effort.' But enlightened masters like Guruji emphasize the inherent potential of each person who can exploit the potential of the human mind by sincere devotion and the grace of God and Guruji, to reach higher levels of spiritual attainment.

The book is divided into five parts, each part delving into a particular theme. The first part contains a single chapter, describing the life journey of Guruji from the pristine land of rural Punjab to the modern settlements amongst the ruins of the seven cities of Delhi in medieval India. There is a curious link between the wanderings of Guruji and the symbolic remnants and lineage of several saints and spiritual traditions of this land. The other significant aspect is the need for healing of places with a collective wounded psyche of the civilizational soul from a highly evolved spiritual master.

The second part is devoted exclusively to the various manifestations of divinity of the enlightened Guruji. The first chapter for this part focuses on the various yogic supernatural powers of Guruji involved in healing people of their physical, mental, and physiological sufferings and deformities, including chronic and fatal diseases. The second chapter depicts the other yogic supernatural powers exhibited by the mahayogi as an analogy to the pinnacle of yogic attainments described in the Vibhuti Pad of Patanjali's Yoga Sutra. Both these chapters contain real-life experiences and eye-witness accounts of the author, his family members and other devotees from whom such renderings were heard in person, either in small informal settings or in the presence of Guruji. These are a few satsangs and not an exhaustive list pertaining to the manifestation of supernatural powers and divinity of Guruji.

The third part of the book deals with Guruji's ways—his *leela* and *mauz*. It deals with the institutions of sangat and satsang in the first chapter and *langar*, a practice introduced by Guru Nanak but elevated to a higher notch by Guruji, in the second chapter of the third part. The third chapter of this part depicts the humane aspects of Guruji. These activities unfold the splendor, beauty and wonder of an unconventional personality like Guruji, portraying him as a fine human being without mitigating his divinity.

The fourth part deals with the universal spiritual traditions of this great land to provide the contextual background for many activities and spiritual tenets espoused by Guruji. This part contains three chapters devoted to the great Indian universal spiritualism, the Guru Tattva, and the tremendous potential of humans to attain enlightenment and supernatural powers through yogic practices as per Patanjali's Yoga Sutra.

In the fifth and last part, the author makes a humble attempt to present a rudimentary outline of the social and spiritual (or metaphysical) essence of Guruji. The emphasis is that Guruji belongs to the great Indian spiritual tradition. He has enriched this tradition by making these spiritual essences relevant to the present-day social and spiritual life. The spiritual tradition is a continuum and each incarnation of a saint, sage or divinity enriches this tradition by retaining the core universal themes while simultaneously discarding the outdated concepts that are no more relevant to the contemporary lives of human society. This part contains three chapters—the first deals with Guruji's spiritual tenets; the second deals with his social philosophy; and the third provides an insight into the pitfalls of misinterpreting the great sayings of Guruji by adopting a literal interpretation without linking the sayings to the spiritual core principles espoused by him. The guru and his disciple have their connections or communions. Anything told by the guru to the disciple, in private or public, has to be interpreted and understood in the contextual plane of that 'guru–shishya connection'. Let the individual disciple interpret and analyse the hints and communion between them. Otherwise, the guru himself would guide the disciple to internalize the true meaning of their communion. Hence, just quoting what the guru has said to somebody, taking the literal meaning and generalizing the same for the mass of followers is not going to unravel the deeper spiritual or philosophical meanings of the great sayings of Guruji and his aphorisms.

The descriptions and analyses of the book may be at odds with the framework of rationalism and prism of the scientific method. There is a tendency to put forward a deterministic framework that the scientific method is the only way to understand the universe. If you want to know and appreciate the spiritual experiences of seekers, you have to believe in the system of intuitions and experiences of the spiritually elevated sages who have steadied their minds, have attained the higher state of *nirvikalpa samadhi* and a vision beyond the ordinary sensory inputs. The tremendous potential of the human beings to attain supernatural powers through yogic practices and the grace of god cannot be discounted by merely stating that these things cannot be proved or analysed through scientific methods. Moreover, the relevance of scientific methodologies for all systems is questionable. For measuring length, one cannot use a decibel meter. Scientific methodologists justify their arguments based on principles that cannot be applicable in matters relating to spiritualism. But denouncing others for following the spiritual path and looking down on spiritual methodology is inappropriate and even borders on deterministic arrogance.

Guruji was the epitome of universal love. He abjured preaching. It is only through subtle hints and small utterances that he spoke of profound things for the discernible sangat. He, as a true master, would lead by his own example. He was not in favour of the dogmas and rigidity in organized religion, and he emphasized on the positives of an individual. He implored a person's own godliness (Lord Shiva within oneself) to cleanse the self. It echoes with the great invocation of the ancient sages of this land in their famous shlokas like 'Shivoham' or 'Brahmasmi'.

When we neglect the finer social and spiritual (metaphysical) essence of Guruji by highlighting only the supernatural powers through which his sangat attained materialistic gains, we are relegating our great and universal guru to a mere cult figure and an ordinary *sadhak*. There is a need to channelize the beautiful renderings by the sangat and the aphorisms of Guruji into structured, thematic ones to highlight the elevated level of divinity of revered Guruji. The author has made a humble attempt in that direction.

The inspiration for writing this book came directly from Guruji and not through telepathy or dreams. It was Guruji who inspired the author to write a book about him on 25 August 2001. That day, the author presented a copy of his first book, *Bitter to Better Harvest,* to Guruji. While using his typical signature to sign on the dedication page by writing 'Blessings Always, Guruji/25.08.2001', Guruji said, '*Rahul* [the name Guruji used to fondly call the author] *mere vare v ek kitab likhega* (Rahul would also write a book about me).' After 20 years, I could finally muster up the courage, under his inspiration, to attempt to write this book.

Part I

The Life Journey of the Mahapurush

1

A *Beautiful Journey*

MALERKOTLA: THE LAND OF PIRS AND SAINTS

Malerkotla is famously known as the 'island of peace and harmony' as there was complete absence of communal strife on the eve of Partition in the erstwhile princely state. Although Malerkotla was predominantly inhabited by Muslims, the Hindus and Sikhs of the state did not face any communal retribution. Rather, the Muslim majority of the state preferred to stay in secular India than migrating to Pakistan, whose border lies at a distance of 160 km. Almost all of Punjab, except the towns of Kadian (the seat of the Ahmedian community) and Malerkotla, the land of pirs and saints, witnessed communal conflagration. The communal harmony witnessed in Malerkotla owes to the Sufi tradition of the land. People from all communities pray together at Sufi shrines throughout India and Pakistan.

Malerkotla is the land of Haider Sheikh, a Sufi saint and founder of the town and forefather to the princely rulers of the state of Malerkotla. Haider Sheikh was originally a Sawani Afghan whose ancestry is traced to Daraband in Khurasan province of Afghanistan. Born as Sadruddin, he was also popularly known as Sheikh Sadar-i-Jahan.

In 1450, Bahlol Khan Lodhi, the then governor of Lahore and Sirhind, under the Delhi Sultanate, was on his way to Delhi. Enroute, he took rest at Bhumsi on the banks of the river Sutlej near the resting place of the pious man Sadruddin. He was thoroughly impressed with the latter's spiritual and worldly wisdom. Legend has it that Sadruddin prophesized that one day, Bahlol Khan would become the sultan of Delhi. Bahlol Khan promised that once he became the sultan of Delhi, he would offer his daughter's hand in marriage to Sadruddin. In 1451, circumstances were such that Bahlol Khan took over the reins of the Delhi Sultanate. As promised, he solemnized the marriage of his daughter, Taj Murassa Begum, to Sadruddin. The Sultan gave Sadruddin a tract of land containing 12 large and 56 small villages, including the villages Bhumsi, Maler and Kotla in addition to ₹3-lakh dowry. Sadruddin founded a large settlement in the villages of Maler and Kotla to which the present city and former princely state of Malerkotla owes its name. The present city of Malerkotla has two prominent parts—Maler and Kotla, united by the construction of the Moti Bazaar.

Sadruddin, the powerful spiritual leader, attracted devotees from all walks of life and from all religious communities—Hindus, Sikhs and Muslims. The *mazar* of Sadruddin in Malerkotla is the epitome of religious harmony. Every Thursday, a fair is held at the mazar. The 1904 *Malerkotla Gazetteer* mentions: 'It is strange that these fairs are mostly attended by Hindus, though Sadruddin was a Muslim saint.'

The princely state of Malerkotla was ruled by the descendants of Sadruddin till 1947. The Sufi culture influenced the lives of the princely state of Malerkotla and the neighbourhood. Guru Gobind Singh, the tenth guru of Sikhs, blessed Nawab Sher Mohammed Khan, a descendant of Sadruddin, with a *hukamnama* and a kirpan (presently in the possessions of the descendants of the Malerkotla household) as a token of gratitude to the nawab who had objected to the inhuman bricking of the Sahibzadas, the two sons of the Guru, Zorawar Singh and Fateh Singh, by the governor of Sirhind. He walked out of the durbar of the Sirhind governor while the bricking was ensuing. Prior to that, he had also written a letter of prayer to Aurangzeb to spare the innocent lives of the Sahibzadas.

Malerkotla is full of shrines dedicated to both Hindu and Sufi saints, as well as Sikhs. The shrine of Gugga at Himatana,

Gurudwara Teg Bahadur in village Mullowal, Tomb of Pir Badu at Banganwadi, Tomb of Pir Nana at Monnam, Samadhi of Baba Sidh at village Asal, Samadhi of Baba Gajjan Singh at village Phalmad and Samadhi of Baba Sidh at Nano Majra village are the prominent ones. Annual fairs were held regularly at these shrines in which people from all walks of life participated. The famous multi-religious festival was the Gugga Naumi held in the months of August–September every year when thousands congregated. Similarly, the Shivratri celebration at village Ranike attracted thousands—again from both the Hindu and Sikh community.

Dugri, the ancestral village of Guruji, on the Nabha–Malerkotla Road is 11 km away from the city of Malerkotla and was part of the princely state of Malerkotla. The flexibility of religious identities and the spiritual traditions of the land finds its place in this small village. The important landmark of this place is the village dera, which was the resting place of pious mendicants and wandering sadhus in the earlier days. Today, it has a small shrine and the ambience is suitable for contemplation and mediation.

Tapa, the ancestral town of Maata Surjit Kaur (Maataji—Guruji's mother), is named after Tapa Ram, a disciple of Baba Sukha Nand. Tapa Ram was a pious man who spent his life in meditation. Thousands gather once a year when a large fair is held at the *samadhi* of Tapa Ram.

According to Maataji, Guruji used to go to the dera in village Dugri to study or meditate as was his mood. This is a place where saints and sadhus used to come and stay periodically. The villagers would come and provide food to the saints. According to a school friend of Guruji, 'Nirmal [Guruji's formal name was Nirmal Singh] used to spend more time in the dera meditating than studying. More often than not, they would find him holding a book upside-down, indicating Nirmal was contemplating on other things than mundane subjects.'

THE UNSPOILED RURAL PUNJAB OF THE 1950s

After Partition, the eight princely states of Patiala, Jind, Nabha, Faridkot, Malerkotla, Kapurthala, Kalsia and Nalagarh were combined to form a single state of the Patiala and East Punjab States Union (PEPSU) on 15 July 1948. Later in 1956, PEPSU merged with the state of Punjab.

The rural landscape of Malerkotla, PEPSU, or even that of Punjab in the 1950s, was of communal harmony, peace and relative prosperity due to the alluvial loamy fertile soil of the Indo-Gangetic plains and the availability of water from canals, dug wells and tube wells. Those were the days when the boundaries of agricultural fields were full of trees and bushes, unhampered by artificial boundaries as a result of land consolidation that took place in the late 1950s and early 1960s. The boundaries of fields, canal bunds and road berms were full of *kikars*. By the early 1950s, with the extension of cultivation and liberal gun licences, the nilgais, blackbuck, the riverine deer and wild pigs went nearly extinct from rural Malerkotla and its neighbouring areas. However, the village folks would rejoice with frequent sightings of jackals, foxes, hares, wild cats, peacocks, partridges, quails and sandgrouses. The communal harmony of rural Punjab is found beautifully expressed in the famous folk song of Sukhi Brar, an ardent devotee of Guruji:

> *Ae Punjab di mitti sundari hai, chitti hai.*
> *Ae nnu maili naa karana.*

> The Punjab is pristine pure and beautiful.
> Do not spoil it.

Those were the days when rural Punjab was not devastated by the paddy-wheat monocropping. Farmers were cultivating multiple millets, pulses, wheat, cotton, sugarcane and a small sprinkling of paddy. Wooden ploughs were the predominant agricultural implements with only eight tractors in Malerkotla tehsil. The *ghanis* were extracting oil, and the donkeys, mules and camels were the draught animals used for transportation.

It was during the early 1950s that Nirmal Singh was born to Mast Ram (Bapuji) and Surjit Kaur (Maataji). In one of the relaxed sessions of free-flowing conversation with a senior civil servant, Guruji asked him his date of birth. The gentleman mentioned his official date of birth and also stated that his parents were not educated enough to keep an exact record of the date and time of his birth. At the time of his admission to the village school, it was the school teacher, who, after brief enquiry about his age, put the date of birth as per his volition. Guruji immediately said, '*Sadda ve oi haal hai* (My case is the same).' Guruji's parents fondly called him Billa. He studied in the government primary school in Dugri till the fifth standard. He then took admission in a government high school in Bhurthala Mander near Dugri and passed his matriculation in 1969. He joined Government College, Malerkotla, for his higher studies, completing his pre-university (1970), and getting his BA degree (1973) and MA degree (1975). However, it is well known and accepted by sangat that Guruji celebrated his birthday on 7 July every year.

A lot of the early life events of Guruji are attributed to the testimony of someone claiming to be his school and college buddy. As per the claim by this buddy, which is not confirmed independently, Nirmal Singh and this buddy spent a lot of time together.

This gentleman describes two incidents from Guruji's school days.

One day, Nirmal along with this buddy, went to the wheat fields surrounding the village to study there in the shade. As it was the practice, they would sit at a considerable distance from each other, so that one was not disturbed by the other. After some time, Nirmal's friend got up as it was getting dark and approached Nirmal. However, he found that the field was flooded with water from all sides. Though the field was levelled, the water had not touched Nirmal. The friend had to shout at the top of his lungs to get him out from his contemplation. Generally, it would take some time to get him back to normalcy before they could depart for home. Most of the time, Nirmal would be engrossed with something else other than studying.

Another incident described by this friend is the materialization of ink in a dry fountain pen. They were appearing for some test when one of their classmate's fountain pen ran out of ink. Thinking that it was malfunctioning, they tried to tinker with it, so that the ink would flow again. When they realized that the pen had run out of ink, Nirmal came to their rescue. He tinkered with the pen and lo and behold, it was full of ink!

One time, Nirmal's classmates challenged him to jump into a village well. The well was deep enough to drown a person. Nirmal did not know how to swim. His classmates thought that by forcing him into the well, he would learn how to swim. Thinking this, they pushed him into the well. They were taken by surprise when they saw Nirmal come out of the well without getting drenched. It seemed as though he had simply been standing on the water.

Maataji used to describe snippets of Guruji's childhood to Urvashi, my wife. She vividly recollected that after the birth of Guruji, a saint visited their ancestral house in Dugri. The saint was rendered the usual hospitalities with the utmost respect. Maataji was a pious lady, and she would never allow saints and sages to go without being served properly. While blessing Maataji and the infant Guruji, the saint told Maataji that the boy had telltale indications of reaching great heights. He advised Maataji to allow the boy to be on his own and never force anything upon him. A day would come when lakhs and lakhs would worship him.

Another incident described by Maataji to Urvashi and me relates to Guruji's lack of interest in the usual domestic affairs. Bapuji used to pester him to help in managing the household affairs, but Nirmal would not have any of that. One day, Bapuji sent him to the fields to look after some agricultural activity. Instead of devoting time on that, Nirmal sat in meditation. When Bapuji found him in that condition, he dragged him out of the field, causing a strained muscle. Maataji advised Bapuji to desist from forcibly engaging Nirmal in such activities and allow him to be on his own.

The incidents described by the school buddy (sometimes in the physical presence of Guruji) neither overawed his friends nor could they visualize the miraculous powers and spiritual attainment of Guruji. For them, these were aberrations or deviations from the normal and were not of much significance. It was only after Guruji openly met sangat and started exhibiting great miracles and supernatural fits that Guruji's friends could relate their childhood experiences to his greatness.

Mrs Pannu, wife of Prof. Pannu of Government College, Malerkotla, describes an incident from the time Guruji was studying as an undergraduate student (BA second year). Prof. Pannu was newly appointed to the college and was teaching political science to the second-year students. He found two students (Nirmal Singh and one of his friends) engrossed in conversation while he was delivering a lecture. The professor ordered both the students to get up and asked them to describe what he had been teaching. None of them was able to respond. Then, the Professor told them that if they were finding the lecture boring, they could go out of the class and should not disturb others.

After the period was over, as the professor was going out of the class, Nirmal Singh followed him outside and said, 'You ordered me to stand up in the class and asked embarrassing questions. This is not fair.'

Prof. Pannu could not digest the audacity of the student who was advising him what was to be done in the class. In the staff room, he described the incident to his fellow colleagues who informed him that Nirmal Singh was not a serious student and is known to have his strange and mysterious ways. Some informed him that the boy behaves like a fakir and it was advisable to ignore his antics.

Prof. Pannu got curious and wanted to know more about Nirmal Singh. He started interacting with him and realized that the boy had different qualities. Both the academic guru and his student developed good rapport thereafter, and it continued even after Prof. Pannu got transferred to Amritsar, then Ludhiana and back to Malerkotla. Guruji would find his whereabouts and land up at his college or residence from time to time. When Guruji's supernatural powers were revealed and he had a sizable following in Jalandhar, Prof. Pannu, the erstwhile academic guru became an ardent devotee of Guruji, his erstwhile pupil.

Guruji's knowledge of economics was tremendous. Sometimes, it was demonstrated to some sangat. One time, a devotee came to Empire Estate (Sultanpur, Delhi) to pay his respects to Guruji and sought his blessings for his daughter who was to appear for her examination the next day. Guruji tested the daughter's knowledge of economics by asking a few questions. He suggested her to prepare specific chapters and questions for the macroeconomics exam. The next evening, the father–daughter duo rushed to Empire Estate to thank Guruji. The daughter found in the question paper the same questions from the specified chapters as had been mentioned by Guruji.

Prof. Khera was another professor from Government College, Malerkotla, who also served as a lecturer in the college while Guruji was a student. However, he had no extraordinary or noticeable events to describe. He, like Prof. Pannu, became an ardent follower of Guruji in the mid-'80s.

Narinder Dhand describes another incident about Guruji during one of his relaxed conversations with a small band of sangat. There was another professor from Government College, Malerkotla. He had three daughters and wanted a son. The academic guru who had become a disciple of the academic shishya prayed for Guruji to bless him with a son. Guruji repeatedly told the couple that they should not pray to God or seek the indulgences of the true guru for things not part of their destiny. If God had ordained them not to have a son, they should be satisfied with that. But, after observing the supernatural feats of Guruji, the lady of the house was convinced that they could have a son if Guruji would bless them. After much persistence, Guruji one day took the professor aside and told him that he was blessing the couple to have a son. But since it was against nature, the boy would die an untimely death at the age of 12. The professor should not tell this to his wife, as she would live a miserable life for the 12 years and would trouble Guruji day and night.

The couple had a son. They celebrated each of his birthdays with fervour and gusto. On his thirteenth birthday, they kept a *path* and after the *bhog*, they distributed the prasad. After consuming the prasad, the son got ill and became unconscious. All efforts to revive him were in vain, and they lost the boy at the age of 12 as prophesized by Guruji.

THE WANDERINGS

Chandigarh, the city of gardens, symbolized the modern city. The foundation stone of the city was laid by Jawaharlal Nehru in 1952, the year Nirmal Singh was born in Dugri. The tricity of Chandigarh, Panchkula and Mohali (Ajitgarh) epitomizes the vision of aspirational India. With a picturesque location at the foothills of the Shivaliks, Chandigarh boasts of the famous Leisure Valley that runs through the heart of the city, taking various avatars like Bougainvillea Park, Zakir Rose Garden, Shanti Kunj, Hibiscus Garden, Garden of Fragrance, Botanical Garden, Smriti Upavan, Topiary Garden and Terraced Garden. Sukhna Lake provides the most idyllic scenery throughout the year. The broad avenues of the tricity boasts of tastefully chosen 22 species of evergreen trees representing various parts of the country.

Mansa Devi Mandir, located in Panchkula, is one of the seven *shakti pithas* of North India, the other six goddesses associated with Goddess Shakti are Naina Devi, Jwalamukhi, Chintpurni, Brajeshwari, Chamunda Devi and Jayanti Devi.

The tricity is planned in such a manner that the places and buildings provide adequate space for all human activities—being harmonious and one with nature and the heart. No wonder, Guruji chose the tricity for spreading the message of love and healing to the suffering humans for a considerable period.

Guruji moved to Chandigarh in 1976 to a house owned by a relative of his school buddy. After a lapse of nearly two months, some close relations of Guruji, came and fought with his friend that Nirmal was wasting his time with him. They accused this friend of spoiling Nirmal's future. They advised that Nirmal should look for some job or assist the family in its affairs. They wanted to take him back to Dugri, to which Guruji refused. After this bitter exchange, Guruji left that house. The friend of Guruji did not see Nirmal again for considerable period, till 1980. A mahapurush was destined and ordained for far higher mission in life than getting involved in mundane family affairs!

The latter part of 1976 to the mid-1980s became a period of unknowns to the devotees and the public, as not much is known about the whereabouts and activities of Guruji during this time. There may be people or sangat who could have come across Guruji during this period. Such sangat should come forward to provide authentic information about Guruji's wanderings.

Guruji used to tell some sangat that he went to undertake austerities and deep meditation in the dense forests of the Himalayas. He also begged on the streets of Mumbai as an ordinary mendicant/yogi. What can we make out of such sayings? Guruji sometimes used to transmigrate through various births and describe the relations and events with certain devotees that are specific to those previous births.

But there is a curious turn of events relating to the penance story. A lady came to Empire Estate to have Guruji's darshan after she heard about his miraculous powers. When she paid her respects to Guruji, he told her that they have met earlier, to which the lady flat-out denied. Guruji gave a wry smile and described an incident that took place a long time back. He reminded her that she once went to meet a yogi doing penance in a dense, forested area in Uttarakhand. She offered the sadhu, who was in deep meditation, some fruits. She also took home two oranges offered as prasad. Guruji mentioned that the yogi was none other than himself. The lady recollected the incident and nodded in agreement. But she was equally dumbfounded realizing that the yogi did not open his eyes but could still describe the exact happenings of that day and recognize her. Such was his capability of extra-sensory vision!

It is difficult to put events and relations uttered by Guruji in respect of time and particular birth or life. Sometimes, such divine persons transmigrate from births to describe events and relations. Such utterances of mahapurush could not be ordinarily comprehended with our limited vision and experiential understanding of events and relations of our present life.

Guruji was reticent and rarely undertook preaching, pravachan or satsang himself. However, it was his mauz, and sometimes, on his own volition, he would start a satsang with the limited sangat present after a majority of them had left. Narinder Dhand of Ludhiana describes one such satsang rendered by Guruji himself relating to his wandering days in erstwhile Bombay (now Mumbai). Guruji used to tell that he was wandering as a mendicant in the streets of Bombay. Hardly any sangat had any inkling regarding such a life of Guruji.

A middle-aged lady once came to pay her respects to Guruji, seeking his blessings. She had been suffering from some chronic ailment for the last 22 years. When she finished paying her respects, Guruji said, 'Aunty, we are meeting for the second time.' The lady vehemently denied that she had ever met Guruji. After langar prasad, while Guruji was distributing the sweets, he again told the lady that it was their second meeting. The lady strongly denied that they had any previous encounter. Guruji said that the lady was staying in a particular locality in Mumbai in a gated colony. He pointed out her exact flat and floor number. Then he described the incident when a sadhu knocked on her door begging for alms. The lady had rebuked the sadhu saying that he was strong and stout, and there was no need to beg from others. She chased the sadhu away without giving anything except a sound rebuke for not working hard. Guruji described the dress the lady was wearing and the date and time of her encounter with the sadhu. The lady recollected the incident and agreed that such an event took place. Guruji told her it was he who had come to her place to bless her. She earned that visit by her good deeds, but she had sent back the sadhu empty-handed. She did not realize that there was no chance a sadhu could enter the gated community, and that too for a flat on the sixth floor without her permission. The lady repented her behaviour of that day, 22 years ago. Nevertheless, Guruji blessed her to lead a better life, bereft of her great sufferings.

~

Bapuji used to tell Urvashi and me that he would send *panjiri* to Guruji's residence for his personal use. Panjiri is a winter delicacy made of wheat and channa flour, mixed with liberal quantities of dry fruits and nuts, and fried in a lot of ghee. It is still believed in rural Punjab that panjiri is the best diet that provides enough energy to fight the severe cold wave that afflicts Punjab every winter. One day, Bapuji found that instead of keeping the panjiri for future use, Nirmal was distributing the entire lot among his mates and children in the neighbourhood.

~

As per some of his earliest acquaintances, Guruji joined as an assistant in Punjab School Education Board's (PSEB) Sangrur Depot in 1980. This could be cross verified from the official records of the PSEB. He worked there for some time. This is the time when the old school buddy of Guruji re-established contact with him at Sangrur. Guruji expressed his dissatisfaction regarding the job. He submitted his resignation letter and came back with the friend to Chandigarh.

The friend was getting married in 1980. He was contemplating sending the invitation for Guruji to his village address, as he did not know his exact place of residence. To his surprise, Guruji came to meet him the same evening. When the friend mentioned about how he was intending to send the invitation to Dugri, Guruji told him there was no need for it and would have been an exercise in futility as he would not have received the letter posted to Dugri, since he had left the village for good.

This friend got married in the month of March in 1980. By that time, his schoolmate Nirmal had acquired the reputation of exactly telling about the past, present and future of people. But the friend was not convinced about the latter's extraordinary feats. He jokingly asked Guruji when he would have an offspring. Guruji replied that they would be blessed with a newborn in October, 1982. The friend did not believe it. His wife had an abortion in December 1980 and true to Guruji's words, a son was born to them in 1982. In friendly banter, the friend asked about the arrival of the next offspring, to which Guruji said they would have one more son in 1986. His second son was born in 1986.

In 1980, this friend was taking Guruji for a scooter ride around Chandigarh. After a while, the scooter developed some technical snag. He felt dejected, as the trip was getting cut short. Guruji consoled him and told him not to worry. Guruji asked the friend to wait for some time, and he would provide him with the pleasure of a car ride. After 10 minutes, a car stopped in front of them. A sardarji came out and asked Guruji politely to get inside. Both the friend and Nirmal dropped the scooter off at a nearby repair shop and hopped into the car. The gentleman then took them for a lengthy drive in and around Chandigarh.

~

Vimal Kapoor met Guruji for the first time in 1979. It was during the time when he was serving as an assistant in the Department of Housing and Urban Development, Punjab, with the office located in Sector 22, Chandigarh. One of his colleagues knew about Guruji. One day, Guruji came straight to his office and started interacting with him. Guruji was staying in the official residence of some assistant in Sector 32 who was working at the Punjab Civil Secretariat. His wife was working in the estate office of Chandigarh Administration.

After his brief disappearance in 1980–81, Guruji came back to Chandigarh. In 1981–82, he was staying in the house of Sardar Harbans Singh Sidhu, the then chairman of the Punjab Staff Selection Board (17 August 1981 to 30 June 1985) in Sector 36. Mr Sidhu subsequently rose to become the Minister for Public Works and Animal Husbandry in 1992. Guruji would meet small groups of people or individuals seeking his advice. He used to suggest people remedies for their ailments. He would tell people of their past, present and future just by looking at them. He would produce things out of thin air. It is during this period that a lot of civil servants of Punjab, Haryana and Chandigarh came in contact with Guruji.

Vimal Kapoor was his constant companion. This is the time when Romila Dubey and Ashok Dubey, the IAS couple from Punjab, Mr Rajput (Judicial Magistrate), Justice Khichi, the family of Umrao Singh (Congress Member of Parliament from Jalandhar) and many other politicians and civil servants came in contact with him. He had become a spiritual advisor for them and demonstrated his uncanny ability to cure people of their ailments. Because of his supernatural powers, people also started consulting him regarding their worldly affairs. When they were in a confused state of mind or were indecisive, they would seek his advice. And for this, people started calling him Guruji, the name that stuck with him. Billa and Nirmal Singh of Dugri, Malerkotla, lost his original identity for good and willingly embraced the new identity of Guruji.

There was a time when Vimal Kapoor and others persuaded Guruji to get a steady job, and at that time, the Punjab Mandi Board was recruiting fresh graduates as mandi supervisors in the Agricultural Produce Marketing Committees (popularly known as market committees) in Punjab (1982–83). They made Guruji apply for the job. After going through the formalities of a job interview, Guruji was selected for the post of mandi supervisor. Vimal Kapoor and the other well-wishers got his joining letter typed and signed from him. They suggested a meeting with the then Secretary of the Punjab Mandi Board, the boss of all the market committees. They went to the meeting where Guruji was supposed to discuss his employment matters as a provincial cadre employee of the Mandi Board to be deployed to a particular market committee.

After some considerable time passed and Guruji did not come outside from the meeting room, Vimal and the personal assistant of the Secretary gently knocked on the door, and with permission, Vimal entered the room. He found the officer on the carpet and Guruji on the sofa. Vimal had no guts to ask Guruji about the state of his probable employment as a subordinate to the boss of Mandi Board.

Romila Dubey, a civil servant of Punjab, was at the helm of affairs as the secretary of the Mandi Board during 1982–83. According to her, Guruji entered her spacious office without an appointment. She was surprised by the entry of the gentleman, partly balding in the front, sporting spotless white trousers and a bush shirt with yellow boots. The gentleman had an unusual demeanour. She could not shout at him as to why he barged into her office without an appointment or permission. The gentleman made himself comfortable on the sofa and suggested that she come and sit beside him. Mrs Dubey complied with his request. Then he exchanged pleasantries and engaged in a conversation relating to the people she knew. In the course of the conversation, she mentioned to him about a nagging pain at the bottom of her neck. Guruji then suddenly got up and, out of nothing, produced a prasad, some sort of mixed mishri and sweetmeats, and offered it to her, assuring her that the nagging problem would soon disappear. Later on, sangat would call that prasad as *sachkhand prasad*, and only a few lucky ones would be blessed to get it. Mrs Dubey was floored by the supernatural feat demonstrated and sat on the carpet in reverence while Guruji was on the sofa. That is the time when her personal assistant and Vimal Kapoor entered the room.

One time, Vimal accompanied Guruji to the government employees' residential quarters in Sector 27. Guruji went there to bless one of the occupants, perhaps an assistant or a Group D employee. Guruji travelled with Vimal on the latter's scooter.

After reaching the gentleman's house and sitting comfortably for a while, Guruji suddenly raised his arm and a beautiful stalk of rose appeared in his hand. He gave it to the gentleman as a gift for the special occasion. Vimal was thinking that Guruji picked the rose from some garden while he was parking the scooter. He went around the premises looking for a rose plantation. He could not find any garden, never mind rose plants. When he came back to Guruji, the latter gave him a wry smile as if quizzing Vimal. The rose was produced out of thin air!

A PLACE OF HIS OWN: THE JALANDHAR HEADQUARTERS

From Chandigarh, Guruji shifted his residence to Jalandhar in 1984–85. Jalandhar, or Andhak as per the Padma Puran and Shiva Puran, was the capital city of the demon king of the same name. Jalandhar, the demon king, was granted boons being blessed by the gods to have enormous supernatural powers and became arrogant and deviant. As the gods could not defeat him, they prayed to Lord Shiva to protect them from the tyranny of the demon. Lord Shiva fought a great battle and killed the demon with his trident, with the help of a little trick executed by Lord Vishnu. The present locality of Jalandhar is the place where the demon met his end. And over time, the place came to be called Jalandhar.

Jalandhar is also associated with *Mahasiddha* yogi Jalandhar (also Jalandharipa or Jalandharpad) under various *Nath* traditions—in the Shaiva Nath tradition of Hinduism and the tantric Buddhist tradition of Tibet. His name is traditionally connected with the practice of Jalandhara Bandha and the invention of Hevajra Tantra.

Others say that it was the city established by Luv, the son of Ram, under the guidance of the sage-poet Valmiki. The marshy area lies between two main rivers—Sutlej and Beas and hence is virtually underwater for most of the rainy season. Since the place is within two water bodies, hence the name Jalandhar (jal: water, andar: within). The term 'Bist Doab' is also used to describe the

Jalandhar area bounded by the two rivers—Beas and Sutlej.

The Rajatarangini of Kashmir and other Puranic literature also refer to Jalandhar as Trigarta—the land surrounded by three rivers: Ravi, Beas and Sutlej. The king of Trigarta participated in the battle of the Kurukshetra, which is talked about in the Mahabharat.

Whatever may be the origin of the present name, Jalandhar (Jullunder for the British) had witnessed important events of Indian history and civilization. It was part of the Harappan Civilization and later an important centre for Buddhism. As per Hiuen Tsang, the Chinese traveller, the Jalandhar area boasted hundreds of Buddhist *viharas*. Jalandhar has witnessed the vicissitudes of history where important battles and conflagrations took place involving the Kushans, Turks, Sayads, Afghans, Moguls, Sikh misls and the British. It had witnessed the mass transmigration of population in the history of mankind on the eve of the partition of British India into two sovereign countries.

~

Initially, when Guruji came to Jalandhar, he settled in Model Town. Subsequently, he shifted to a rented house in Mota Singh Nagar near the bus stand. The owner of the house, an officer of the Department of Food and Civil Supplies, Punjab was not comfortable to rent the house to Guruji for a longer period because of the likely disturbances to the immediate neighbourhood. By that time, Guruji had a number of influential people of the town and Punjab as his disciples. The followers of Guruji arranged Plot No. 300 of Defence Colony in Jalandhar for him. The plot was part of the town planning scheme of the Jalandhar Improvement Trust. They persuaded him to construct a house for his stay and to meet the flow of the ever-increasing followers. While staying in Mota Singh Nagar, Guruji and his followers started the construction, and he moved there after completion. He started attracting scores of devotees after that.

This was the time when Guruji would revel in the company of

a small band of devotees and followers. The setting was informal. The house, later called Jalandhar Mandir, was open 24x7 to the devotees. Anybody can walk in any time for a *darshan*, chat or hold a consultation with Guruji. Nobody would return empty-handed even if Guruji was not present in the mandir. They will be served jal (water), chai (tea) and langar prasad. It was a place where devotees would find peace.

The main hall was aesthetically decorated as per the direction of Guruji. The ornate sofa chair functioned as the *aasan* of Guruji. By this time, a devotee-painter had gifted a painting of Guruji—standing with his raised hand depicting blessings to the world. This, and a couple of photographs, adorn a part of the wall near the aasan (sitting pedestal). A small place to the right of the aasan contained the statue of Lord Shiv and the photograph of Guru Nanak. The mantra 'Om Namah Shivay, Shivji sada sahay', would run through an electronic display system.

Guruji went to Greater Kailash, Delhi, as part of his shifting bases during his wanderings. After a couple of months of holding of sangat at Greater Kailash, the institutionalized sangat came to an abrupt end. It was 3 July 1995 when Guruji abruptly left the sangat and asked Jagi Grewal to accompany him to the army mess in Dhaula Kuan, where he was staying, courtesy General Mohan Singh. He picked up a few clothes and left for Punjab with Jagi and a few others. As was with Guruji's system, the accompanying devotees never ventured to ask about the destination. Guruji was not uttering a word throughout the journey. Near Ambala, Jagi ventured to ask about his unusual silence. Guruji told him about the sudden death of his elder brother Bahadur Singh in a freak accident. A bull ripped his stomach open with its horns, and he was rushed to a hospital in Malerkotla, perhaps a little too late. Due to excessive bleeding, Bahadur Singh succumbed to his injuries.

Guruji attended the last rites of his elder brother. Maataji was inconsolable, as there was none to take care of the two teenage daughters of Bahadur Singh and his widow. Guruji tried to console her, to which she retorted how a yogi who had left his house for good could take on the worldly responsibilities of his sister-in-law and nieces. Guruji promised to take the responsibilities of the two young daughters of Bahadur Singh and left for Jalandhar. Guruji was epitome of love and compassion. Such love and compassion was bestowed on each and every body irrespective of relation, caste, creed and religion. He was loving his biological family as he was equally loving his followers and the humanity at large.

~

When Guruji returned to Jalandhar from Greater Kailash and Dugri in July 1995, he was almost sick to the bone. He had lost considerable weight. He summoned Vimal from Chandigarh to be with him. For a month, he did not meet anybody, and Vimal and two other devotee-sewadars were there to take care of Guruji and the mandir.

One day, Guruji ordered Vimal to bolt his room from outside while he was meditating. Vimal dutifully obeyed and went to sleep. There was no one in the temple except Guruji and Vimal. Early in the morning, Guruji woke up Vimal by shaking him. Guruji told him to prepare tea for both of them. But Vimal wondered how did Guruji manage to come out of his room when he had bolted it from the outside. Guruji looked at him mischievously with a wry smile and Vimal understood. For Guruji, nothing was impossible!

Guruji had the uncanny habit of sitting on the floor along with the sangat and engaging in small conversation with them. The chats were informal, spanning across mundane topics to warm banter and chat between friends. This informality concealed the real Guruji many a time. However, in between these small informal chats, gems of worldly and spiritual wisdom would permeate the discerning sangat. For others, he was a friend and guide in worldly matters.

The formal system of langar started in Jalandhar Mandir. The sangat would initially be offered langar two times—mid-day and late evening. The rest of the time, chai prasad would be served. Guruji used to serve langar himself to the sangat that would be gathered there.

Guruji would take walks in the cantonment area. He would ask a devotee or a small group to drive to the army cantonment. They would disembark from the vehicles at the centre of the cantonment and go for a walk. Sometimes, Guruji would drop by one of the followers' residences and spend considerable time there.

Defence Colony was the place where Guruji attracted scores of defence personnel as his followers. Prominent among the devotees who were regular at Jalandhar durbar were Colonel Joshi, General Mohan Singh, General Deepak Malhotra, General Ahuja, Lieutenant General Kapoor, Mr Prakash Singh

Indian Police Service [IPS], Inspector-General [IG] Border Security Force [BSF] and subsequently Director General [DG], BSF, Director General Police [DGP], Assam, and DGP, Uttar Pradesh), Mr Bhullar [IPS] and scores of other IAS and IPS officers apart from politicians. The extended family of Sardar Umrao Singh, the Agrawals, the Sondhis, the family of Paras from Phagwara were aslo regulars.

Guruji used to visit the salon of Kishorie in Model Town in Jalandhar. Kishorie would offer his services to Guruji dutifully for which he would be paid handsomely. He did not know of Guruji except for the fact that he was a regular at his salon and always in the company of different people fetching him in their vehicles. One day, he tried his best to shave Guruji's head but could not run the razor on his head even after repeated changes. Each time he tried to run the razor, Guruji's head would turn as hard as stone and the razor would not move. He realized that the gentleman was someone with supernatural powers. He fell at the feet of Guruji and prayed for forgiveness for his ignorance. He prayed Guruji to return to normal and allow him the *sewa* of shaving his head and beard. Guruji smiled at him and blessed him. Since then, Kishorie became the official barber of Guruji. When Guruji shifted his base from Panchkula to Chandigarh and then to Delhi, Kishorie would stay with Guruji and render the sewa of shaving his head and beard every day. He was provided space to stay in the same premises. Guruji blessed him for his daughter's marriage and to take care of his finances, as he had neglected his salon to be with Guruji.

Guruji was blessing people through a myriad of ways. A typical method of blessing was dipping his *rudraksha mala* in water and offering that blessed water to the sangat as prasad. Devotees reverently called the blessed water as *amrit*. He had jokingly designated one room in Jalandhar Mandir as the 'operation room'. People with chronic diseases or serious ailments would be taken to that room. Guruji would ask for a spoon and run it on the body or body parts (as if to assess or diagnose the disease) of the ailing person. Then, he would press betel leaves on the body parts affected by the ailment or containing the affected internal organs. Once the operation was over, Guruji in his characteristic way, would say, '*Kalyan kitta, aish kar* (I have blessed you and now you enjoy your life)'. People got cured of serious and chronic diseases in this manner.

~

Initially, when Dr Shashi Ahuja was accompanying her parents-in-law (General Ahuja and Mrs Savitri Ahuja) to Guruji's place at Jalandhar, she had the least amount of devotion to and connection with Guruji. She used to rationalize the miracles as coincidence and happenstances. One day, Guruji asked her whether she was suffering from a stomach problem. She answered in the affirmative. Actually, she had been suffering from a peptic ulcer for the last six years. When Guruji ordered her to fetch 100 betel leaves, she reluctantly proceeded to the nearest market to fetch them. She had always been assuming that there was a big racket of exploitation (marketing the betel leaves) going on in the name of curing people. After she fetched the betel leaves, she was asked to proceed to the 'operation room' in Jalandhar Mandir. She was apprehensive to go alone inside. Guruji read her mind and ordered her to come along with her husband, Arvind. Both of them were asked to lie down—Shashi on the divan and Arvind on the carpet on the floor. The operation of running the kitchen spoon on their bellies and applying the betel leaves after uttering incomprehensible mantras was conducted. The betel leaves were placed on their stomach, and they were told to lie down in that position for half an hour. After passage of some time, Guruji announced that the operation was over and they could now go back to Chandigarh. They were asked to throw the betel leaves into running water, which they did in a canal on the Chandigarh–Phagwara road. Dr Shashi could feel that her pain had disappeared.

Dr Shashi was still reluctant to accept the miraculous healing power of Guruji. She could now eat chutney made from green chilies and spicy langar without any problem. She realized her peptic ulcer had been cured. But she was not yet completely convinced about Guruji's healing powers.

Two years after the 'operation', Dr Shashi developed acute pain in the stomach accompanied by vomiting and diarrhoea. Her condition got so bad that she was admitted to the ICU. An endoscopy revealed that she had a post-surgery fault in her oesophagus. Her vagus nerve had not been correctly attended to. Dr Shashi realized that Guruji had performed the 'operation', but the doubting Thomas in her had created all these complications. She prayed to Guruji to cure her completely. Guruji blessed her in his characteristic way. After conducting a thorough investigation, the doctors prescribed some minimal medication, and she was completely cured of her problem with Guruji's blessings.

~

Jalandhar was practically Guruji's headquarters. He would suddenly embark upon a journey with one or two devotees without mentioning about his destination to anybody. He would settle in a devotee's house in another city. His devotees would get to know about his whereabouts months later. He would not start meeting with people immediately upon his arrival at a new place. By word of mouth, Guruji's *mahima* would spread to the acquaintances of the devotee in whose house he would be staying.

Other times, Guruji himself would remember some old sangat of the town and nearby areas, sharing the memory with the new place of stay. He would selectively allow or send across messages to meet a selected number of followers. Then the torrential flow of the sangat would start. Depending on the suitability of the place, he would hold regular sangat or would move to another place after blessing a large number of devotees.

During his days in Jalandhar, Guruji would embark upon day trips to various places in Punjab. The occasion would be some social function of a devotee, some sort of inauguration, housewarming or wedding in the family, or an occasion to celebrate some achievement. On rare occasions, he would comply with the request of some devotee to inaugurate some business or factory. The houses of Dr Baldev Singh Chahal, a professor at Punjab Agricultural University, Ludhiana, or the Grewals of Mandi Govindgarh were his temporary halts en route to various parts of Punjab and Chandigarh. Invariably, a caravan of vehicles of devotees would follow Guruji, of course with his permission. The devotees would enjoy such short day-trips to other towns and being a part of Guruji's entourage. By this time, Guruji had acquired a Contessa, and Shagan, from Ludhiana, was the chauffer ferrying Guruji from place to place if he was not embarking on a ride with a chosen devotee.

On one of the journeys with Guruji, Sukhi Brar, was part of Guruji's caravan. On the way, her vehicle developed some snag and they stopped. During that period, when the mechanics were attending to the car, she wrote the famous song about Guruji:

Aaj sade Guru Awana jee Guru awana jee,
Aage Aage guru lang gaye jee, guru lang gaye jee
Sayion pichhe Murada, Pichhe murad
Aage Aage Guru Lang Gaye Jee.

Today, revered Guruji would go to meet his beloved Sangat. Guruji has moved ahead, and the caravan is dutifully following him.

The mukhda of the song became the signature tune for Guruji and whenever he entered a formal sangat, this tune was played announcing his arrival.

During his stay in Jalandhar (1984–96), Guruji's following grew in leaps and bounds. Devotees from Jaipur, Delhi, Chandigarh and major cities of Punjab would land up at Jalandhar for his darshan, seeking his blessings and advice. His following among the politicians, higher and subordinate judiciary, bureaucracy, other professions and people from general walks of life grew considerably. The Punjab police had a good number of IPS and Punjab Police Service Officers who frequented Guruji's durbar. Mr Bhullar, who became DGP, Punjab and Mr Joshi, IPS (also DG rank officer), were the prominent ones.

THE ADAB AND TEHZEEB OF LUCKNOW

The Ahujas were staunch followers of Guruji. General Ahuja was a Major General when he was posted at Chandimandir, near Chandigarh. He was to superannuate from the Army Medical Corps within a short period. The military authorities were considering the probable candidates to be promoted from the rank of Major General to Lieutenant General. He was eighth in the list of panel and there were only five vacancies. Being a bit distressed, he went to have Guruji's darshan at Jalandhar. Guruji addressed him as Lieutenant General and suggested that the General should be feted for that. General Ahuja got three extensions in service and during the extension period, he got promoted to the rank of Lieutenant General and was posted at Lucknow, one of the most sought-after posts. He served there from 1993–95. When they were at Lucknow, Guruji was invited by the Ahujas to visit Lucknow and see how they were doing with his blessings. Guruji told them that he would visit them at an appropriate time and they need not remind him.

One fine morning in January 1995, Guruji rang up their residence and their daughter, Geetika, picked up the phone. Guruji informed her that he was coming to Lucknow. The Ahujas had gone to Bareilly for some work, and after getting the message from Geetika, they rushed back. They were happy to host Guruji at their residence.

Lieutenant General Ahuja was retiring in the month of January 1995. Guruji was with them during the last week of his service as if participating in the farewell celebrations of the decorated Lieutenant General with meritorious service in the armed forces.

Through word-of-mouth, the supernatural qualities of Guruji spread to other army and civilian people. Guruji started meeting with the ever-increasing sangat in the drawing room and the lawns of Ahuja's residence and blessed scores of people visiting him.

One fine afternoon, there were a couple of shradhalus in the residence of Lieutenant General Ahuja when the power system suddenly failed. The electricians were summoned and they were working with the main switchboard by switching off the main supply line to the residence to check for any defects in the connections. Inside the house, Guruji ordered Geetika to play the *sabads*. Geetika politely told Guruji that there was no electricity supply in the residence. Guruji again told her firmly to play the music system. By this time, Geetika and the other followers had taken to not contradicting Guruji. She put the cassette in the music player and switched on the system. Lo and behold, the beautiful rendering of a sabad by one famous *ragi* started playing. The entire house was without electricity! Geetika thought that the power supply had been restored to the house and tried to switch on a couple of fans and lights. No, nothing worked. The four electricians were still struggling with the main supply system and the music system played the sabads for four hours without electricity!

ROYALTY OF THE PINK CITY (1994)

Brigadier (subsequently Lieutenant General) Mohan Singh was posted at Jaipur, Rajasthan. One fine morning in 1994, Guruji left Jalandhar and arrived at the Brigadier's residence in Jaipur. The Brigadier's wife was popularly known as Maami because she was called as such by Guruji. He used to tell her that she was his maami in a previous birth.

Guruji's reputation and supernatural powers, including healing the sick and infirm, was the talk of the defence-services circles. As word spread about Guruji, the number of *shradhalus* dropping in at the Brigadier's residence increased by leaps and bounds. One of the dignitaries who came to Guruji's fold was Brigadier Bhawani Singh, MVC (Maha Vir Chakra, the second highest military award) and scion of the Jaipur maharaja Sawai Madho Singh II, and owner–resident of City Palace, Jaipur and other royal estates. He was bowled over by the divinity and love and affection of Guruji. He could notice the immediate change in his quality of life after coming in contact with Guruji. Brigadier Bhawani Singh was suffering from debilitating arthritis and other related problems. He had difficulty in walking and was being supported by at least two people when he first came to meet Guruji, who blessed him, and there was considerable improvement in his condition within a short period.

When Guruji returned to Jalandhar, scores of shradhalus from Jaipur and Rajasthan started coming there. The simple folk of rural and urban Rajasthan hired buses and other modes of transport and landed at Defence Colony, Jalandhar. Guruji told the sewadars there that the people were spending a lot of money to commute to Jalandhar. Instead, he should go to them to bless them. After a month, he again embarked upon his second journey to Jaipur. This time, a small stream of shradhalus grew to become a surging river. The flood of shradhalus engulfed the Pink City.

BIN BADAL BARSAAT (rain without clouds)

One day, Brigadier Bhawani Singh invited Guruji to his palace for an evening satsang and langar. He was like a tourist guide taking Guruji to the nooks and crannies of the palace. He showed him the royal grandeur of the City Palace, particularly the Chandra Mahal, which is not ordinarily accessible to visitors. He even took Guruji to the prohibited sections where even the ladies of royalty were not allowed. By Guruji's grace, the royal ladies also had a chance to enter the prohibited section.

Brigadier Bhawani Singh informed Guruji that the most enjoyable moment for the royals was the advent of rain. The royals would enjoy the rain while sitting on the terrace listening to songs composed with Raag Megh Malhar. He was feeling nostalgic about the moments when the royals would enjoy the rain sitting in a private corner of the royal palace. He pined for the rains. Guruji told him and the few sangat accompanying them, '*Koi gal nahin, barish chheti aa javegi* (Do not worry, the rains will come soon).' There were no clouds in the sky, and the royals and sangat were sceptical about the prophecy. Suddenly, there appeared a lonely cloud, a gush of wind, followed by a mild rain. Everybody was stupefied and fell at the feet of the great guru. It was like the Guruvani saying:

> *Bin badal barkha hoey*
> *Je Satguru nu bhai.*
>
> If the Lord Satguru is benevolent and willing, there will be rains without cloud.

WATER AFTER 80 YEARS

Guruji used to bless several devotees, particularly people suffering from chronic ailments. As the news of his supernatural powers spread far and wide, the elected panchayat members of a village came with a peculiar problem. The village wells for drinking and irrigation had gone dry for nearly 80 years.

Could Guruji resurrect water in the dried wells? Guruji blessed the villagers in his characteristic way, '*Jao, kalyan kitta* (Go, I blessed you all).' After a couple of days, the streets of Jaipur witnessed a strange kind of celebration. The villagers and the Panchayat came out in a procession praising Guruji and shouting '*Guru baba ki jai* (Hail Guruji!).' They shouted that water had reappeared in the village wells after Guruji blessed them. When they reached Brigadier Mohan Singh's residence to thank Guruji for the benevolence showered to the villagers, they were advised that they should never sell water from their wells. The mahima (glory) of Guruji spread like wildfire.

Jaipur is 130 km away from Ajmer, the sacred place where the most famous Ajmer Sharif Dargah of the Sufi saint of the twelfth century, Muʾīn al-Dīn Chishti, is located. Ajmer is one of the most significant places of pilgrimage in the world, not only for Muslims but for people across all religions. Many of the most beloved and venerated Indian Sunni saints were Chishti in their affiliation, including Nizamuddin Awliya (1238–1325) and Amir Khusrow (1253–1325). Muʾīn al-Dīn was a charismatic and compassionate spiritual preacher and teacher who received the gifts of many spiritual marvels such as miraculous travel, clairvoyance and visions of angels. He is also notable for having been one of the first major Islamic mystics to formally allow his followers to incorporate the use of music in their devotions. Additionally, Ajmer Sharif Dargha attracts many Hindus who have also venerated the Islamic saint since the medieval period.

Sufism focuses on the spiritual search for God and shuns materialism, emphasizing asceticism, devotion to God (*Bhakti*), self-discipline and stresses on inner purity. Service to humanity is tantamount to service to God. No wonder Guruji's sayings and activities during his lifetime resonated with these principles and tenets.

PANCHKULA (1996): THE CITY ON THE BANKS OF GHAGGAR

It was usually observed that whenever Guruji cured somebody of any serious disease, he used to get some kind of pain or suffer an impact on his body. Most of the time, such an impact was felt by Guruji internally. It is like taking the pain himself to cure the person of his sufferings. Sometimes, it could have debilitating physical effect on Guruji. This has been corroborated by many devotees through their satsangs. Guruji used to have periods of isolation from holding sangat, so that he could recoup physically and spiritually. Perhaps that was one of the reasons for which Guruji used to change base to different locations without furnishing the details of the next destination. The other reason may be reaching out to the vast mass of suffering individuals at various locations. Yogis have no permanent place of residence, for the world is their abode.

The ever-increasing suffering devotees would reach the new abode within no time to pester Guruji to cure them and their near and dear ones of diseases, solve their personal and professional problems. Guruji used to say that very few come to a *mahapurush* for the real thing—spiritual seeking. Despite their intentions, Guruji would bless them. He used to say that his purpose of coming to this world was to shower blessings and, through that, nudge them gradually towards the spiritual path. Even if one per cent of those who get the blessings thrive to adopt a spiritual journey, he would be a satisfied person.

After staying in Jalandhar Mandir for a couple of months, one fine morning in 1996, Guruji left for an unknown destination—unknown to the Jalandhar and Punjab sangat. It was to the private residence of Lieutenant General Ahuja and Dr Savitri Ahuja. The Ahujas had superannuated from the Army Medical Corps and shifted to their private residence. After a couple of weeks of convalescing, he selectively allowed some sangat located in the Tricity. Colonel Sadhu (popularly known as 'Sadh Sangat') and his wife were a few sangat allowed to have a darshan of Guruji. Urvashi was also allowed to have his darshan in the Ahuja's residence. After a couple of months of allowing a limited number of sangat, it was opened for all. It was the same institutionalized holding of sangat like it was in Jalandhar Mandir. The limited one *kanal* house of General Ahuja would be agog with sangat in the evening. A few were allowed during daytime. The system of distributing chai prasad, sabad, kada prasad or other forms of sweet prasads, and langar started in full swing.

Surinder Kaur, the famous folk singer (some call her the Lata Mangeshkar of Punjab), her daughter Dolly Guleria and granddaughter would visit Guruji quite often. General Guleria, Dolly's husband, was also seen paying his respects to Guruji occasionally. I could vividly recollect the surreal and magical moments when Dolly and her daughter, with their full team of accompanists, rendered the beautiful and soulful bhajan 'Om Namah Shivay' in praise of Lord Shiva in the sangat hall of the residence of General Ahuja in Panchkula.

The residence would be bursting with activities in the evening leading to traffic and other issues in the colony. It was time for Guruji to shift base.

CHANDIGARH (1997): THE CITY OF GARDENS IN THE FOOTHILLS OF SHIVALIK

The Grewals of Mandi Gobindgarh, particularly Shri Harjinder Singh Grewal, his wife popularly known as Sarpanch Aunty, as she was the sarpanch of village Ajnali, near Mandi Gobindgarh, Jagi Grewal, Rimple Grewal, their children, and their extended family members were Guruji's earnest followers. Harinder Grewal had a property lying unoccupied. Occasionally, the Grewals would come and use it temporarily. They never intended to settle in Chandigarh, as they were comfortably placed in Ajnali with their business and establishments.

On the suggestions of some sangat and with request from the Grewals, Guruji shifted from Panchkula to Chandigarh in the early days of 1997. The usual system of holding sangat continued for nearly a year. Guruji blessed scores of devotees and non-devotees and held a couple of big functions like Baisakhi and Gurpurab, there. The adjacent plot was vacant, which was used for parking the vehicles of sangat. The house was facing a park, the inner road was wide enough to prevent traffic jams and the neighbourhood was never disturbed by the sangat activities in the evening.

The prominent sangat who used to have Guruji's darshan are Justice K. Sreedharan, the chief justice of Punjab and Haryana, his son-in-law of the Rajasthan cadre, senior civil servants like Shri S.S. Brar, Shri Ashok Dubey and Mrs Romila Dubey, Shri J.S. Keshar, Shri Miglani, Shri Alok Nigam, Shri A.R. Talwar, Mr R.P.S. Powar, Mr Deep Inder Singh, Mr A.S. Chatwal, Shri Badhan (IRS), Shri D.S. Jaspal, Mr Chhena IAS (Retd), Mr Amit Jha, the son-in-law and daughter of Mr Banshi Lal, Shri Balram Das Tondon (Minister, Local Government, BJP in Akali-BJP coalition), scores of other politicians, Mr Rajput (District and Sessions Judge), Justice A.S. Gill, Justice Khichi, Lieutenant General Deepinder Singh, General Kaushal, General Ahuja, Colonel S.K. Toor, Brigadier Saini, family of General Hoon, Mr Bhullar (IPS), Mr Bhawra (IPS), Dr M.P. Singh, Dr S.C. Sharma, Mr Gogia (IPS), and General Guleria, the Soods, the Bhores, the Grewals of Mandi Gobindgarh, Mr Chopra (Advocate), Mr Harpal Tiwana and Gulab Kaur (theater artists), Mrs Tiwana (poet), the Rais (Ravi Rai and Anu), the Puris, Daljit and Neena Sandhu, Navraj, Vimal Kapur and his extended family, including his elder and younger brothers, were also regulars.

There was a constant flow of sangat from the rest of Punjab and other parts of the country. Particularly, Sudha Aunty, Babbar, V.P. Bharadwaj, General Malhotra, Colonel Joshi and others from Delhi were coming at regular intervals for Guruji's darshan.

Guruji used to have most of the sangat dispersed by 11.30 p.m., by which time a handful of sangat would be left. He used to have small discussions wherein most of his witty comments were heard. Sometimes, he may order a second or third round of chai prasad for the limited sangat left at that time. Some of them will feel sleepy and move to the semi-basement near the hall and make themselves comfortable. Most of the days, it would go on till past-midnight. Guruji would order parathas to be made and served to the sangat (not more than 8–10). Someday, he would take the sangat to Sukhna Lake at around 3.30–4.00 a.m. The peacocks in the nearby Kansal Forest would sing their praise for Guruji in unison. It would be a divine feeling.

Guruji would take a walk on the bund road of Sukhna Lake, where only a few could match his speed and steps.

Then he would give permission to the sangat to leave for their respective homes. We would sleep for a couple of hours and get ready for the next day's business or official work. We would never feel fatigue from a lack of sleep, and it did not affect our efficiency in working.

Towards October 1997, Guruji developed a very unusual kind of physical ailment. He would be in constant pain originating somewhere in his body. All the doctor devotees, such as Dr M.P. Singh, Dr S.C. Sharma and Dr (Brigadier) Saini could not diagnose it. He was taken to the military base hospital in Chandimandir, near Panchkula, where Brigadier Saini was posted. All the tests and scans were conducted. Nothing could be found.

Again back in his house, he would virtually roll over the floor with pain uttering 'Oh Maa, Oh Maa'. I have never seen a person in so much pain. In the meantime, Sudha Aunty and Babbar's family arrived from Delhi as part of their regular visits to have a darshan of Guruji. They persuaded Guruji to move with them to Delhi. Guruji agreed to their suggestion and left for Delhi. The much-needed rest and the sewa of Sudha Aunty helped Guruji to recover from the unknown ailment and pain. That is how Guruji landed up at Empire Estate in Sultanpur, New Delhi.

DELHI, THE WOUNDED COLLECTIVE PSYCHE

Pandit Jawaharlal Nehru, the then Prime Minister (PM) of India, while addressing at the convocation of Delhi University in 1958 stated:

> Here we stand in Delhi city, symbol of old India and the new. It is not the narrow lanes and houses of old Delhi nor the wide spaces and rather pretentious buildings of New Delhi that count, but the spirit of this ancient city. Delhi has been an epitome of India's history with its succession of glory and disaster and with its great capacity to absorb many cultures and yet remain itself. It is a gem with many facets, some bright and some darkened by age, presenting the course of India's life and thought during the ages.
>
> We face the good and the bad of India in Delhi city which has been the grave of many empires and the nursery of a republic. What a tremendous story of hers! Here the tradition of millennia of our history surrounds us at every step, and the procession of innumerable generations passes by before our eyes.[1]

Delhi, housing three world heritage sites (Humayun's Tomb, the Red Fort and Qutub Minar), has nearly 700 heritage buildings comprising tombs, sarais, gates, old havelis, colonial buildings which are several hundred years old, and religious structures like temples, Gurudwaras, Jain temples, churches and mosques. They say if you throw a stone in Delhi, there is every likelihood that it will be hitting a heritage site.

The civilizational history of Delhi is invariably linked with the ups and downs of the entire subcontinent. It was, and still is, the heart of Hindustan, that is Bharat. For most of the history of the country, it is said that whoever rules Delhi, rules India. But Delhi suffers from the civilizational wounds spanning several

---

[1] 'Eight Cities of Delhi', Delhi Tourism, https://bit.ly/3WeS8e0. Accessed on 16 January 2023.

millennia, spanning from the mythical Indraprastha of the Pandavs (Khandava Forest), the unrevealed and unexplored history of the Hindu and Buddhist civilizations prior to the seven cities of Delhi during medieval India.

Delhi has witnessed the rise and fall of several citadels of political power, accompanied by the great wealth and splendour of regimes. The ruins and heritage structures, which have survived the onslaught of successive rulers and adverse vagaries of weather, provide the testimony for such great power and opulence. Art and culture also thrived in the citadels. These are a saga of destructions and creations, of a new city built every time only to be subsumed by a newer one.

The earliest of these is the Lal Kot or Qila Rai Pithora in the Mehrauli complex, which was a citadel of political power and splendour that lasted nearly five centuries, spanning from the eight to the thirteenth. The Qila Rai Pithora citadel of power got replaced by successive rulers and dynasties, each establishing a new city or capital adjacent to or on the ruins of the previous one. The Turkish tribe of Khiljis of Afganistan built the 'Siri' as their capital consisting of the present-day Siri Fort and Hauz Khas area. Alauddin Khilji's General Ghiyasuddin Tughlaq built Tughlaqabad, which was abandoned after being cursed by the great Sufi saint Hazrat Nizamuddin Auliya, who famously said after being harassed by the emperor, '*Ya base gujjar, ya rahe ujjar* (The city will be ruined, and either herdsman will dwell or it will be deserted).'

Muhammad bin Tughlaq, the successor of Giyyasuddin bin Tughlaq, built a smaller city (1324–25), after shifting from Daulatabad, called Jahanpannah (Refuge of the World) between Qila Rai Pithora and Siri Fort. He abandoned the city within a year. Firozabad (Palace of Spirits) was built by Firoze Tughlaq in the fourteenth century on the banks of Yamuna, near the present-day Feroz Shah Kotla cricket stadium, followed by the Lodhis and Sayyids who left their mark in Delhi in the form of beautiful mausoleums and landscaped gardens (Lodhi Garden).

Purana Qila was built by Humayun in the 1530s and named as Dinpanah. Sher Shah, after defeating Humayun, built an ornate fort on the razed capital of Dinpanah and called it Sher Garh. Humayun regained control of the fort in 1555 and added structures and beautification in Sher Shah's fort and ruled from there till his death in 1556.

Akbar's grandson Shah Jahan, who built the Taj Mahal in Agra, also built Shahjahanabad, present-day Old Delhi, in the 1630s. Shahjahanabad was the capital of the Mughal Empire until its fall in 1857. The prosperity and wealth of the empire was unrivalled in the world. India at that time (1700s) was the largest economy in the world, contributing nearly 25 per cent to the global GDP. The splendour of Delhi is beautifully described by Mirza Ghalib:

Ik roz apni rooh se poocha, ke dilli kya hai.
To yun Jawab me keh gayi
Ye duniya maano jism hai aur dilli uski jaan hai

One day I asked my soul, what was the city of Delhi, to which it replied, if the world were a body, then Delhi is its life.

The British East India Company established their suzerainty in most of India after the 1757 Battle of Plassey. They defeated the Marathas in 1803 and occupied Delhi, putting Bahadur Shah Zafar in jail. The power transferred to the British crown after the mutiny of 1857.

New Delhi was built by the British (by 1911) and the Vice Royal Lodge (present Rashtrapati Bhavan); the central secretariats and the India Gate are part of the Raisina Hill; and the present Central Vista (renamed as Kartavya Path) and the residential and office complexes are the contributions of the British.

These successive citadels of power exemplify the sacrifice of lakhs in the battles and the internecine succession wars. The ruins and the structures standing today testify the exhibition of the worst of the base traits of humans. Alauddin Khilji defeated the successors of Mongol-raider Genghis Khan at the present-day

Mangolpuri and established the fort by putting the decapitated heads (*sir*) of 8,000 Mongols as the foundation of the new fort (hence, the name 'Siri').

The famous gate of the old fort is called the Khooni Darwaza. After defeating his elder brother Dara Sheikh (Dara Shikoh) during the battle for succession in Shah Jahan's old age, Aurangzeb displayed the severed head of Dara at the gate. Subsequently, three princes of the last Mughal king, Bahadur Shah Zafar (sons Mirza Bahadur, Mirza Khizr Sultan and grandson Mirza Abu Bakht) were shot by the British major William Hodson on 22 September 1857, who displayed the dead bodies at this gate (following the footsteps of Aurangzeb), a symbolic show of authority after the great mutiny of 1857.

Present-day Delhi has not overcome its civilizational grief and wounded psyche. It is etched into the collective DNA of Delhites. Periodically, it erupts in the form Hindu–Muslim or anti-Sikh riots (1984). It has permeated the polluted air and smog of Delhi (termed as the most polluted capital in the world), depicting the poverty of management skills in tackling environmental issues and finding ad-hoc alibis by blaming the stubble burning of paddy straws, which lasts only for 15 days. The mindless pursuit of wealth and power has obliterated the age-old pursuit of civilized conduct (*tahzeeb*), propriety and decorum (*tamadun*). The predicament and anguish of Delhi is beautifully depicted by Urdu poet Jaan Nisar Akhtar in the following couplet:

> *Dilli kahaan gaii teri koochon ki raunaqe*
> *Galiyo se sar jhuka ke guzarne laga hun main*

> Delhi, where are the glories of your famous streets, I have
> to lower my head while passing your lanes now.

Delhi needed the compassion and love of a highly spiritually elevated soul to heal its wounded psyche and intergenerational karmic fault lines. The presence of saints like Khwaja Qutbuddin Bakhtiyar Kaki (thirteenth century) or the annual festival of fans (Pankha Mela) as well as the festival of flowers (Phool Walon Ki

Sair), could not imbibe the spirit of universal brotherhood and humanism in the political citadel of Delhi. Similarly, the humanism of Sufi saint Hazrat Nizamuddin Auliya in the fifteenth century was not adequate to bring solace, peace and harmony to Delhi. It is no doubt that Hazrat Nizamuddin Auliya and his disciple, the mystic poet Amir Khusrao were the foremost contributor to India's composite culture. Amir Khusrao's poetry is still sung throughout the subcontinent with great passion and fervour. The legendary beneficent spirits (*jinns*) of Feroz Shah Kotla also couldn't alter the base characteristics that are the essence of the heritage of Delhi.

Guruji used to tell that Delhi has not been visited by a mahapurush epitomizing love and compassion to heal the civilizational wounds and psyche of the city. Delhi needed the benign presence of such a mahapurush. Recounting what he said, '*Delhi'ch kade mahapurush aye nahin. Delhi nuu mahaprukh di sakht lod hai.*'

THE SOJOURN IN GREATER KAILASH–HEALING THE WOUNDS

Kailash Colony is a residential neighbourhood in South Delhi. Greater Kailash is an extension of this place. Present-day Greater Kailash lies between the ruins of Daulatabad and Siri Fort, the medieval Delhi. Greater Kailash was originally a plotted development by DLF through the Public Private Partnership or PPP mode. Right next door is Kalkaji, which is a resettled colony originally for the immigrants from West Pakistan. And the next neighbourhood is CR Park, whose residents comprise migrants from the then East Pakistan (now Bangladesh).

By the end of 1994, Brigadier Mohan Singh, being promoted to Major General, got posted at the army headquarters in New Delhi. He was residing in the allotted quarters at Dhaula Kuan. One fine morning, Guruji, with a couple of devotees, left Jalandhar and landed at General Mohan Singh's residence. After a couple days of convalescing (not allowing any sangat), he started meeting a limited number of people from the sangat. As the number of devotees started increasing, some devotees persuaded Guruji to have a place of his own where he would give darshan to the ever-growing sangat. They purchased a basement in S-Block, Greater Kailash and it was converted to a sangat hall. Only one or two sewadars were allowed to stay there. They were assigned the task of looking after the property, cleaning it and getting it ready for holding the sangat in the evening. The institution of holding sangat was the same as it was in Jalandhar Mandir. The sangat will be allowed to reach the mandir around 6.30 p.m. Sabad will be played from a music system. Chai prasad and langar would be served and then most of the sangat would leave. With a couple of devotees left, Guruji used to have his small witty sessions, or an impromptu programme to some destination in Delhi or someone's house. Due to his irregular timings, he shifted from General Mohan Singh's official residence to the army mess in Dhaula Kuan. During this period, Guruji attracted a large number of devotees from the National Capital Region and other cities. Guruji had, among his following, many bureaucrats, politicians, industrialists, journalists and people from other walks of life.

In the year 1995, Air Marshal Chopra, the then Wing Commander, was diagnosed as suffering from Hepatitis-B, a serious form of hepatitis and a complicated liver infection. The doctors in Army Research and Referral Hospital, New Delhi, diagnosed that it was approaching a dangerous and chronic phase. Moreover, they found that there was no readymade medicine for this kind of infection. He was advised by well-wishers to seek alternative systems of medicine. Chopra tried all other systems of medicines, but the infection was not subsiding. A wife of one of his seniors, a devotee of Guruji, suggested him to seek the blessings of Guruji. That time, Guruji was holding sangat in the basement mandir in Greater Kailash. He went with the senior's wife to Guruji's sangat. When he just paid his respects to Guruji by the usual bow of his head, Guruji uttered, '*Chopra, tera kaliyan kitta* (Chopra, you are blessed).' Guruji was distributing amrit and Chopra was given eight glasses of it. In normal course, it would have been difficult to drink that much water, but Chopra, with full reverence, drank all the eight glasses (about two litres) without hesitation and discomfort. When langar was served (that time each person was given one thali), Guruji came to Chopra and enquired how many chapatis he had already eaten. Mr Chopra had taken the two chapatis given to each sangat and told about the count. Guruji himself got one more chapati and handing over to him said that he should eat it considering as prasad. When he finished his langar, Guruji told him that his infection had been cured. Nevertheless, he should go for a medical test to confirm. Mr Chopra went for testing the next day and the results the subsequent day showed his infection had been cured. That was the miraculous healing experienced by Wing Commander Chopra.

And after a couple of months of holding sangat at Greater Kailash, the institutionalized sangat came to an end abruptly. It was 3 July 1995 when Guruji abruptly left the sangat that day and asked Jagi Grewal to accompany him to the army mess in Dhaula Kuan, where he was staying, courtesy of General Mohan Singh. He picked up a few clothes and left for Punjab. After attending the last rites of his elder brother in Dugri, he left for Jalandhar.

EMPIRE ESTATE, BADE MANDIR AND DELHI (1998 ONWARDS)

By the end of October 1997, Guruji shifted from Sector 33, Chandigarh, to Empire Estate, Sultanpur, New Delhi. Sultanpur is an urban village in South Delhi and lies at the edge or rather a part of the old Qila Rai Pithora complex of the original Old Delhi.

Guruji rested for a couple of months there and by March 1998, he allowed some sangat to have his darshan on the first floor of Sudha Aunty's house, which was a duplex bungalow.

Guruji used to meet a limited number of the sangat in the living room of the first floor. He used to sit on a sofa and the sangat on the carpet. Sometimes, some of the VIP sangat, while having his darshan for the first time, would sit in another corner of the same sofa. Some of them, who became genuine followers, would later realize their folly and the importance of divinity. On subsequent occasions, they themselves would sit on the carpet.

Guruji started meeting the sangat openly after some months. It was four days in a week—Thursday to Sunday. The sangat would start at 6.30 p.m. However, sometimes Guruji used to call a few sangat during the daytime on sangat days and on non-sangat days (Monday to Wednesday). But they were very few in number—not more than five to six—Dr S.C. Sharma, Brigadier Saini, Colonel Joshi, the Sabharwal (Arjun) family, Roma Sapra, Vipi Bhardwaj, Babbar Uncle, Vini Kapur and few others.

When I was posted in Delhi, my brother-in-law Mr Maheswar Sahu joined as Joint Secretary in the Department of Telecommunications. We were both fortunate to have this privilege. Singla Uncle used to prepare langar for the sangat and didn't have to seek any permission for coming regularly to Empire Estate for a consultation with Guruji. When Bade Mandir was under construction, Raghubir Uncle of Jalandhar and his better half used to stay in Empire Estate. Sometimes, Guruji would call over some others during these restricted hours.

When Guruji started the open darshan for the sangat, the living room of the first floor was found to be too small a place to accommodate the sangat. So, the ground-floor living room was cleared of the furniture, except for the dashboard along the wall to the kitchen. An ornate single-seater sofa with carvings was procured to serve as the aasan for Guruji. Guruji would come down to the sangat hall after the sangat would be settled with chai prasad. He used to wear his *chola*, mostly of silk fabric and with beautiful borders and knitting. He would use them for a couple of days or weeks and then give away to one of the sangat as his blessings.

The sangat hall with Guruji seated on his aasan, filled with bright lights and devotees, would provide a majestic ambience. The aura of divinity would radiate and resonate throughout the entire place. Sitting there and listening to sabad or satsang was the experience of a lifetime. The place was full of energy and vibrations emanating from the divinity. It was a blessing to the sangat, who could realize, feel and bask in the aura of divinity. Of course, for the nay-sayers, the non-believers and persons coming to test Guruji (Guruji used to call them 'let-us-try types') and the people from the intelligence bureau, the vibration of the divinity was perhaps as remote as Mount Kailash.

By this time, Guruji had a strong following among the higher and lower bureaucracy, politicians of various hues and parties, higher and lower judiciary, industrialists, journalists, academicians, intellectuals and other walks of life. I had the opportunity to witness four former PMs—Mr Deve Gowda, Mr V.P. Singh, Mr Chandra Shekhar, and Mr Atal Bihari Vajpayee—who had come to Guruji seeking his blessings. Maheswar Sahu, my brother-in-law, was present when Mr Modi, the then chief minister of Gujarat, came to pay his respects to Guruji. In one of the satsangs held in one of the former PM's house, there are photographs of Mrs Sonia Gandhi and Mr Manmohan Singh paying their respects to Guruji.

Among the politicians who were seen in Guruji's durbar at Empire Estate were Mrs Maneka Gandhi and Mr Varun Gandhi, Mr Murli Manohar Joshi, Mr Krishna Tirath, Ms Uma Bharti, Ms Mayawati, Mr Pranab Mukherjee, Mr L.K. Advani, Mr Arun Shourie, Ms Meira Kumar, Mr Arun Nehru, Mr Sekhawat, Mrs Rama Pilot and Mrs Jaya Jaitly and the family members of Pratap Rudy, Ram Vilas Paswan and Syed Shahnawaz Hussain. Among the top industrialists, Mr K.K. Birla was a frequent visitor. Mr Ajay Piramal and Mr Nusli Wadia were reported to have come to Guruji's durbar. Mr Verma, promoter of RD City, Mr Sharma of Sita Travels, and the family of Raunak Singh, the promoters of Heritage Resorts, are some of the prominent personalities from the business and industry sector (whose names I could recollect) who were seen in Guruji's durbar. There were scores of senior civil servants like Mr Satyananda Mishra, Mr Sujit Mitra, Tinno Joshi and her husband, Mrs Neera Yadav, Mr Sahani, Ms Amarjeet Ahuja, Mr Ajay Vikram Singh, Ms Gurjot Kaur, Mr S.D. Mathur, Shri

R.P.S. Powar, Mr R.I. Singh, Mr D.S. Jaspal, S.S. Brar, Sandeep Dave, Mr Jagdishan, Shri A.S. Chhatwal, Mr Mehta Mr Miglani, Mr Sudhir and Mr Satish Lamba who were also seen frequenting Guruji's durbar. The senior police officers include Mr K.K. Paul, Mr Gogia, Mr Prakash Singh, Mr Bhawara and Mr Pankaj Singh. From the higher judiciary, Justice Verma (Supreme Court of India), Justice Malhotra (Delhi High Court), Justice S.K. Singh (Former Chief Justice, Supreme Court of India), Justice Khichi (Punjab and Haryana High Court), Justice Amarbir Singh Gill (Punjab and Haryana High Court) were also seen in Empire Estate and Bade Mandir. There were several civil servants belonging to the central services and the Indian Foreign Service who were also seen at Empire Estate and Bade Mandir. They include Mr M.S. Badhan, Mr M.S. Narang, Mr Jagtar Singh, Ms Omita Paul and Mr Prem Singh, who were seen frequenting Empire Estate and Bade Mandir during major functions. Among the defence personnel, Lieutenant General Mohan Singh, Lieutenant General Verma, Air Chief Marshal S. Ramaswamy, General Deepak Malhotra, General Grewal, Brigadier Saini, Colonel Joshi, Lieutenant General Kapur, Lieutenant General Deepinder Singh, Air Commodore Chopra, Commander Sharma, General Ahuja, Major General MPS Sandhu and General Harinder Singh were found to have visited Guruji's durbar. There were also sports personalities (Mr Ravindra Jadeja, Mr Navjot Singh Sidhu), journalists (Ms Madhu Kishwar, Editor at *Manushi*), actors (Mr Chandrachur Singh, family members of Anil Kapoor), singers (Hans Raj Hans, Daler Mehndi, Sukhi Brar, Dolly Guleria), famous photographer Raghu Rai and his family, the family members of Mehbooba Mufti, classical dance exponents like Radha Reddy and Raja Reddy and their family, and designers like Madhu Jain, were blessed by Guruji at Empire Esate and Bade Mandir. Apart from them, there were scores of other bureaucrats, businessmen, professionals, politicians and common men and women who were enjoying the divine presence of Guruji at Empire Estate and during special functions at Bade Mandir. It is difficult to recount and recollect their names.

Sometimes, people would wonder how the small hall of the villa in Empire Estate could accommodate such a rush of sangat. Guruji was the supreme manager. He used to tell some sangat to come after a period or just once a week. Generally, there would be no issue of shortage of langar for the sangat.

It is not that the neighbourhood was always tolerant. The sangat were not allowed to drive to the villa from the gates of the Empire Estate. The guards were strictly instructed to allow only the vehicles of residents and their authorized guests. The sangat used to park the vehicles on the kerbs of MG Road. The vacant plot in front of Sudha Aunty's bungalow, owned by the Mehras (who are ardent followers of Guruji) was used for serving jal prasad after langar. Mr Vini Kapoor (the next-door neighbour of Sudha Aunty) and Roma Sapra, residents of Empire Estate, became ardent followers of Guruji.

Guruji used to go for satsangs or social functions organized by the sangat. He would direct a couple from amongst the sangat to come to Empire Estate and then 10–15 vehicles would accompany Guruji's to the place of the sangat. It could be some wedding of a son or daughter of a devotee, or a plain sangat and satsang organized by devotees. I had the opportunity of attending such a sangat in the residences of Mr Pranab Mukherjee, Mr Pankaj Singh (son of Mr Chandra Shekhar, former prime minister), Mr L.K. Advani, Justice Verma, Lieutenant General Mohan Singh and Mr Suman, Indian Railway Accounts Service (Member of Finance, Railway Board).

Guruji used to take a few devotees, after most of the sangat was allowed to go home, to various places in the city. It was his mauz or leela. He would take them to five star hotels like Sheraton in Saket, The Bristol in Gurugram (a favourite place), Le Meridien, the Claridges, the Janpath Hotel, the Ambassador Hotel, ITC Maurya, the Taj Mahal Hotel, and so on. It would be midnight or in the early hours when Guruji would call the chef and order soup or chai. The rest of the sangat (10–12 of them) would be ordering snacks like pakoras and tea, coffee, cold coffee, etc. Some of the executives and chefs became followers of Guruji. Shri Dipak Haksar of ITC is an ardent follower. From the coffee shops, Guruji loved to take the sangat to the paan shop near The Claridges for the benefit of the sangat, not for himself. I have never seen him consuming paan. There were sometimes midnight langars and post-langar walks in the lawns of the India Gate.

On other days, Guruji would go for a walk after most of the sangat had left. Mrs Maneka Gandhi would be a constant companion. Mr Pankaj Singh and Rasmi Singh (Pankaj's wife), Sudha Aunty, Roma Sapra, Colonel Joshi, V.P. Bharadwaj, and myself included, had the privilege of accompanying Guruji on such walks. He would go to the lanes and by-lanes of the farm houses on MG Road off Sultanpur on such walks.

On many occasions, we would find that our shoes would be full of dirt or dust, depending on the weather and season, but Guruji's sneakers would have none. Was he walking or floating above ground? This was invariably noticed by the sangat who accompanied him on such walks. On some days, Guruji would take some sangat to Bade Mandir. Particularly, some of the new devotees who had come for the first time were taken to Bade Mandir.

THE RAMGARH HEIGHTS

The Sharmas (Mr Mahinder Sharma and family) of Punjabi Bagh, Delhi, and a devotee of Guruji had a property on the hilltop of Ramgarh, a small habitation on the Nainital–Mukteshwar Road. With Guruji's blessings, the Sharmas developed the property as a tourist resort and named it The Himalayan Heights. The resort is spread over a sprawling 72 acres, at an altitude of 7,800 feet above sea level. One can have a picturesque and spectacular view of the Himalayan ranges and snow-clad mountains from the resort. The pleasant surroundings are full of small streams and orchards of plums, peaches, apricots and apples. On the way to Ramgarh from Nainital, one can get the opportunity of visiting the ashram of Neem Karoli Baba reputed to have performed many miracles throughout his life.

Once the resort became functional, the Sharmas requested Guruji to bless the resort. Guruji took a group of 15 odd devotees and stayed there for a week. When Guruji was at Ramgarh, by word of mouth, some people of Nainital came to know about his supernatural powers. A Muslim named Naseer came all the way from Nainital to have darshan of Guruji at the resort. When Naseer was paying his respects, Guruji surprised him by stating that he had three wives—with none able to bear a child, and he had come to seek Guruji's blessings for a child. Naseer could not believe his ears; Guruji knew his details by reading his mind. On the next visit at Empire Estate, Naseer was alone. When Guruji enquired about his wife, he mentioned her sudden illness from a headache and stomach pain. Guruji told him that his wife was faking the ailment and that she had conceived. Naseer had not heard from his wife whether she had missed her period. He went back, half in doubt and got the pregnancy test done the next day. The couple was blessed with a son, after 15 years of marriage and confirmed infertility by the medical fraternity.

HARIDWAR AND RISHIKESH

A senior IPS (Indian Police Officer) of Uttarakhand and her sister, a well known TV actor were ardent devotees of Guruji. When this officer was the IG of Haridwar, she invited Guruji to visit Haridwar and Rishikesh. Guruji accepted her invitation and stayed three to four days in a guest house on the right bank of the Ganges. Guruji would take regular baths in the river at the VIP ghat on the opposite bank of the river. He would hold impromptu sangat in the guest house and take the accompanying devotees to the by-lanes of Haridwar to treat them with the famous Chotiwala puris and potato curry.

BADE MANDIR

Guruji's Bade Mandir lies near Bhatti village, close to the northwest edge of the Asola Bhatti Wildlife Sanctuary. This sanctuary lies at the far southern edge of the city of Delhi, at Asola near Tughlaqabad in the Delhi–NCR region. This protected area contains one of the last surviving remnants of the Delhi Ridge.

Guruji built the Bade Mandir under his constant supervision. He would take interest in minute details of the construction. Raghubir Singh of Jalandhar was overall in charge of the construction. Mr Bharadwaj, father of V.P. Bharadwaj and renowned architect, was in charge of the architectural aspects. The other people who were assisting or facilitating Shri Raghubir were Sudha Aunty, Mammi, Babar, etc.

After the construction was complete, Guruji was asked why he was not shifting to the Bade Mandir and holding sangat and satsang there. He said that the mandir was for the sangat and not for mahapurush. A mahapurush has no fixed place of residence or attachment for a particular place. It is only for large gatherings during functions that he used to hold sangat at Bade Mandir.

Wherever he used to stay, he would describe the place as a mandir. He would call the villa at Empire Estate a mandir. When Guruji visited Guruji Ka Ashram at Bhatti mines, he would call it Bade Mandir. Following that, some sangat started designating the villa as 'Chhota Mandir'.

Guruji would go around Bade Mandir, showing every bit of the place—the rooms, the parking, the langar hall, the kitchens—to the accompanying sangat. Chai prasad would be served or ladoo/ mishri prasad would be distributed in the main hall. He would not sit on the aasan meant for him. Usually, he would sit on the carpet reclining on the wall. Most of the time, he would have changed to his informal trousers and shirt, or into his walking gear, like shorts and sneakers, for these visits. He would hardly go in his formal robe (chola), which he wore while giving darshan to a sangat in Empire Estate. He would be found in cholas in Bade Mandir only on special functions.

At other times, he would go to Bade Mandir with only one or two of the sangat like Colonel Joshi or Sudha Aunty. He would discuss the affairs of the mandir with the *mali* (gardener) Ram Avatar and give him instructions. He once blessed Malan (Ram Avatar's wife) to have a baby girl. He would ask their welfare not only regarding their stay at Bade Mandir but also their kith and kin in their ancestral villages. He would sit on a charpai brought by Ram Avatar. An appliqué umbrella from Pipili (near Puri, Odisha) would be used to provide shade from the sun.

The landscaping and the surrounding constructions bear the divine signature of Guruji. He was the architect-in-chief, imbibing the essence of divinity in each and every aspect of the temple's architecture, landscaping and structures. Each plant, each blade of grass and each stone was blessed by Guruji under his temporal and divine supervision. There are stories abound (you may refer to *Light of Divinity* and other write-ups like those from Bambi Singh) regarding the divine touch Guruji provided during the construction of the temple. The fountain above the *kutiya* (meditation hut) was designed to flow like the Ganga from the matted hair of Lord Shiva. This was Guruji's own idea. He used to tell some sangat that the kutiya was for his meditation, but during which birth? Only he would know and could say. Sunny, the late son of General Mohan Singh, and Maami used to spend the entire day at Bade Mandir while it was under construction. He assisted in the landscaping, beautification and cleanliness of the premises while the finishing touches were being given.

Guruji, the divine guide, would show each room and describe their purpose. The first room on the left when you enter from the hall is supposed to be the resting place, when Guruji would visit the mandir. But he had hardly used it on a few occasions. He preferred the hall or the lawns to relax whenever he visited the mandir. Of course, during annual functions like Shivratri, Baisakhi, New Year's Eve, Guru Purnima, Diwali and his birthday on 7 July, he would be in his chola and sitting on the designated aasan to bless the sangat. The driveway had an entrance to the anteroom or living room as Guruji used to describe it. He would describe how the stationary car would rotate 360 degrees, so that you would not need to reverse the vehicle. A rotating platform with a motor on the floor of the parking had been installed for this purpose.

THE FUNCTIONS

Guruji revelled in holding special functions on a grand scale. Thousands of sangat would land up for his darshan and blessings on such auspicious days. The mandir would be decorated in a majestic manner with lights, flowers and coloured cloths. Special caterers would be engaged (mostly Sardar Harjinder Singh from Punjab) for preparing the langar. It would be served individually in disposable plates (deviation from the norm during normal sangat days). Guruji would distribute ber, mangoes or dry fruits as prasad. Famous singers, mostly his devotees, like Gurdas Maan, Sukhi Brar, Hans Raj Hans, Dolly Guleria and others, would be called to perform. A special pandal would be erected on the vacant plot adjacent to the mandir (the vacant land is used as parking by the devotees). Guruji would come out of the mandir hall and listen to the devotional, Sufi and folk songs rendered beautifully and reverentially by these famous singers.

The mandir has its aesthetic and spiritual significance. From a distance, you can have the view of the majestic Shiva Linga projecting to the sky. The entrance of the mandir hall with its arches symbolizes the open arm of the Lord welcoming the devotees. The surrounding landscaping provides a soothing and serene calmness matching the divinity. We would sit in the lawns, close our eyes and contemplate on the Lord whenever we visit Bade Mandir during the non-function days. What an ambience to connect with the Supreme Self!

It is no wonder Guruji used to say to some sangat that he had put the divine energy of 12 *Jyotirlingas* here in Bade Mandir. The

Shiva Swaroop statue in the fountain near the driveway added additional spiritual significance to the place. You cannot help but contemplate on the Supreme Self in such a beautiful, serene and calm place. You automatically bow your head to the Lord for the opportunity provided to connect with Him.

MAHASAMADHI

Guruji took *mahasamadhi* or left his chola on 31 May 2007. It was just unbelievable to the sangat. The emotional turmoil, the feeling of loss of everything and the void left behind in the lives of the sangat would have to be seen to be believed. Almost all the sangat felt that it wasn't yet time for Guruji to leave this world and his beloved sangat, since at the time Guruji was just 52 years old. But the fact is, enlightened masters (mahapurush) like Guruji know when to leave the world. Some say they embark upon *iccha-mrityu*. Guruji used to say, '*Asi to light to aye hain, light nuu chal jawange. Sada maksad tuhannu rab de naal jodna.* (I have come from Light, the Supreme Divine, and will go back to Light. My purpose is to connect the sangat to the Lord.)' Guruji did not have any serious co-morbidity factors except high-sugar levels. There were no known adverse cardiovascular indicators, but he left this world due to a myocardial infarction, in laymen terms, cardiac arrest or heart attack.

Guruji had sent me to Dugri on 30 May to follow up on certain matters relating to the construction of a hospital at Dugri in memory of Maata Surjit Kaur. I had to follow up on this matter with the Department of Health and Family Welfare, Government of Punjab, and with the district authorities at Sangrur. Vicky Chopra was with me, as Guruji had ordered that he would be my companion on this tour. We had a couple of meetings with the health department officials and then proceeded to Sangrur to follow up on the matter with the deputy commissioner and civil surgeon at Sangrur. After finishing the day's work, we proceeded to Dugri to stay with Guruji's family as had been directed by Guruji at the time of our departure from Delhi.

We reached Dugri late in the evening. Guruji had the uncanny way of excellently following up on the task given to anybody. He would take stock of our minute-to-minute reports regarding the progress of the task (where have you reached, whether the meeting with the officials took place, etc.) and periodically would call to confirm whether everything was going smoothly. But on 30 May, Guruji did not call a single time to know the progress of the task given to us. It seemed strange to me and I thought he would call late in the evening.

We enjoyed the hospitality of Gaurav's mother in the company of Bapuji, and Roopi Bhai Sahib (Gaurav's father). I always loved the simple but tasty food cooked by Gaurav's mother.

Before retiring to bed, I thought I should call up Guruji and furnish him the day's progress of the task assigned to us, as he had not taken stock of the matter. I rang up Chhoto (Sudha Aunty's domestic help who was rendering sewa to Guruji) and requested him to connect Guruji. Chhoto informed that Guruji was not feeling well for some time. Nevertheless, he passed on the phone to Guruji. Guruji was sounding low when he talked to me. His warm, sweet and somewhat deep voice was missing. Nevertheless, I furnished the day's progress and asked whether we would go back to Delhi next day. He just said '*phir milenge*'. I could not understand what that meant. I thought, as Guruji is not feeling well, I should not bother him then. It was 11.15 p.m. We retired to bed.

At around 11.30 p.m., I got a call from Sudha Aunty. She was barely saying anything; she was just crying. She managed to say, 'Rahul, Guruji is not well. Please rush to AIIMS, and tell Mr Sahu (my co-brother-in-law) to come with you. We are taking him to the emergency room.' She did not know that I was in Dugri, a 6-hour drive from Delhi. She thought I was in our Delhi residence in R.K. Puram. Before I could say anything, Sudha Aunty disconnected the phone. I again rang up Chhoto. He informed that Guruji was in a serious condition and Dr Khilnani and Sudha Aunty had rushed him to AIIMS.

Realizing that the matter was not normal, I decided to return back to Delhi immediately. On any other occasion, I would have first taken permission before returning to Delhi, but I thought that the circumstances were not normal. I woke up Vicky and told him to get ready for immediate departure to Delhi. I just informed him that Guruji was not well and we should reach Delhi as soon as possible. Bapuji, Roopi Bhai Sahib and Gaurav's mother, got to know our untimely departure and we had to tell them that Guruji was not well and we had to go back immediately. We did not have any knowledge about exact ailment of Guruji and we could not furnish any more details to them. We left Dugri around 12.15 a.m.

Vicky was half asleep. He managed to drive till Khanna up to GT Road. The four-laned road and smooth drive with low volume of the night traffic made Vicky dose off intermittently. I had to take over the wheel pushing him to the passenger seat to sleep. I had not had the practice of driving long distances due to a bad habit of depending on official drivers. I managed to drive the entire distance from Khanna to Delhi, in between attending phone calls from Singla Uncle, informing us about Guruji's health and also directing me not to divulge exact details to Bapuji and the others in Dugri. Before leaving Dugri, I had informed Mr Sahu about Guruji's health and, as requested by Sudha Aunty, told him to rush to AIIMS.

We reached Delhi around 5 a.m. I rushed to the ICU and talked to the attending doctors. They had informally declared that he had left this world. But they had not disconnected the ventilator keeping the sentiments of the sangat. We were devastated—as if the sky had fallen on us. Regaining composure, I asked the doctors regarding the formalities. They said that it would take some time. I rushed back home and informed Urvashi, Jenny (my daughter), Jyoti and Sonia (Guruji's nieces), my sister-in-law (Mrs Sahu), Babbu and Shilpa. It was Guruji's blessing and desire that both families could stay together in the same block. They had been earlier asked to pray for Guruji and they were praying throughout the night, without taking any breaks. Nobody had informed them about the exact situation in AIIMS.

After freshening up, I rushed back to AIIMS after telling the others to rush there in another vehicle. By this time (6.30 a.m.), news about Guruji had spread like wildfire. Scores of sangat had landed up in AIIMS and the ICU was full of devotees. They were all in despair and surcharged with emotion. Even Brigadier Saini, who was an army medical doctor, said, 'Rahul, Guruji will resurrect, ask the doctors not to disconnect the ventilator.' It was the voice of unison. The AIIMS doctors were in panic and informed that they had to clear the ICU of the sangat as it was disturbing other patients. The sangat was asked to make room for the doctors and nurses to attend other patients. But the corridor leading to the ICU and the waiting area outside the cardiac ward was agog with hundreds of sangat. It was decided that we should wait till Bapuji and Krishna (Guruji's sister) reached AIIMS before further activities would be taken up. The AIIMS authorities were tolerant finding the huge following and emotional outpour of the sangat.

By 7 a.m., Brigadier Saini and I went to Dr Khilnani's residence in AIIMS to know the exact nature and the sequence of events leading to his last moments. Dr Khilnani informed that Guruji had already had one heart attack by the time he reached Empire Estate at the frantic request of Sudha Aunty. Gaurav and the sewadars at Empire estate were at loss as to what is happening to Guruji. When Dr Khilnani heard the details from Sudha Aunty, he advised them to immediately rush Guruji to the AIIMS emergency room. But Guruji did not listen. He told them to wait for the arrival of Dr Khilnani. After his preliminary examination, Dr Khilnani persuaded Guruji that he should be taken to AIIMS immediately. Guruji was put in the backseat so that Dr Khilnani could tend to him. Gaurav also rushed to AIIMS. On the way to AIIMS, he suffered a second attack. A team of doctors were waiting in the emergency room. They tried their best by following the required protocols of emergency treatment. He was briefly revived, but by 3.30 a.m., Guruji departed from this world.

We came back to the ICU from Dr Khilnani's residence. Still, many devotees were adamant that Guruji would resurrect. The AIIMS doctors were feeling jittery. Bapuji and Krishna had arrived around 8.00 a.m. After their consent, the doctors removed the wires from the ventilator and the beautiful body was taken to mortuary for further proceedings. Singla Uncle was given the charge of following the proper procedure of cleaning the body. All arrangements were made to put his *sharir* (mortal body) in Bade Mandir for a last darshan by the sangat. Due precaution was taken so that the mortal body remained fresh for sufficient time before the appropriate decision was taken regarding cremation or *bhoo Samadhi* (burial) . There was no unanimity regarding the practice to be followed.

It was a chaotic scene. Guruji had not nominated anybody as his spiritual inheritor nor there was any known syndicate to take decision on his behalf when he would be no more available for physical consultation. It is different matter that Guruji had established a Public Charitable Trust in the name of Guruji Ka Ashram. However, the details about the Trust and its managing body (which was limited to Guruji himself as founder Trustee and Bapuji, who was added as additional Trustees after death of Maataji) was not known to many except a few who were instrumental in getting the Trust deed and subsequent amendments executed. Disparate views were emanating from various quarters. By this time, Bapuji had informed, prodded by some sangat, that Guruji would be taken to Dugri for the last rites. We rushed to Bapuji, and with much difficulty, persuaded him that Guruji did not belong to Dugri or to the family. He was/is above these narrow confines. I reminded him the divine nature of Guruji and suggested that he should not be treated as an ordinary son of Dugri, and Bapuji and Maataji. The mahapurush who left the family and Dugri for good should not be treated as an ordinary human being. I told him that thousands of Guruji's devotees from Delhi and different parts of the country as well from foreign lands would be visiting his last place of rest. Hence, it would be appropriate that his last rites were performed in

Delhi where an appropriate structure could be hoisted for the sangat to pay respect to Guruji. With much persuasion, Bapuji agreed to the proposal that the last rites should be held in Delhi.

Dr S.C. Sharma who, along with his guru (he used to address him as Gurudev) from Jaipur, had just returned that morning from a pilgrimage to Kailash Mansarovar. I wanted to consult his guru as to what should be the appropriate way of disposal of the mortal remains of a mahapurush. Are there any prescribed methods for such divine souls? Gurudev is also a realized soul. He is well-aware of Guruji and used to tell Dr Sharma about the elevated divinity of Guruji. I went to Dr Sharma's residence and asked the same query to this enlightened soul. He gave a beautiful response: 'The Soul has gone to the Supreme Soul. It is the *lokachar* which matters. If the sangat decides on a particular manner of disposal of the mortal body (*mara sharir*), it is up to them.' But how does one find the views of the sangat? I rushed to Bade Mandir. A group of us—a couple of the sangat, Sudha Aunty, Singla Uncle, Colonel Joshi, Brigadier Saini, Rasmi and Pankaj Singh, Deepak Chopra, V.P. Bharadwaj and others whose name I could not recollect—held a confabulation and decided, in conformity with Bapuji, that Guruji's body will be cremated and it would be in the front lawns of Bade Mandir, where a samadhi would be built for paying respect by the sangat. His ashes would be kept in urns and would be put beneath the ground on which samadhi would be built. The *asthis* with ashes would be immersed in the Ganges at Haridwar.

A round-the-clock guarding of Guruji's body was arranged. It was feared that some *tantriks*, from amongst the sangat and others, may dismember a part of his body for tantrik purposes.

Guruji's mortal remains were cremated around 3.30 p.m. the next day. Bapuji, assisted by other family members including Gaurav and sangat, performed the last rites of Guruji. Some devotees reported that an 'OM' symbol formed in the pyre fire, with some even taking photographs of it.

Along with Bapuji and Gaurav, we rushed to Haridwar the next morning to immerse the asthis in the Ganges at Kankhal Ghat.

Sudha Aunty, Singla, Colonel Joshi, Babbu, Arvind (Singla's son), Ravi Rai and Arjun Sabharwal were accompanying us. After the immersion of the ashes and leftover bones (asthis), Singla Uncle, Gaurav and Bapuji left Haridwar for an unknown destination. The rest of us decided to return to Delhi. On the way, we stopped at a dhaba for dinner. By the time we resumed our journey back to Delhi, it was 8.30 p.m.

We had not had proper sleep for the last couple of days. Arvind was driving a car in which Arjun was also present. It met with an accident in Ghaziabad; the car banged into an electric pole head-on. By Guruji's grace, Arjun escaped with a fracture on one leg, and all the others had minor scratches. We rushed them to the nearest hospital and after they had been attended to properly by the doctors, we left for Delhi. Babbu (my nephew) was the one drivng, and near Akshardham, I found him dosing off behind the wheel. The vehicle was moving in a zigzag fashion, almost hitting the divider. I shouted at the top of my voice and Babbu gained control of the vehicle. I told him that I was taking over the wheel.

At the T-junction on GT Road, I took the right turn and drove towards Pragati Maidan. I had to, with due indicator, overtake a truck from the right going at a precariously low speed. From nowhere, a three-wheeler rushed out from our right and slammed straight into our vehicle. We stopped and inspected the vehicle. By that time, the three-wheeler had sped away. The silencer and mudguard of our vehicle was damaged and it could not be driven. We could manage to take the vehicle to the kerb near the overbridge. I called my official driver who reached within half an hour. He drove us home while the vehicle was towed to the garage.

All of us, with Guruji's blessings, could escape with minor consequences, except for Arjun, who took a couple of months to walk normally. The lack of sleep from two-to-three nights could have resulted in major accidents. Though Arvind's accident was a major one, none of Guruji's sangat had to face any extreme situations. Guruji used to say, 'I save my sangat with minor problems when they are destined to suffer significantly.'

Part II

Manifestations of Divinity

2

Manifestation of Divinity

The discernible disciples ascribe (attribute or impute) Guruji as divinity incarnate. It is up to the spiritually surcharged devotee to elevate him or ascribe his divinity to that of God incarnate or puran guru or an enlightened master. As one spiritual research organization puts it, the devotees of a spiritually enlightened Guru have different levels of spiritual attainment. Most of the devotees have an average of 20 per cent level of spiritual attainment. When such devotees attain a spiritual level of 50 per cent or more, or such a spiritual level has been inherited by birth due to good deeds (karma) of their previous birth(s), having been blessed by the grace of God, they can recognize a true Guru.

THE MAGNETIC PULL OF DIVINITY

It is the grace of God that we had the blessings to have had the association, *sansparsha* (contact) and darshan of Guruji in his enlightened form during our lifetime. The serenity, calmness and peace of mind we experienced in Guruji's presence are reflective of his spirituality and divinity. Whether Guruji would be seated on his aasan or elsewhere, there was the radiant engulfment of positive energy. This energy would transport the sangat to a different state characterized by happiness, bliss, peace and calmness. That is the beauty of being in the spiritual zone of a *nitya siddha*. The ever-perfect soul is born a *siddha* and all his activities or exertions, after attaining perfection, are for the sake of setting an example for humanity. Such a mahapurush is immersed in perfect bliss from within. It is like the waves of a large body of water, a lake or an ocean, ruffled and rolling on the surface, but the deep expanse of water underneath lies placid. Such bliss is infectious, and it transforms the devotees and the surroundings to a magnificent spiritual plane.

The discernible devotees, blessed by his grace, could find an aura around Guruji's crown. It is no wonder that we have occasionally witnessed the symbol OM on the left and right side of his cleanly shaved head, in the region between the ear and the area slightly above his forehead. It is not always manifested and not visible to all devotees. (Many a times, while doing acupressure, I would be curiously looking at his head to find the OM. Guruji used to look at me and give his enigmatic smile.)

Patanjali, in his Yoga Sutra (Vibhuti Pad III.41) says:

> The blazing radiance or inner energy is the outcome of the mastery of the trinity of Dharana, Dhyana and Samadhi by the enlightened Yogi or Sadhak. Self-effulgent radiance shines forth by itself when the yogi masters the knowledge and awakening of the energy located in the Manipura Chakra in the navel region.[1]

Can we ascribe the inner energy being reflected in Guruji's presence to such an outcome of God's grace or the years of *sadhana* during the many births or his current life? Guruji only knows!

The divine peace, calmness and serenity that epitomize Guruji would draw us to his place of stay like a magnet. Every day, we would look forward to finishing the day's engagements and rush to his abode. We would not think of any other engagement except going to Guruji's place. The friends, the kith and kin, professional colleagues, clubs and socialization would assume least importance. The unavoidable social engagements would be attended after taking leave from Guruji. Once, while Guruji had gone for his midnight walk in the by-lanes of the farmhouses of Sultanpur,

[1]'Yogasutra-3.34-pratibhadva', Shlokam, https://bit.ly/3jWO7xl. Accessed on 4 January 2023.

Deepak Chopra, the private secretary to Mr. L.K. Advani said, 'It is beyond our intelligent capacity to understand Guruji. Rather, we are quite confused about who he is. Nevertheless, every day, we are attracted to his presence, like a huge magnet pulling us to him.'

The Mumbaikar

One day the sangat hall in the villa at Empire Estate was full to the beam. DJ Uncle (Late Sardar Rajinder Singh, who oversaw the sound system to play the sabads, was fondly called by Guruji as DJ Uncle), was playing sabads one after another. A gentleman, who was not seen earlier in the sangat, was sitting in front of the washroom. I was sitting next to him. He was in meditation throughout. Suddenly, he shouted at the top of his voice as if he was Archimedes discovering the principles of floating. Everybody in the sangat got startled. However, Guruji was in his iconic serene and calm state, satchitanand manifested, sitting quietly. The gentleman regained his composure and requested to say something. Guruji hinted DJ Uncle to stop the playing of sabads. The gentleman said, 'Sangat ji! You are all blessed souls. Guruji is *sakshat parabrahma* (God incarnate). I could see him being surrounded by all the gods and demigods. I request you all to never ever leave such a mahapurush. I had heard about him from a devotee. I came all the way from Mumbai to have his darshan. I got his divine darshan here amongst you.'

Guruji listened to his satsang quietly without reacting. Langar was served and the gentleman left the hall after having langar and taking Guruji's permission. He was never seen again in Empire Estate or Bade Mandir, as far as my knowledge goes.

FRAGRANCES FROM THE TEN DWARS

Guruji's divinity always manifested in multifarious ways. It was universally experienced by most of the sangat that Guruji's body exudes beautiful fragrances. The sangat, who had the grace to press his feet or do acupressure on his palm, had the blessings of retaining Guruji's body fragrance in their palms and hands for a long time. A gush of fragrance would linger around each time Guruji would pass by someone; and this fragrance would stay for a considerable time.

Guruji used to say, 'My body has ten *dwars*, and you would find ten different fragrances for each part.' When Guruji would be in his mood, he would direct or allow a devotee to smell a part of his body to get the feel of the typical fragrance of that part of his body.

Abundance of Fragrances

The surge of the sangat was enormous for the narrow lanes surrounding the house of General Ahuja in Panchkula. For better facilitation of the sangat, Guruji shifted from Panchkula to Sector 33, Chandigarh, in the year 1997. Guruji allowed the institutionalized sangat system only a couple of days in the week. There were a few of them who were allowed every day. Similarly, a few would be allowed during the off-sangat hours. On one of those off-sangat moments, we were called to Guruji's place. When we reached there, a civil servant couple was already present there. The four of us were comfortably sitting in the retiring room of Guruji. While we were rendering sewa, Guruji engaged us in small talks about matters of government and other aspects of daily life. After a moment, Guruji got up and asked the female civil servant to smell a particular part of his body. She was surprised to get the fragrance of different kind than the usual fragrance of Guruji—a kind of a mix of a rose essence. Then Guruji asked us, one by one, to smell the same part of his body and savour the fragrance. That was not all. He directed us to smell various parts of his body. Each part was emitting a different fragrance. We had our heart's content in getting the essence of the distinctly different fragrances from several parts of Guruji's body.

When any devotee, far away from the physical presence of Guruji, genuinely sought his divine guidance and blessings, or connected with him by sincere reverence, the puran guru made his presence felt by sending (dispatching, radiating, remitting or broadcasting) a whiff of his body fragrance. This is an experience of many devotees and may be taken to be near universal. A typical fragrance (a kind of essence largely of rose) denoted his remote presence. It was not only a specific individual devotee for their exclusive internalization, but a group of family members or sangat that would get a chance to experience the fragrance. It was not an imaginary phenomenon or hallucination; rather, it was a real sensory experience mediated through the olfactory system. Later on, Guruji would corroborate his remote presence by telling during subsequent darshans that he was there present at that moment to bless or grace the sangat. Many a time, he would tell the sangat, '*Dekha, Guruji nuu yad kitta te main tohade kol haajar hoia* (See, you hailed Guruji, and I could not help but appear at your location),' or '*Main bhi uthe haazar si* (I was also present there).' It was common knowledge to the sangat that Guruji would be present anywhere through his strong will, and that presence would be in the form of his beautiful divine fragrance.

Guruji's body fragrance would have a lingering impact on his clothes and other accessories (shoes, socks, jutis, etc.) that he wore. He used to give away all his clothes, chola, T-shirts, kurta-pyjama, shirts, jutis, sneakers, among other items, to the blessed sangat. His fragrance would be felt on those clothes for years. Whenever he materialized sachkhand prasad, it would emanate a beautiful fragrance. If the blessed devotee is allowed to keep the prasad at home, the fragrance would be intact till it dematerializes, degenerates or gets used up.

Guru Nanak has described five realms or domains in Japji Sahib, a section of the Guru Granth Sahib. The five realms are Dharam Khand (the realm of righteousness), Gian Khand (the realm of right knowledge), Saram Khand (the realm of spiritual endeavor),

Karam Khand (the realm of grace) and Sach Khand (the realm of truth). Sach Khand is the final stage in the five realms, which is the realm of God—the Nirankar.

Pauri 37 of Sri Guru Granth Sahib (p. 8) states:

Sach khand vasai nirankra. Kar kar vekhani nadar nihal.

In the realm of Truth, the Formless Lord abides.
Having created the creation, He watches over it.
By His Glance of Grace, He bestows happiness.

The followers of Guruji have variously described a special kind of prasad produced out of nothing and distributed to the devotees present as a sachkhand prasad. It may be noted that Guruji might have materialized many things for his devotees as part of his supernatural powers or sidhis, but all such materializations are not deemed to be a sachkhand prasad; these are simply called Guruji's prasad.

Guruji would call one of the blessed devotees and ask him/her to open their palm. Guruji would open his palm that contained a small ball of a crystal-like *murabba* (marmalade). It is generally made of suji (semolina), mishri (rock sugar) and the like. The small ball of prasad would grow to completely cover the palm of Guruji within no time. The joined palms of the devotee would barely suffice to contain the entirety of the prasad. Such a prasad is full of a special kind of fragrance that lasts for eons. Guruji used to distribute a small piece of such a prasad to each of the sangat present.

There are numerous instances narrated by individual devotees how they could actually experience Guruji's presence in the form of his typical fragrance at locations far away, even in foreign countries, away from Guruji. And such a presence was not only because of the prayers of the devotees; it was Guruji's own volition (his leela, mauz, love and affection for the devotee) as to where and when he would make his presence felt to individuals or a group of devotees. This unique ability of a puran guru of being physically present simultaneously at more than one location is described as *Manaḥ-javah (manojvitva)* by the ancient sages. Even after Guruji had left his physical body on 30 May 2007, several devotees still experience his divine presence in the form of his fragrance, confirming Guruji's cosmic presence.

Bhavesh's Realization of Divinity

Bhavesh Pandey, Colonel Joshi's nephew, was initially cynical about the supernatural powers of Guruji. He was a regular at Empire Estate and was enjoying the serene atmosphere in the company of devotees with a positive vibe, the soothing sabads and the cocktail of prasads. Though he enjoyed the satsangs rendered by the devotees describing the blessings and supernatural abilities of Guruji, he was sceptical about them, rationalizing these as coincidences and happenstances.

One day, he was returning home from his office in Manesar. It was late in the night and the Delhi–Jaipur highway was full of long-haul-goods trucks from far-off places like Mumbai, Surat, Nasik and Pune. Suddenly, a street dog darted out of nowhere and collided with his bike. Despite the impact, he did not lose balance and managed to steer ahead. Had he tripped, it could have been fatal, as heavy trucks were speeding on both sides. At that moment, he felt a draught of Guruji's fragrance and could feel it for a couple of minutes. He could sense Guruji's presence in the hour of reckoning. Was it Guruji who steered him to safety? Bhavesh was sure it was Guruji; and since then, his cynicism about the supernatural powers of Guruji dissipated and Bhavesh had no doubt about the divinity of Guruji.

HE IS THERE; HE IS NOT THERE

Most of the time, when Guruji would not be engaged in conversation with any sangat and the hall would be riveting with the sabads of Gurbani, with the sangat engaged in their own way of contemplation or wavering thoughts (depending on the level of spiritual maturity, devotion and sincerity), it would be observed that Guruji would be in a different world. It was like he was there (his physical body) and also not there (mentally, he would be engrossed elsewhere), as if he was in constant communion with some higher authority—the Supreme Being—while his presence would be radiating the divine light in its entire splendour. The atmosphere would be radiating with high-octane energy filled with love and divine benevolence. The sangat used to relish this spark of divinity and its resonance. Guruji has been the manifestation of the divine light to the world in this exciting time. He raised the spiritual level of humanity under a new paradigm of living.

DIVINE LOVE AND COMPASSION

Guruji is the embodiment of the enlightened soul that radiates divinity all around. The divinity is not a momentary state but perpetual, which is the essence of Guruji's existence. It is the constant state of an enlightened soul in communion with the Supreme Soul in all states of consciousness—awake, sleep, dream and samadhi. Such an enlightenment is characterized by pure awareness that is free from the chattering mind, constantly connecting with the infinite. Here, he is the embodiment of love, joy, gratitude and truly living in a beautiful state. In this state, he radiates divine energy like the bright morning rays of the sun falling on everything, without discrimination. It is like the *paavan* (sacred) Ganga of love and affection emanating from the head of Lord Shiva, multiplying into thousands of divine streams reaching to sangat, near and far.

Patanjali, in Yoga Sutra (Vibhuti Pad III.34) says, '*Pratibhad va sarvam*', which translates to 'By the power of Pratibha all knowledge.' The meaning given is, 'When a person has risen to a high state of Pratibha (enlightenment from purity), then he has that great light. All things are apparent to him. Everything comes to him naturally, without making samyama on anything.'[2]

When a spiritual seeker attains Kaivalyam Samadhi (as per the Yoga Sutra) or the *kundalini* rises and resides in the Sahasrara Chakra (Crown Chakra, located at the top of the head), eternal bliss is realized by the sadhak. Such a realized soul is the embodiment of godliness and is free from the illusion of the duality between the *atman* and *Paramatman*. He identifies himself with the Lord. Jagadguru Adi Shankaracharya succinctly puts it through his composition of Atmashatakam when he describes the perpetual state of such a realization. The enlightened person loses his individuality as it has merged with the Supreme Soul. At that stage, he does not identify himself through his intelligence, ego or sensory inputs mediated through the five elements (*panchtattva*) which constitute the material existence. He has risen beyond hatred, attachment, greed, infatuation, pride, envy and jealousy. At that stage, he is neither bound by righteousness (*dharma*) or material wealth nor does he desire anything—including liberation. He attains the stage of *sthitaprajna* when he is not bound by the dualities of joys and sorrows, merits and demerits, objects to see and be seen, and the like. For him, the sacred hymns, the sacred pilgrimage, the sacred scriptures or austerities hold no meaning or importance. He has risen above the phenomena of death, fear and worldly distinctions of caste, community and race. He has no family, no birth, no friends, no guru. He identifies himself with the Eternal Being who is without any variation, and without any form, neither attached to anything nor detached from anything. Such a mahayogi is the realization of the *'cidānandarūpaḥ śivo'ham śivo'ham* (ever pure blissful consciousness)'

As Ramakrishna Paramahansa says, 'As the glow of dawn heralds the rising sun, unselfishness, purity and righteousness announce the advent of the Lord (within oneself).'[33]

Guruji, the enlightened mahapurush, was born with

[2]Ibid.

[3]'Sayings by Sri Ramakrishna—Chapter 19: The Man of Divine Realization', GreatMaster.Info, https://bit.ly/3X7SQKZ. Accessed on 5 January 2023.

spiritual attainment and supernatural powers. The supernatural powers were never demonstrated by effort. Those manifested spontaneously by divine volition. Because of this enlightened state, he remains in a relaxed heartfelt authentic communication with everyone he met, in a way that is grounded in compassion, love and a state of emotional liberation. In this enlightened state, he feels, sees and experiences a divine quality in everything and everyone, because he is living in deep spiritual connection with the Divine Universal Intelligence. The most important divine powers of 'love and compassion to all' and 'alleviating the sufferings' (physiological, material and psychic) of mankind are amply evident from numerous satsangs rendered by devotees who come into contact with Guruji by his divine grace.

Whenever the devotees or others went to Guruji to pay their respects, Guruji would greet them with a *namaste*, which is the recognition of the divine in the person you are greeting. God resides in everybody. When you do namaste, it is as if you are uttering, 'I honor the divine in you. I see that you are a unique expression of God and that we are one.'

The enlightened Guruji radiates great warmth towards everyone. Every word spoken by him and every action taken by him comes from his heart beaming with love, peace and empathy because he is always connected with the Infinite Spiritual Essence. This manifests in his usual saying '*Kalyan kitta* (blessings always).' In the Yoga Sutra (Vibhuti Pad III.23), it is said that the enlightened person, through his yogic attainments, gets the unique qualities like friendliness, compassion or sympathetic joy, and he also imbibes the same traits in others. Guruji is the embodiment of all these traits on account of his spiritual and yogic attainment. He could imbibe the same qualities and traits.

The Vibhuti Pad of the Yoga Sutra describes various supernatural powers acquired by mahayogis due to their sadhana (grace of God). Guruji's sangat have witnessed such expression and exhibition of supernatural powers on numerous occasions. With the pinnacle of spiritual attainment, Guruji, the enlightened master, has the supernatural ability or power to read what is going on in the minds of the suffering person, the ability to have the extraordinary visualization of the tiniest cells and organs inside one's body; the extraordinary power of destruction and regeneration of the cell bodies and organs; the supernatural power of healing and the like. These are in conjunction with the extraordinary and godly qualities of empathizing with others and extending the divine grace to alleviate the suffering of humanity and living beings. As it has been stated in the Bible in Matthew 8:16–17,

> They brought to Him many who were demon-possessed. And He cast out the spirits with a word, and healed all who were sick, that it might be fulfilled which was spoken by Isaiah the prophet, saying: 'He Himself took our infirmities and bore our sicknesses.

The compassion and empathy of Guruji manifests in alleviating the physiological (ailments, disease), physical (deformities) and mental sufferings of people. There are innumerable accounts given by the sangat on how they have been blessed by Guruji and recovered from their physiological, physical and psychological sufferings. We will describe some of our own experiences in the next chapter.

Guruji's blessings are non-discriminatory; the universal Divine Love is for everybody. This results in a beautiful phenomenon—each and every one would feel that Guruji is too close to them. His blessings are for all the children of God—the sinners, the powerful, the weak, the rich, the poor, the man of the street, the yogi and the like.

GURUJI, THE MAHAPURUSH

Guruji would never say directly that he is a mahapurush or puran guru. But he would indirectly impute their characteristics by making statements like:

> *Mahapurush ki honda hai, tuhanu ki pata?*
>
> What do you know who is a mahapurush?
>
> *Mahapurush aimei hunde hai? Pooran Guru ki honda hai? Tuhanu na Mahapurush na Pooran Guru pehchan hoia.*
>
> Do people become a mahapurush like that? What do you know about puran guru? The sangat here do not recognize a mahapurush or a puran guru.

He would also invoke the Avatar Principle, dropping hints in third person:

> *Asi to light to aye hain, light nu chal jawange.*
>
> We have come from the Divine Light and we will go back to that divinity.
>
> *Mahapurush da maksad hai lokanu rab de naal jodna.*
>
> The purpose of a mahapurush is to connect people with the Supreme Godhead.

Guruji was neither used to preaching nor was he a verbose master in love with his own voice. There were rare occasions when he would be at his spontaneous best and would say a few pithy words and sentences. However, the discerning devotees could impute the true meanings of such pithy hints. Just because a million followers believe that he is divinity incarnated, the world at large would not accept that. His utterances apart, the exertions, the life of Guruji and his ways amply demonstrated his divinity. It is only the true seeker of spiritual enlightenment who could recognize him as a mahapurush.

THE PURUSHA TATTVA

Purusha is the Cosmic Being, the Absolute or the Supreme Self. The concept of the purusha has been elucidated in the Rig Veda, the Upanishads and the Bhagavad Gita, as explained below:

> Purusha Suktam is an important part of Rigveda (10.7.90.1–16) and is often recited during the worship of the Sri Vishnu or Narayana. It is also mentioned in the Taittiriya Aranyaka (3.12,13), the Vajasaneyi Samhita (31.1–6), the Samaveda Samhita (6.4), and the Atharvaveda Samhita (19.6). Some parts of Purusha Sukta are also explained in the Shatapatha Brahman, the Taittiriya Brahmana, and the Shvetashvatara Upanishad. Purusha Sukta is also mentioned in the Bhagavata Purana (2.5.35 to 2.6.1–29) and in the Mahabharata (Mokshadharma Parva 351 and 352).[4]

The purusha in the Vedas refers to the Cosmic Man, Super Consciousness or the Universal Principle.

In the Samkhya School of theology, there exist two original principles whose interrelations is the cause of the universe—purusha, the inactive, and prakirti, the active. Purusha is the immobile, immutable and self-luminous 'pure consciousness of being'. Prakriti is the divine energy and its process. Purusha is not involved in any activity but reflects the action of energy in conscious activities and phenomena like creation, conservation, dissolution, birth and life, death, consciousness, unconsciousness, sensory knowledge, intellectual knowledge and ignorance, action, inaction, happiness and suffering.[5] Prakriti is everything that has changed, can change and is subject to cause and effect. Purusha is the unchanging and uncaused Universal Principle.

The Mandukya Upanishad beautifully talks about the purusha and prakriti by citing the famous parable of two birds perched on the same branch:

> *Dvā suparṇā sayujā sakhāyā samānaṃ vṛkṣaṃ pariṣasvajāte.*
> *Tayoranyaḥ pippalaṃ svādvattyanaśnannanyo abhicākaśīti.*

> Two inseparable companions of fine plumage perch on

[4]Ramesh, 'Purusha Suktam Explains the Nature of Purusha or Cosmic Being', VedicFeed, 10 April 2020, https://bit.ly/3QlBY12. Accessed on 5 January 2023.
[5]Aurobindo, Sri, *Essays on the Gita: Volume 19*, Sri Aurobindo Ashram Trust, 1997, p. 70.

> the self-same tree. One of the two feeds on the delicious fruit. The other not tasting of it looks on.[6]

Swami Krishnananda explains the shloka beautifully:

> There are two birds in this tree of life. This tree of life may be either this body of the individual, or it may be the entire creation itself.
>
> Ishvara (God) and Jiva (living beings) are present in the world of creation as well as in the human body. They are friends. They are inseparable siblings, one connected with the other perpetually. These are compared to birds living on a single tree which is this vast creation. And they enjoy their existence on the tree.
>
> The only difference is, one of these birds is busy enjoying the delicious fruit that is of the tree and the other bird is not interested in eating anything. It is merely looking on, unconcerned and unattached.
>
> This unattached bird is God, Ishvara, seated in your own heart and everywhere in this world. The bird that is eating the sweet fruit of this tree is the individual soul, the mind-body complex. So there are two phases of experience going on in one's own body: a consciousness that is totally detached, and a consciousness that is very much involved.[7]

The purusha in the Gita is also the Lord of nature; he is Ishvara. If the operation of intelligent will belongs to nature, the origination and power of the will proceeds from the conscious soul—the Lord of nature. He is not only the witness, but the Lord and knower, master of knowledge and will. He is the supreme cause of action of the prakriti and the supreme cause of withdrawal from action. Purusha is the universal principle that is unchanging and uncaused but is omnipresent, omnipotent and the reason why

---

[6]Sastri, S. Sitarama, *Mundaka Upanishad with Shankara's Commentary*, Wisdom Library, 1905, https://bit.ly/3Qg8u4Z. Accessed on 5 January 2023.

[7]'A Story of Two Birds—Quote from Mandukya Upanishad', ReSankrit, 16 May 2019, https://bit.ly/3WR5JcO. Accessed on 5 January 2023.

the prakriti changes, evolves throughout time and why there is a cause and effect. Purusha, whose greatness for all this creation can be described as *Brahman*—the *Purushottam*.[8]

Hence, from the inactive, immobile, immutable and self-luminous 'pure consciousness of being' of the Samkhya theology, the Bhagavad Gita has succinctly elevated the purusha to being unchanging, uncaused but omnipresent, omnipotent and the Lord of nature—the reason why the prakriti changes, evolves all the time and why there is a cause and effect.

When Guruji used to refer to the mahapurush, should we have interpreted as per the spiritual traditions mentioned above that which purusha refers to the Cosmic Self or Cosmic Consciousness, or are we to take the literal meaning of a great personality? It is up to the devotees to accept him as they find appropriate.

SHIVOHAM

Patanjali's Yoga Sutra talks about the pinnacle of yogic spiritual attainment variously called Nirbikalpa or Kaivalya Samadhi. Once a person reaches this stage, he attains godliness—eternal bliss and freedom from the illusion of duality—the distinction between the individual soul (*atman*) and the Supreme Soul (*Paramatman*). He identifies himself with the Lord. As Hymn 16 of Isha Upanishad says, '*Puruṣaḥ so'ham asmi* (I am He, the purusha within thee; or I am the Param Purusha who resides in you).'

The ardent followers of Guruji consider him as an incarnation of Lord Shiva. Should we literally or figuratively put him as Lord Shiva or should we ascribe many of the divine manifestations of Guruji as akin to Lord Shiva—the mahayogi or *adiyogi*?

The true guru or puran guru is equated with God (Lord Shiva). The Guru Gita (Shloka 20) says:

[8]'Sankhya and Yoga', Bhagavad Gita, https://bit.ly/3GL7jYb. Accessed on 5 January 2023.

> *Yo guruḥ sa śivaḥ prokto yaḥ śivaḥ sa guruḥ smṛtaḥ.*
>
> He who is the Guru is Shiva Himself, so declare the scriptures, and the fact that Shiva is the Guru, is reminded to us in all the Smritis.[9]

Adi Shankaracharya begins Guru Paduka Stotram (verses to the Guru) with equating the Guru to the trinity of Brahma (The Creator), Vishnu (The Preserver) and Maheshwara (The Constructive Destroyer). Further in Atmastakam, he states that the yogi or guru, who is fully liberated and has realized God, attributes himself as:

> *Cidānandarūpaḥ śivo'ham śivo'ham.*
>
> I am the Ever Pure Blissful Consciousness—I am the eternal Shiva, I am the eternal Shiva.

All the characteristics of a realized soul are found in Guruji. The testimonies are the satsangs of numerous sangat who came across Guruji during his lifetime. So, can we interpret the saying of Guruji in the sense the Guru Gita equates a puran guru with Lord Shiva? Or can we interpret it from Adi Shankaracharya's invocation that a realized soul does not find the duality of the self and Supreme Self (Lord Shiva)? Again, it is left to the discerning disciples and readers to put context to the invocation of the concept of mahapurush by revered Guruji.

---

[9]'Who Is the Guru? Who Is Worthy of Receiving Brahma Vidya?' IndiaSpirituality, 4 June 2013, https://bit.ly/3vFbLBk. Accessed on 4 January 2023.

3

Assuaging with Compassion and Healing

Guruji is the human manifestation of the healing power of compassion. He cures the individual of his sufferings in the blink of an eye. The relieving compassion manifests in a split second. Such healings include alleviating the physiological ailments and disease, remedying physical deformities and eliminating mental sufferings of people.

When Guruji's grace falls on a person, it be a devotee or non-devotee, all the power which are integral to Guruji's essence, flow like streams of the pure Ganges, purifying the person beyond his own imagination.

Such a true spiritual healing is the reflection of the grace of a highly realized and enlightened spiritual master. It embodies a process involving invocation of a number of supernatural powers. Guruji, the Enlightened Master, has several extraordinary or supernatural abilities and powers as described in the Vibhuti Pad of Patanjali's Yoga Sutra. These include, among other things, the power to read what is going on in the minds of the suffering individual; the ability to have the extraordinary visualization of the tiniest cells and organs inside one's body (microscopic vision); and the supernatural power of destruction and regeneration of body cells and organs (materialization and dematerialization). All these powers, in conjunction with the godly qualities of empathy, love and compassion, are arrayed as an assortment to be termed as the supernatural power of healing.

The invocation of these supernatural powers for healing may be in singular form, a combination of some of the powers or may be a combination of all. It depends on the specific ailment, level of suffering and, of course, the grace of the Enlightened Master.

THE PROFOUND STILLNESS

An important factor for the healing to occur is the vital process of making the mind still. A healthy mind is a prerequisite for a healthy body. But at the same time, the mind is the nest for all the ghosts, the wavering thoughts, which lead us to poor physical and mental health.

For ages, spiritual masters have advised devotees to attain stillness of the wavering mind. Stillness may be attained in a fraction of a second by a spiritually elevated soul like Guruji, or by years of sadhana comprising austerities, disciplines, yoga, pranayama, meditation, etc.

By the grace of Guruji, the devotees and non-devotees are guided to a degree of stillness which, in turn, helps accelerate the healing of their bodily and mental ailments. But it sometimes manifests in a simpler and less spectacular manner. The complete surrender, sincere devotion and the grace of Guruji's divine energy create the positive valence (because an entity that attracts the individual has positive valence, whereas one that repels has negative one) for connection with the Supreme Lord.

The divine energy, the flow of love and compassion of Guruji, the cocktail of blessings comprising chai prasad, soulful sabads from the Gurubani, langar prasad, satsangs, and the light mood from the folk and Sufi songs during the langar and afterwards deliberate the wavering minds to a certain degree of stillness and connectivity with the divinity. Like an enhancing tool, a positive frame of mind under Guruji's fold enhances the efficacy of the medicines that are at times not effective. The assurances of the enlightened master that nothing untoward would happen create the protective umbrella for the suffering soul. '*Kalyan kitta* (you are blessed)', '*Jaa aishe kar* (go and enjoy)' are some of the reassuring words that fill the mortal soul with vigour and energy to revive.

THE UNCONDITIONAL AFFECTION

People suffering from physical and physiological ailments and diseases often also suffer from a lack of love and affection from their near and dear ones. The inadequacy of a social support system compounds the physical sufferings. Ailments and diseases may be considered from a biopsychosocial perspective, where within the systemic framework, any modifications in one dimension may lead to complications in others.

A suffering individual needs love and affection, and the inadequacy of such psychosocial support may lead to negative emotions, like anxiety, rage or sadness and depression. Even a normal and healthy person may develop emotional problems due to the lack of love and affection. It often leads to psychological stress impacting in physical ailments, like hypertension, psychosomatic disorders like alexithymia or a deterioration, in already existing physical ailments. It also leads to the ineffectiveness of medicine, in any system. Be it Allopathic, Ayurvedic, Homeopathic, Unani, or any other traditional system, every therapy is bound to be influenced by this factor. In other words, the suffering individual encounters a psychosocial void—not to mention a spiritual void, depending on the spiritual orientation and attainment.

Guruji is the epitome of love and affection to all—irrespective of the devotion or the absence of it, and irrespective of their social standing. This love is irrespective of caste, creed or religion. An elevated master like Guruji and the associated systems readily fill this vacuum. Here, we are not speaking of the spiritual or supernatural powers of such elevated masters as yet.

Guruji used to say, '*Doctor apna kam karanga, main apna* (Let the doctors do their duty, I will perform mine).' Essentially, his gift for us includes his blessings, love and affection.

COMPASSION, THE HEAVENLY VIRTUE

The spiritual healing witnessed with Guruji's blessings is beyond the so-called commercial practices peddled by many spiritual marketers today. It is far above, and far sacred than the profane, mundane and commercial healing practices hawked in the form of Reiki, Shiatsu, Acupuncture, Acupressure, Healing Touch, Therapeutic Touch, Faith Healing, Aura Healing, Past Life Therapy, Visualization, Kinesiology, Hypnotherapy, Psychotherapy and other such plethora of methods.

The suffering may be physical, psychological or both. Guruji touches the soul of the suffering individual and works towards alleviating the suffering. The phenomenon is something akin to reading the suffering individual's mind. It is like having the microscopic vision of each and every healthy or diseased cell. The feats of regeneration of cells, like creating fallopian tubes not existing earlier, materialization of cells and tissues, destruction of diseased cells, like the dematerialization or destroying of cancerous cells, superfluous growths in ears or lumps anywhere in the body, are few of the manifestations of divinity witnessed by many.

The omniscient guru does not need the suffering individual's actual verbal rendering of the accounts of his sufferings. He knows. He understands.

Highly evolved souls like Guruji feel a sort of spiritual calling to ease the sufferings of people, animals and nature. Such enlightened persons are able to shift unseen divine energy for the greater good of the collective. They are people who allow the energy of divinity to flow through them in a way that guides, rejuvenates and empowers others.

THE MYRIAD DIVINE WAYS OF HEALING

Healing without Medical Interventions

Operation Room, Spoons and Betel Leaves

From the early days of the manifestation of divinity, Guruji had used various methods of treatment for suffering individuals. During his days in Jalandhar, Guruji jokingly designated one room in the mandir as the 'operation room'. The suffering individual would be taken to that room and made to lie on the bed. Guruji used to get a spoon and run it through the ailing body part of the individual. He would utter some mantras and then go on to prescribe some remedies or prescribe nothing at all, depending on the state of the ailing person. And his words would prove prophetic every time: '*Jao, kalyan kitta* (Go, you are blessed).'

Another method used by Guruji was the application of betel leaves on the suffering individual. He would direct the person or the family members to fetch a specific number of betel leaves. He would combine the process of running the spoon on the body and then apply the betel leaves on the affected part, invoking or uttering his silent prayers or mantras. The following are some instances of the application of the non-amusing ways of Guruji's treatment of the body and soul of the suffering individual.

Gitan Grewal, Jalandhar (1996)

Gitan was the daughter of Mrs Nirmal Kaur and granddaughter of Late Sardar Umrao Singh, Member of Parliament, from Jalandhar. Gitan's family members (parents, grandparents and others from the extended family) were the earliest devotees (early 1980s) of Guruji.

Gitan was 15 years old in 1996. One fine morning, she felt excruciating pain in her abdomen. It was unbearable and she was unable to remain stable in one place. The family tried locating Guruji as a first resort and traced him to Panchkula. They immediately planned to visit Guruji. Before that, they had gone through medical investigations at PGI, Chandigarh, and private labs as advised by the doctors. It was found that she had a cyst in her ovary and it had burst, spreading abscess all around and it could have led to blood poisoning.

The doctors at PGI advised her to undergo a surgery to remove the remainder of the cyst and also to drain out the abscess. But Guruji had his own ways of blessing his devotees. He ordered five betel leaves and placed them on her abdomen, uttering silent mantras. She was told to lie down in that position for 15 minutes. After Guruji's procedure, they were ordered to carry out the tests again. The doctors in PGI were astonished to find no trace of the abscess inside her abdomen. They heard about the grace and blessings of Guruji, and the doctors became keen to have Guruji's darshan. Subsequently some of them came to Guruji's sangat and became his ardent devotees.

Dr Shashi Ahuja (1995), *Ms Anita Verma* (1992) *and Mrs Lalita Mathur* (1998)

There are several testimonials of devotees getting cured of ailments during the Jalandhar and Panchkula–Chandigarh days of Guruji by similar methods. We have already described the treatment using betel leaves for the suspected peptic ulcer of Dr Shashi Ahuja in the mid-1990s in the Jalandhar 'operation room'. Mrs Anita Verma, who developed chronic knee pain, could not be cured through the application of medications from all the known systems of medicine. When she went to Guruji and prayed for relief, Guruji brought a spoon and placed it on her knee. The pain vanished instantaneously, and it never came back. Similarly, Mrs Lalita Mathur, spouse of Mr S.B. Mathur, IAS of J&K cadre, was suffering from low-grade fever for a considerable period, and the doctors were suspecting cancer or tuberculosis. Guruji blessed the betel leaves in his characteristic way and advised them to put these on the forehead of Mrs Mathur to keep them overnight. The low-grade fever disappeared overnight, and there was no need for any further medical procedure.

Kiran Sood (1997)

The Soods are ardent followers of Guruji. At a time when hardly any sangat were allowed to have the darshan of Guruji, they were the only few who rendered daily sewa to him.

One day, just before the rush hour of sangat, Guruji was sitting on his aasan in the sangat hall. A couple of the sangat had already taken their positions, reclining against the walls to make themselves comfortable. He signalled Kiran to come close to his aasan. Suddenly, he got up and ordered a spoon. The spoon was promptly fetched from the kitchen. He ordered her to lie on her back, and asked her to raise the kameez from the waist and untie the string of her salwar. She was feeling embarrassed and her face turned pink. Nevertheless, she did as Guruji ordered. Guruji held the spoon and moved it on her belly at the navel region a couple of times and then said, '*Jao, kalyan kitta* (Go, you are blessed).' As she confided with us, the problem was serious. That is the way Guruji used to conduct 'operations' to cure ailments. A spoon and the betel leaves were his instruments of diagnosis and treatment. Many a sangat and non-sangat have been blessed by Guruji this way in Jalandhar and in the tricity of Chandigarh-Mohali-Panchkula.

Pouring Salted Water through the Nose

Colonel (Retd) Chatterjee, Gurgaon

On one occasion, Colonel Chatterjee was running a high fever, with a headache. Guruji used to drop in at their place occasionally. It was a coincidence that when Guruji came to their house, Colonel Chatterjee had already summoned a doctor. The doctor prescribed some medicine and told him that it would take a couple of days for his recovery. However, Guruji asked for a spoon, salt and water. The salt was mixed with water in the spoon and the solution was poured into his nose. The impact was the instantaneous cleaning of the nasal passage by draining the liquid out of his nose. After Guruji's procedure, the doctor was asked to take the Colonel's temperature again. To everybody's surprise, the temperature reading came out normal, while moments earlier the doctor had recorded 103-degree Fahrenheit. The running nose, nausea, headache and fever disappeared within no time.

Rudraksha Mala and Amrit

Mrs Gill, Spouse of Justice (Retd) A.S. Gill (1987)

In 1987, Mrs Gill was diagnosed with an internal tumour that was suspected of malignancy. The doctors advised for immediate operation to remove the growth and prevent further malignancy. The operation date was also finalized. As ardent devotees of Guruji, the Gills came to Guruji's durbar seeking his blessings for a successful operation. However, Guruji gave amrit to Mrs Gill to drink and told them that there was no need for any operation. He blessed her and told she would be all right. The Gills had full confidence in him. They did not go for the surgery. Instead, they enjoyed the satsang with the Divinity and savoured the offering of prasads in Guruji's durbar. Mrs Gill did not have any problem thereafter. The tumour neither grew in size nor replicated elsewhere and gradually disappeared. After two years, when she had a stomach pain, the Gills went for a repeat test to ascertain whether the tumour had resurfaced. But the test results came out negative. By Guruji's blessings, Mrs Gill was cured of the suspected cancerous growth.

Eating the Blessed Chapatis from the Hands of Guruji

During the Jalandhar and Greater Kailash days, Guruji used to bless the suffering individuals by serving langar, particularly chapatis, himself. Sometimes, it was an extra offering of chapatis even after the regular langar. There are several testimonials of devotees who were cured of chronic and serious ailments by this method.

Ms Joga Cheena, the daughter of Mr Cheena, a senior bureaucrat from Punjab, was regularly visiting Guruji at Jalandhar Mandir. They would drive down to Jalandhar from Chandigarh and return back after the darshan of Guruji and having langar. Ms Joga was suffering from severe migraine from early childhood, and it persisted till adulthood. One day, when she was in Jalandhar Mandir, she had a severe migraine attack. She prayed silently to Guruji to cure her of the debilitating migraine. Guruji read her mind and fetched four chapatis. Handing over the chapatis to her, he told her that she should eat the chapatis and her migraine would disappear for good. Ms Joga was not in any condition to consume the chapatis in the midst of the migraine attack. She managed to eat three and put the fourth one surreptitiously in her purse while Guruji had gone to his resting room for a while. When Guruji returned to the sangat hall, the Cheenas took leave from Guruji and proceeded to Chandigarh.

They came back to Jalandhar Mandir after a couple of weeks for Guruji's darshan and blessings. Guruji asked Ms Joga how her migraine problem was. She replied that it was 90 per cent cured. Guruji rebuked her that it could have been 100 per cent had she eaten all the four chapatis. Why did she put the fourth one in her purse without eating it in the mandir as was told by Guruji? Ms Joga was stupefied as to how did Guruji get to know that she had put the fourth chapati in her purse, as he was in his resting room when she did it surreptitiously. Guruji knew about it all this time.

Drinking Water from a Blessed Copper Tumbler

During the Chandigarh and Empire Estate days, Guruji would prescribe the method of the copper tumbler, called *lota* in Hindi, for curing diseases. He would invariably ask the suffering individual to bring a copper tumbler, purchased with their own money. Guruji would bless the tumbler by invoking some mantra only known to him. The suffering individual would be asked to fill the tumbler with water every night before going to bed. Next morning, the first thing he had to do was to drink half of the water from the tumbler. The remainder half was to be used for bathing purposes. The tumbler was to be properly cleaned, not with soap or detergent, but with ash.

There are numerous testimonials in the book *Light of Divinity* compiled and edited by Jitendra Pant (Jeetu), a devotee with the blessings and knowledge of Guruji. These testimonials have been heard by the sangat, including myself, in the presence of Guruji. The testimonials of Colonel Madan regarding the opening of a blocked artery; Mrs Lamba, spouse of Mr Satish Lamba (Retd IAS), describing the opening of a blocked artery of Mrs Singh, spouse of Mr Ajit Singh (IPS) obviating open heart surgery; the cure of the severe back pain of bedridden son of Shri B.B. Chaudhuri; curing of severe knee pain and rheumatism of the mother-in-law of Mr Kanwar Lal; and the curing of severe depression of Mrs Kanwar Lal are a few examples of the healing of serious ailments and sufferings through the tumbler treatment by Guruji. Here, I describe testimonials of two devotees whom I know quite intimately.

Usha Singh, Singapore/USA (1998-99)

Mrs Usha Singh and her family were residing in Singapore. Their daughter was suffering from chronic asthma. It was so severe that they could not have any flowers in their house. The child would get serious asthmatic attacks if she played outside (she was allergic to pollens or spores from grasses and flowering trees). She was almost deprived of a normal childhood. Most of the time, she was on steroids and nebulizers. The doctors told them that there was no permanent solution to this kind of asthmatic problem. They tried all medicines prescribed by the experts of alternative medicines including homeopathic, ayurvedic, etc. They even went for fish therapy propounded by one Hyderabad-based *vaid*.

On one of their visits to India, they came to know about Guruji from Mr Prakash Singh (IPS), their own relative. They accompanied Mr Prakash Singh and his wife to Empire Estate and paid their respects to Guruji. When Mrs Usha Singh was paying her respects, to her astonishment, Guruji himself opened up about her family's details. When she broached the subject of her daughter's suffering, Guruji said, '*Jaa, teri beti da kaliyan kitta* (Be happy, I have blessed your daughter).'

Mrs Usha Singh was not convinced. How come without even examining the child, without doing anything, Guruji could just said that? They were advised to get the copper tumbler. After blessing it, they were told to follow the usual procedures—pour water in the tumbler before going to bed; drink half the water from the tumbler in the morning after getting up from bed; use the remainder for bathing; and clean the tumbler without using soap or detergent. They were also advised to get a pendant in the form of the 'Om' symbol. Guruji blessed the pendant and advised their daughter to wear it for 51 days. The daughter had full confidence in Guruji. She knew she had found the right person and understood that her salvation from disease and psychological trauma laid with Guruji. She dutifully observed the directions. When she forgot to take away the pendant after the completion of 51 days, the pendant kept falling off automatically, despite her repeated attempts to fix it. Then she realized, after looking at the calendar, that 51 days had already elapsed.

They had Guruji's darshan in December 1998. By the first week of January 1999, there was considerable improvement in her asthma problem. Even the daughter, who was earlier not allowed outdoor activities, went on a school tour to Australia and enjoyed all the activities, without any recurrence of asthmatic attacks. After the trip, the Singhs found that the asthma had been taken care of completely. It never came back.

Disappearance of Asthma of Amlaan (Mumbai/USA)

Amlaan (Richie, to family members) was suffering from asthma for a long time. He was in Singapore for nearly five years before relocating to New Delhi to take admission in a CBSE school. His father was about to complete his foreign posting at SBI, Singapore, and Richie had to come earlier to be at his uncle's place in Delhi to enable him for school admission. During his stay in Delhi, he developed a serious asthmatic problem. After his parents came to Mumbai, Richie joined them there. But his problem became so severe that he had to be hospitalized in a nursing home. He had to be administered oxygen and a nebulizer to relieve him of the discomfort from having severe breathing problems. Despite hospitalization, Richie's condition was not improving significantly. When Mr Sahu (his uncle) mentioned to Guruji about Richies's problem, he suggested remedies, and Richie got the relief from the illness and was soon discharged from the hospital. During one of the darshans, his mother again mentioned about the recurring asthmatic problem to Guruji. Guruji asked them to bring the copper tumbler and blessed it in his usual manner. Richie followed the procedure for a month and his problem, boiling over many years, finally disappeared.

Chai Prasad, Nimbu Paani and Sweets

On other occasions, Guruji would direct a suffering individual just to have chai, langar prasad or other form of prasad like sweets, dry fruits, mishri, berries, etc., being distributed by him. They would be told that their ailments would disappear.

The Divine Chai Prasad (1996)

One day, I had to go to Delhi for an official meeting. My wife Urvashi expressed her desire to accompany me to meet her sister. Before embarking on the journey, we thought it would be appropriate to seek the blessings of Guruji. That day, I had a hectic schedule in the office, as I had to complete a number of tasks. So, when I reached home, and since it was already late, I hurriedly finished lunch. We rushed to the Ahuja's residence in Panchkula to seek Guruji's blessings. By the time we reached Guruji's place, I had already developed a severe headache. I was worried that the headache might turn into a migraine and would persist during our journey to Delhi and the journey would be a nightmare. I had had similar experiences of road sickness and vomiting on several journeys in the past.

Guruji was resting in a room on the ground floor. He asked me to come to sit beside his bed. He entreated Mammi (General Mohan Singh's wife) to prepare tea and offered the chai prasad to us. I was sipping the chai slowly and could feel the headache receding gradually. By the time the tea was finished, the headache was completely gone. Guruji looked at me and gave his laconic smile. We took permission from Guruji to leave and had the most pleasant road journey to Delhi.

Chhavi and Sumeet Jethra (2005)

Chhavi and Sumeet, after two years of their marriage, planned to start a family. After failing to conceive, Chhavi and her husband went for all sorts of medical examinations. She had some problem with her fallopian tube, giving her only a 25 per cent chance to conceive. The problem was compounded when it was found that Sumeet had a low sperm count. They were contemplating IVF, but not proceeding with the procedure yet because of the low success rate. They went to seek Guruji's blessings where he emphatically suggested to go ahead with the procedure with divine assurance of definite success. On the New Year's Eve of 2005, when Guruji was distributing sweet prasad in Bade Mandir, Chhavi was told, *'Ja, tainu dawai ditti* (I have given you my medicinal blessings).' On 13 February 2005, Chhavi got the good news that the treatment was successful. She went through some trouble like haemorrhaging, for which the doctors prescribed heavy doses of medicine. She also contracted jaundice. Despite all these, by Guruji's grace, her pregnancy went well. Guruji predicted that she will deliver on 21 October, contrary to the dates given by the doctors. She delivered beautiful twins on that appointed date! They went to Guruji, seeking his blessings. Guruji named the twins, Arjun and Gauri.

Mrs Krishna Sethi, Vasant Kunj (2000)

Mr Gopal Sethi was working as a senior executive in one of the premier textile companies in India. Mrs Krishna, Gopal

Uncle's wife, was suffering from tubercular infections, which had compounded her physiological and physical health. It had developed into a cocktail of health issues, including peptic ulcer, gall-bladder stones, hiatus hernia and tumours on the eardrum, leading to hearing loss. The Sethis had tried all the medical procedures and prescriptions from all systems of medicine, including Ayurvedic and Unani systems. But, her problem was persisting without much improvement. She could barely eat anything. She went through five major surgeries during the period from 1987-99.

They happened to know about Guruji and his blessings, and how he alleviated the sufferings of people. They went for his darshan in February 2000. She dutifully savoured the chai prasad and the spicy langar. To their surprise, she did not develop any after-effects from taking the milky tea and spicy langar. Prior to that, she could barely take tea and any spicy food for years.

On the day of Mahashivratri, the Sethis visited Bade Mandir and were blessed to have Guruji's darshan, and had the usual chai prasad and langar. That day, Mrs Krishna felt as if an energy current was passing through her body while taking the prasad and as if being in the divine aura of Guruji. The next day, the Sethis discovered that she got back her hearing, as she found the TV volume to be too loud; and after a couple of days, all her ailments subsided and she led a normal life. The Sethis were full of gratitude for Guruji who was benevolent to cure the problems of 18 years within 18 days.

Green Chillies as Paracetamol

Urvashi Roul

When Guruji shifted to Empire Estate, Sultanpur, we were in Chandigarh. However, Guruji's magnetic pull would drive us to Delhi on one pretext or the other; and we would rush to Empire Estate for Guruji's darshan and be part of the sangat, which had become our true family.

It was Shilpa's annual examinations. We did not want to disturb her. So, we decided to stay in Punjab Bhawan instead of staying at Urvashi's sister's place. While we were putting our luggage in the room, Urvashi was already running a mild fever. But she decided to go to Empire Estate. When Guruji occupied the majestic aasan, Urvashi felt too uncomfortable to sit as her temperature was running high. She went to the first floor and Maataji, who was temporarily staying there, guided her to be comfortable on the carpet of one of Sudha Aunty's retiring rooms. But Maataji could feel the high fever when she touched her forehead. She rushed downstairs and announced to Guruji, '*Kudi nuu tej bukhar hai; kutch to karo* (The poor girl is running high fever; do something). Guruji instructed Maataji to tie five green chillies on the five fingers of Urvashi and allow her to rest for 15 minutes. Maataji rushed upstairs and tied the green chillies as directed by Guruji. Urvashi started sweating profusely, and then after 15 minutes, her fever came down. After lying down for a while, she felt normal and went downstairs to be a part of the sangat. Guruji got up from the aasan and sat on a sofa in front of her. He beckoned Urvashi to come near and politely asked whether her fever had subsided. Urvashi answered in the affirmative.

The green chillies treatment has been prescribed to many a sangat suffering from high fever.

Sprinkling Water on the Chest to Treat Cardiovascular Disease

Justice A.S. Gill, Chandigarh

Justice A.S. Gill had a fall in the bathroom while he was posted as Justice of Allahabad High Court in the Lucknow Bench. He broke a couple of ribs. The doctors in Lucknow conducted all the tests to know the state of his heart. It was found that he had suffered a heart attack and there was partial damage to his heart. The tests were repeated in R & R Hospital, New Delhi, and the damage to his heart was confirmed. Justice Gill went for Guruji's darshan and talked about his heart condition. Guruji ordered a glass of water. He asked Justice Gill to unbutton his shirt and sprinkled the water on his chest. Then he pronounced that Justice Gill has fully recovered from the heart problem and his heart would be normal. Not to leave any doubt in the devotee's mind, he ordered for a retest. It was conducted in the same hospital again and the doctors were surprised. The improvement in the condition of his heart was surprising as it was medically not possible to have such regeneration within that short a period.

Crushed Samosas and Cure of Heart Ailment

Colonel (Retd) H.S. Tur, Panchkula

Colonel (Retd) H.S. Tur was having heart problems for a long time. On one occasion, his heart rate reached 180 beats per minute. He consulted the doctors, who after all investigations and diagnostic tests advised him for open-heart surgery. A date was fixed for the procedure. But, as Guruji's devotees, his family members wanted to seek Guruji's blessings before going for this major surgery. They went to Guruji's place in the evening. He was in his resting room and a couple of sangat were sitting in the sangat hall. Before they could broach the subject to Guruji, a devotee came out of Guruji's room and conveyed Guruji's message that Colonel Tur should not bother about his heart problem, Guruji would take care of that. They felt assured and savoured the offerings of various prasads.

A devotee had brought samosas for Guruji, who usually would distribute them as prasad. He crushed five samosas and gave them to Colonel Tur to consume. He ate them all with much trepidation, as samosas are fried in oil and not good for heart patients. After he finished the samosa prasad, Guruji again gave him two more samosas and blessed him. Next day, when Colonel Tur went through the medical procedure prior to the surgery, his heartbeat had come down to 80. The doctors further conducted tests and came to the conclusion that there was no need for any surgery.

Almond Oil and the Cure of Auditory Ailment

Son of Colonel (Retd) H.S. Tur

Colonel Tur's son lost his hearing due to some infection or congenital factors in his early childhood. The problem persisted for 25 years. The Turs had approached all sorts of methods and adopted procedures and medicines prescribed by the doctors from all systems of medicine. But the problem remained the same. The Turs happened to learn about Guruji from their extended family who were regulars at Guruji's durbar. They went for Guruji's darshan and sought his blessings to alleviate the suffering of their son. Guruji blessed the family and suggested a remedy for their son. Colonel Tur was asked to put one drop of Badam Rogan, an Ayurvedic almond oil, in his son's ear every day. After 10 days of this procedure, when the son had a severe earache, they approached Guruji. He assured them that the healing process was ongoing and that their son would regain his hearing soon. They were advised to consult an ENT specialist to conduct an audiometric test. When the audiometric test was carried out, the son could not bear the sound and took away the headphone claiming that the sound was too loud. The ENT specialist declared that the auditory functions were normal now. With Guruji's blessings, the young Tur regained his normal hearing after 25 years!

Pomegranate Juice and Low Haemoglobin

Sardar Santokh Singh, Chief Engineer (Retd), Chandigarh

In the year 1997, Sardar Santokh Singh was experiencing severe pain in both his ankles. He consulted a series of specialists and they prescribed a host of tests. His haemoglobin reading was as low as 7.2 and his ESR value was as high as 105, against the normal range of below 20 for his age. He consulted some renowned specialists in Delhi who suggested for bone marrow tests suspecting cancer due to the prognosis of low haemoglobin. The mere suspicion of the dreaded disease made Santokh Singh dread for his life. Terrified, he deputed his son to go to the Sector 33 abode of Guruji to seek his blessings. Guruji told his son emphatically that all the test results would come out normal and that there was nothing to fear. True to his words, the results came within three days and all samples showed normalcy. The doctors prescribed some vitamins and other medicines considering his clinical history.

Santokh Singh went to Chandigarh for Guruji's darshan. Guruji told him to stop taking the medicines and advised him to take pomegranate juice and go for a daily walk in the morning. Santokh Singh dutifully carried the remedy prescribed by Guruji, contrary to the advice of the doctors. As his parameters improved significantly, Guruji told him to even stop taking the pomegranate juice and advised him to take his usual two pegs of whisky every evening. Santokh Singh led a healthy and normal life thereafter.

Cocktail of Prasads and Blessings

There were other times when people had been cured of their chronic health problems by savouring the cocktail of prasads—chai, jal, langar, sweet prasad, etc., served to the sangat. Guruji would advise the suffering individual to attend his durbar regularly and enjoy the soulful sabads, listen to the satsangs rendered by devotees and cherish the cocktail of prasads served to the general sangat; and that is their remedy for their serious health issues.

There are thousands of testimonials of devotees in that respect. Mrs Chhavi Jethra got rid of her insulin medication permanently. Mrs Sushila Kapur's sugar levels dramatically came down from 200 and stabilized at 107. Mrs Sandhu was suffering from Ménière's disease (imbalance of fluid in the inner ear) for more than a decade and half. After 15 days of coming to Guruji's durbar and savouring the cocktail of Guruji's divine benevolence and presence, chai prasad, sabads, langar and satsang, Mrs Sandhu discovered that her ailments had disappeared. The shattered lives of many due to psychological and physical sufferings were rebuilt, and these devotees led a more balanced, and professionally and personally creative as well as fruitful life with the blessings of Guruji. The instances are many. Here, we have given a few examples for highlighting the divine spiritual healing of Guruji.

Arjun Sabharwal, Gurgaon

Arjun Sabharwal, Gayatri's husband, and their son Udhav were suffering from asthma for a considerable period. It was a sight to watch Arjun when he was initially coming to Guruji's sangat at Empire Estate. He would be covered in a monkey cap in mild winters or even on rainy days. Arjun was blessed by Guruji and the remedy was the blessed copper tumbler. This was a standard remedy Guruji prescribed to many a devotee who had physical and physiological ailments. The Sabharwals got the opportunity to render sewa to Guruji and his sangat. They were one of the few who had the opportunity of coming on non-sangat days and hours. The entire family was savouring the cocktail of sabad, chai prasad, satsang, langar, etc. After drinking the water from the blessed tumbler for a couple of weeks, with Guruji's benevolence, Arjun's asthma of years disappeared and it never came back.

Ms Anita Kumar, Delhi

Anita was diagnosed as suffering from a rare kind of skin disease. In her own words:

> By July 1997, my skin that was already flaked up with severely unsightly eczema manifested into something far more grave, more psychologically damaging and more physically deteriorating.
>
> In August, 1997, my skin broke out like never before with pus and intolerable burning sensation. It would bleed and constantly red, inflamed and blotchy and unbearably itchy.[1]

[1]Kumar, Anita, *Turning the Page*, Om Books International, New Delhi, 2012.

Anita dared not look into her bathroom mirror as her beautiful face had turned into an unbearable, unsightly mess. She would switch off the bathroom lights, lest she would catch a sight of her own face.

After savouring the divinity of Guruji for two seasons, Anita was praying for Guruji's blessings to get rid of the scourge of the skin disease. Guruji was testing her devotion and told her one day, 'I have tried and tested you ceaselessly, squeezed you like a lemon and now you go and see your reflection without switching off the bathroom lights.'[2]

Anita observed that her reflection miraculously began to alter. Within weeks of receiving his divine blessings, her inflamed, unsightly and red blotchy skin first turned pink and then almost normal. The pus reduced as did the severe flakiness, making her face less nasty. The rashes on the skin also reduced though it did not disappear altogether. Within a year of his blessings, Anita had a fairly healthy skin and the disease disappeared forever.

Niki Malhotra, Delhi

In 1997, the Malhotras met with a serious road accident. Though the family was saved, Niki, the young daughter of the family, was badly injured. She was in coma for two months. After she regained her consciousness, it was a long road of treatment full of severe doses of steroids, several medicines, frequent diagnostic tests, periodic hospitalization and long physiotherapy sessions. Young Niki was deprived of her schooling and the joys of childhood and adolescence. She was a psychological wreck.

They came to Guruji's fold at his abode in Jalandhar. Before they could tell their woes and seek his blessings, Guruji opened their life history, personal details known only to them. He blessed the family on their first visit. Niki improved significantly thereafter, both physically and mentally. She regained her confidence and got rid of the regimen of medicines against the advice of the doctors.

---

[2]Ibid.

Within two months of having Guruji's darshan, the darkness of despair, the lingering physical ailments were things of the past. Niki could now look forward to a normal life with a purpose of serving the sick and the infirm. She embarked on the mission of becoming a physiotherapist herself. She did her bachelors and subsequently masters in physiotherapy from prestigious institutions and found a life partner. Such was the grace of Guruji's blessings!

Mrs Anita Shourie

Arun Shourie, a former minister in Prime Minister Vajpayee's cabinet, journalist, author and scholar, was a regular at Guruji's sangat at Empire Estate. Anita, Mr Shourie's wife, was suffering from Parkinson's disease. The first time she was brought to Guruji's durbar, she was supported by at least two people as she was not steady to stand or walk. Guruji advised her to savour the blessings embodied in the chai prasad, langar prasad and other prasads distributed by Guruji. She and her family were advised to come to the sangat regularly and enjoy the entire proceedings. After a couple of months coming to the sangat, it was observed that Mrs Shourie had improved to such an extent that Guruji ordered her to serve langar. She did serve it to a couple of sangat holding the langar thali. Such was the miraculous power of Guruji and his blessings to take the pain from the suffering people in the world!

A *Touch of Blessings*

My Account: Rectifying High Blood Pressure (2004)

We were blessed to have had the opportunity of spending considerable time with Guruji. He allowed us to be with him during non-sangat days and the after-hours on sangat days. It was sometime in 2004 that Guruji called me to Empire Estate on a holiday. When I landed there, I found Dr S.C. Sharma, was also already there. We were rendering sewa to Guruji, pressing his palm (acupressure) most of the time and engaging with him in small talk. After some time, Guruji went for a bath and both of us were sitting in the sangat hall. Dr Sharma, being an ENT specialist, noticed my red eyes. My family and near ones have also noticed this for a considerable period. But thinking it to be temporary, we did not pay much attention to it. Now, Dr Sharma advised me to consult a cardiologist and he referred me to one of his colleagues at AIIMS. The next day, I consulted the cardiologist who, after the usual investigation, declared that I have borderline hypertension. He prescribed medicine to control my blood pressure. In a couple of days, the matter was brought to Guruji by one of his nieces. I was again pressing his palm. Suddenly, Guruji took my hand and like an expert doctor, examined my pulse and said, '*Jao, tera blood pressure thik kar dita* (I have controlled your blood pressure).' He took my arm and pointing to the forearm said that I have excess fat and like an expert cardiologist, advised me to go for regular morning walks. In due course, I was blessed with his walking shoes and a couple of his walking gear (shorts and T-shirts) with advice on how to use them for morning walks. Till today, my blood pressure remains in the range that will not qualify me to be termed as the hypertension-type.

Mrs Umrao Singh, Jalandhar

Gitan Grewal's paternal grandmother and Mr Umrao Singh's wife was having heart problems. In 1989, she suffered a massive heart attack. She was rushed to Christian Medical College & Hospital (CMC), Ludhiana. The cardiologists were not very hopeful of a full or partial recovery. Her parameters were deteriorating day by day. Her pulse rate was quite high, and there was accumulation of liquid in the lungs. She was barely able to respond to outside sensory inputs. In those days, Guruji used to stay in Jalandhar. Mr Umrao Singh's family was contemplating to dash to Jalandhar to seek Guruji's blessings. The entire family prayed to Guruji for the old lady's welfare. Before they could embark upon the journey from CMC to Jalandhar, they suddenly found Guruji in the hospital. He went to the ICU, held the hand of Mrs Umrao Singh like an expert doctor, reading her pulse. Guruji sat by her bedside for a couple of hours. The doctors were surprised. The pulse rate came down to 90 from a high of 160 and the patient regained her consciousness. She recovered within no time and her heart rate remained as normal as any other normal person at 90 beats per second.

Dr Savitri Ahuja, Panchkula

Guruji was staying with the Ahujas and holding sangat regularly. Lieutenant General Ahuja was a golf enthusiast and after his retirement, his passion was to golf during the day and cards in the evening. However, his golf sessions resulted in pressure on his right knee. Being an army doctor himself, he consulted his colleagues in the Army Medical Corps. They suggested a medical procedure involving surgery. When the matter was brought to Guruji, he advised to not get surgery. He put his hand over the swollen knee and gently brushed it. The pain disappeared instantaneously and it never came back.

Dr Shashi Ahuja, Pudducherry

Dr Shashi Sharma (subsequently Shashi Ahuja) was married to Shri Arvind Ahuja, son of Lieutenant General Ahuja and Mrs Ahuja of Panchkula. As the Ahujas were ardent devotees of Guruji, Shashi and her husband tagged along with the parents to have Guruji's darshan at the various abodes of Guruji. After a couple of years of her marriage, she observed some sort of spots on her body. Her gynaecologist advised her to take an ultrasound and urine test to rule out pregnancy and other associated issues. They were suspecting a tubal pregnancy. After a couple of tests and ultrasound, pregnancy was ruled out. After a couple of hormone tests and DMC (Detailed Marks Certificate), she was diagnosed as suffering from uterine cancer. She was advised chemotherapy. But she stoutly refused to undergo such a treatment. She never mentioned to her parents-in-law about her medical situation. She carried along hoping some miracle would happen.

At the time, Dr Shashi was a senior resident in GB Pant Hospital, New Delhi. One day, she accompanied her parents-in-laws to Empire Estate. Her parents-in-law had come from Panchkula to have Guruji's darshan. When they were taking leave (*agya*), Guruji told Dr Shashi, '*Shashi Untie, sare test dobara kar lena* (Do repeat all the tests).' Her parents-in-law could not understand as to which test and for what reason. They implored her persistently, but she kept quiet. The next day, she went for a repeat test in Dr Lal PathLabs. The results showed no presence of the indicative value for cancer. Her gynaecologist doubted the efficacy of the lab and ordered another repeat test; this time, in another hospital. Again, none of the tests showed presence of cancerous cells. Her gynaecologist informed that though her uterine cancer had been cured for whatever reason, she would not be able to bear any child. By the earliest opportunity, Shashi rushed to Guruji's durbar to thank Guruji for the miraculous disappearance of her uterine cancer. Guruji was in his jovial mood and asked her jokingly: 'What did your gynaecologist say? You will not have any children? Your firstborn will be a son.' And after a couple of years, the young Ahujas were blessed with a son and subsequently a baby girl.

A Train Journey and Disappearance of Chronic Spondylitis

Colonel S.K. Joshi, Gurgaon

Colonel Joshi was commanding a National Security Guard (NSG) unit at Manesar during the period of 1995–98. In 1996, he got a message from Guruji to come to Chandigarh to stay with him for a couple of days. He took leave and landed at Chandigarh. He was suffering from severe spondylitis causing acute pain in the arms. After spending a few days with Guruji, he was asked to take a train journey back to Delhi. He was apprehensive that his spondylitis may aggravate if he would not get a proper berth and reservation. He managed to get a sleeper berth in an ordinary train. The journey was an overnight one. Colonel Joshi, to his surprise, did not feel the shooting pain during the entire journey and he slept throughout the night as the train was to arrive in Delhi in the morning. After getting down at Delhi, he found his spondylitis was gone. That was the way Guruji cured his ailment even without being prayed to. The Omniscient Guru knew his problem, and his love and affection for the devotee was manifested in alleviating his painful suffering.

Ms Bhavana, Niece of Colonel S.K. Joshi

Colonel Joshi's niece, Bhavana, was suffering from severe depression, and she was admitted to a hospital in Jaipur. Her mental health was going from bad to worse, and as a last resort, Colonel Joshi's sister implored him to seek Guruji's blessings. Colonel Joshi could not muster the courage to do so since Guruji was not feeling good that day. But after the langar session, Guruji himself hailed Colonel Joshi, and in his own volition, described the state of affairs of his niece. The Divine Incarnate read what was going on in his mind. Guruji ordered Colonel Joshi to fetch some medicine from one of the 24x7 pharmacies near AIIMS. To Colonel Joshi's bewilderment, when he got the medicine, Guruji threw them into the dustbin. Instead, he asked Mrs Joshi to proceed to Jaipur the next morning. Later on, Colonel Joshi got the information that while Guruji was keeping him busy fetching the medicine, the mental situation of his niece was improving simultaneously. When Mrs Joshi reached Jaipur, her niece was about to be discharged from the hospital as the girl had regained normalcy.

A Vacation in Singapore, Satsang and the Disappearance of a Gynaecological Problem

Sabina Kochhar, Delhi

Sabina Kochhar had the problem of irregular periods and associated heavy bleeding. The doctors had advised her to undergo a hysterectomy. During that period, she was observing the direction of Guruji that she should not come to Guruji's durbar for five years. After the period of 'no darshan' elapsed, they went to Empire Estate to seek Guruji's blessings. Guruji told her that he had blessed her and she would be alright. With Guruji's permission, she went for the hysterectomy. Her gynaecological problems did not revisit her. However, post-surgery, Sabina was in a state of osteopenia. Her hip joint and femur bone were giving her intermittent pain. Her bone density showed declined levels of calcium. Meanwhile, Guruji ordered the Kochhar family to take a holiday to Singapore and do satsang with sangat there. While she was doing satsang, she could realize that her pain in the hip joint and femur bone was dissipating. Once they were back in Delhi, they went to Guruji's durbar. Guruji told them that her haemoglobin and calcium levels had returned to normal and she was not having any more problems. They took Guruji's word as gospel truth and never conducted any tests to cross verify. And, true to Guruji's word, Sabina led a normal, healthy life thereafter.

Treating Rubella Syndrome through Surya Namaskar

Ms Aditi Mathur

Aditi Mathur was affected by rubella syndrome from birth. She developed a host of problems like congenital cataract, micro-thalamus, micro-cornea, nystagmus and glaucoma. All these led to significant visual impairment. She went for five surgeries to rectify these impairments. The doctors at AIIMS could restore her vision only to a limited extent and opined that she had to live with this problem forever. Because of this and other factors, Aditi also had low comprehension on matters of interest, with psychological tests showing her IQ in the seventies.

Word of mouth about Guruji's miraculous healing powers brought the Mathurs to Guruji's place of stay in 1995. After a couple of visits, Guruji asked Aditi, then 12 years old, to start doing *surya namaskar*, a yogic aasan, and to take a glass of milk mixed with peanuts and mishri given by Guruji. Aditi was asked to adopt this procedure for 51 days. After following this regimen for 51 days, Aditi could notice that her vision has improved considerably.

Guruji left Delhi for Jalandhar and the Mathurs waited three years to have Guruji's darshan again in 1998, when Guruji came to stay at Empire Estate. The Mathurs again started savouring the cocktail of Guruji's divine presence, sabads, satsang, chai prasad and langar prasad. They prayed for the further improvement of Aditi. Guruji answered their prayers and graced their home in June 1998 and blessed the entire family. The next morning, Aditi could read the newspaper. Subsequently, she passed her 10th and 12th board examinations satisfactorily and graduated from Delhi University in Social Work in the first division.

Listening to Satsang, Problem of Yore–Gone

Dr Gurvinder Singh, Malerkotla

Dr Gurvinder Singh was posted in Civil Hospital, Malerkotla. In 2004, he treated Guruji's father for some ailment. Narinder Dhand of Jalandhar was attending Guruji's father. He extensively talked about Guruji to Dr Gurvinder. The doctor, being a medical practitioner, did not have much belief in the supernatural powers of saints to heal people. He was sceptical of Guruji's healing powers, too. Subsequently, he came to Delhi on a professional tour and had the opportunity of having a darshan of Guruji. He came to Guruji's sangat for two consecutive days. While he was given permission to leave for Malerkotla, he was told that he would reach Malerkotla within five hours. The normal time taken to reach Malerkotla at that time was eight hours. The doctor reached Malerkotla in exactly five hours!

When he reached Malerkotla, Guruji asked Narinder to call up the doctor and tell that his daughter would be alright. She would get rid of her mental problems. Narinder called up the doctor to convey Guruji's message. Dr Gurvinder was surprised. Guruji knew his daughter's problem (that was not known outside from close family members) and also read his thoughts/concerns about her. He was again surprised to notice that after his return from Guruji's durbar in Delhi, his daughter's problem was cured to a large extent. Guruji's grace fell on her without even being told about her problem by anybody.

Remote Blessings

Mr David Harrison, Dublin, Ireland

In the early part of 1996, Sukhi Harrison's husband, David, fell ill. He was rushed to the hospital with chest pains and a suspected heart condition. The initial ECG suggested a heart attack. Sukhi prayed to Guruji and gave David the pendant with Guruji's swaroop to keep on his bedside. The observations and further tests continued. David, after receiving the pendant, could smell the fragrance of roses in the emergency room and he slept peacefully. Sukhi later told David that it was Guruji who came to the emergency room to bless him.

Sukhi called Guruji's place to have a direct conversation with him. Guruji himself picked up the phone. Guruji told Sukhi, 'My dear child, I have been with David. Do not worry, everything will be fine.' The medicos ran further tests and found the ECGs had returned to normal and they declared that David's heart had no serious damage. Since then, David has been leading a healthy life without any serious heart problems.

A Garland of Flowers

Father of Mr Baksi Singh, Dugri, Malerkotla

Bakshi's father was suffering from a severe pain in his right leg. Bakshi approached Guruji for curing the old man from the ailment. Guruji blessed him by offering a flower garland placed near his feet by a devotee. Bakshi was asked to dip the garland in a bucket of water and his father would take a bath with that water. They complied with Guruji's remedy and the pain of years was gone forever.

Lentils into River Yamuna

Nibedita Sahu

The Sahus had their first darshan of Guruji when he was in General Ahuja's place in Panchkula. They enjoyed the ambience of spiritual moorings in the serene milieu of Guruji's durbar at Panchkula. They started visiting Panchkula and Chandigarh at regular intervals. One time, they were staying in Netaji Nagar, New Delhi on account of Mr Sahu's central deputation. In the meanwhile, Nibedita, my sister-in-law, was diagnosed with ovarian cyst. The doctors at Apollo Hospital in New Delhi prescribed medicines as a remedial measure. But the problem did not improve, rather it deteriorated and she suffered from irregular periods and heavy flow. The Apollo doctors were contemplating surgery as a last resort.

Subsequently when Guruji shifted to Empire Estate, the Sahus were also regulars at Guruji's durbar. One evening, Mr Sahu missed the usual darshan of Guruji. Guruji rang him up and asked as to the reason for his absence from sangat. Mr Sahu replied that Maasi (Guruji used to call Nibedita as Maasi) was in a precarious state of health due to the aggravation of her cyst problem. Guruji asked him to come to Empire Estate immediately and have langar. After langar, Guruji prescribed the remedy of offering black chana (lentils) into a flowing water body. The suggestion of Guruji was executed without hesitation. Maasi, on learning about the remedy, stopped taking all the medicines prescribed by the Apollo doctors. Her cyst-related problems eased considerably and after some days disappeared entirely.

Utilizing the Unused Ayurvedic Medicine

Tanya Bhardwaj, Daughter of Neeru Bhardwaj, Satbari

Tanya, the youngest daughter of the Bhardwajs, also developed the problem of psoriasis like her father. After a couple of weeks, they reluctantly mentioned to Guruji about Tanya's psoriasis. The usual remedy of copper tumbler was prescribed for young Tanya and the standard practice was to be followed. But, even after drinking the water from the copper tumbler and taking bath with the remainder water, Tanya's psoriasis did not subsidize. Rather, it got aggravated. They could have Guruji's darshan only after a couple months due to Guruji's absence from his place of stay. When Guruji was told about Tanya's aggravated state of psoriasis, he advised them to utilize the ayurvedic medicines he had ordered for himself through the Bhardwajs, but did not consume after taking just one tablet. The remainder tablets were with the Bhardwajs. After 40 days of taking the medicine, on the day of Shivratri, Guruji told them to stop it's usage. The Bhardwajs had complete confidence in Guruji and they scrupulously followed his instructions. After a couple of days, Tanya's psoriasis symptoms disappeared and she could lead a normal life.

Peanuts and Post-Surgery Trauma

The Vegetable Vendor of Chandigarh

A poor vegetable vendor (who was selling vegetables in a vending cart) at Sector 22, Chandigarh, was suffering from a serious kind of malignant brain tumour, which was creating the problem of double vision. The tumour was surgically removed by the doctors. But after six months, the tumour resurfaced. A second surgical operation was conducted and the tumour was removed. But the patient went into a coma. After regaining his consciousness, the doctors told the family to take the patient home as nothing could be done and that they should reconcile for his end, which may come any day. The mother heard about Guruji from someone and came to his abode in Sector 33. She prayed to Guruji, seeking his blessings to save the only earning member of the family to come out of comma. Post recovery, the man had been suffering from double vision. Guruji ordered the mother to fetch some peanuts and blessed them with his characteristic uttering of some mantras. He said that the kernel of the nuts must be eaten for 10 days and the cells be put on his eyes. After 10 days, the vendor got back his normal eyesight (double vision disappeared), and his test and retest confirmed that there was no malignancy left in the body. The malignancy or tumour never returned and the vendor led a normal life.

Darshan of Guruji: Child Suffering from Cerebral Palsy Speaks Their First Word

Sukhi Harrison, Dublin, Ireland

Sukhi and David were married for several years, but they did not have any child. After many prayers to Waheguru and the Lord of Lords, they had a baby girl, Sheena. But Sheena did not show any signs of normal behaviour expected of a child her age. CT scans, brain scans, ECGs, etc., were conducted and repeated to find the exact prognosis. Finally, Sheena was diagnosed with cerebral palsy. They were warned that Sheena would be unable to sit and walk properly and her face may get distorted. By God's grace, these prophesies by medical experts were proved wrong. But Sheena was not able to talk till she was three years old.

In the early months of 1995, Sukhi, along with Sheena, went to India to attend her ailing mother. It is another story that by Guruji's grace, her mother's operation of her uterine growth went smoothly and the growth was found to be benign. On her sister's insistence, Sukhi went to have a darshan of Guruji. Before her actual arrival, Guruji was stating to the sangat present there, '*Beti ayi hai* (My daughter has come).' After paying her respects, she received the prasad distributed by Guruji. After distribution of the prasad, Guruji got up and sat beside her. He recounted her entire life story—her ailments, operations, her home and its detailed decoration back in Dublin, each item like toys, cutlery, dinner set, etc. Guruji asked her to bring Sheena the next time. Sukhi was reluctant in the first instance fearing she would be unmanageable in the sangat. Nevertheless, she brought Sheena to

Guruji's durbar the next day. On entering Guruji's durbar, Sheena left her mother's hand and ran to Guruji. Sheena, the three-year-old who never spoke a word, fell at Guruji's feet and uttered her first word 'Waheguru'. Thereafter, Sheena had a normal physical and psychological develolpment.

Holding the Hand for a Smooth Medical Treatment and Recovery

Cancer patients usually have feelings of guilt of needing to depend upon others, loss of control, fear of recurrence, uncertainty about the future, body image issues, reduced self-esteem, and feelings of loneliness and abandonment; they also face problems in returning to work; there is marginalization and even stigmatization. All these lead to depression, anxiety, and mood and adjustment disorders characterized by communication problems.

The trajectory of the disease also has serious impact on the cognitive faculties of the suffering individual, such as difficulties in attention, concentration, working memory, information processing speed, sequencing ability and visual-motor integration.

A cancer patient faces altered states of time, space and existence while passing through various phases of the disease. Spiritually, the concept of time (the past, present and future) acquires different meaning for them. They revaluate their space (home and the rest of the world) and the microcosm of close relationships, and in social and community relationships in the macroscosm of broader work. The person encounters the existential confrontation with altered morality.

Considering the range of implications related to physical, emotional, spiritual and interpersonal difficulties experienced by a patient with cancer, it becomes the responsibility of the family, friends and medical professional to help patients attain sound mental health. But such a social and professional support may not be readily available to all suffering cancer patients.

Under such circumstances, the satsang, along with Guruji, fulfils a lot of psychosocial and spiritual void. The mere mention by the medical fraternity that the physical and physiological parameters may point towards suspected cancer leads to panic, fear, anxiety in many an individual. The protective umbrella of assurances by Guruji (*Jaa, kalyan kitta*; Go, you are blessed) removes a morbid psychological impact.

During the trajectory of the disease, treatment and therapies in confirmed cases, the blessings of Guruji and the associated systems of the sangat and satsang provide the psychosocial and spiritual succour to the individual to work through the suffering with fortitude. The helping hand of Guruji leads the individual to a faster course of recovery and long-term survival. Guruji not only reduces the suffering or makes the person emotionally strong to go through the trajectory of the disease, he also eliminates any such sufferings altogether by his grace. The cancer may completely disappear by Guruji's grace; the suspected cancer would be reported negative; the therapies may turn out to be manageable with little physical and emotional discomfort; and the person in post recovery would survive much longer than the prognosis of the medical fraternity.

Brigadier Saini

Brigadier Saini (a professional medical doctor of the Army Medical Corps) underwent a thorough investigation for a suspected cancer in 2003. It was found that he was suffering from NHL, a severe kind of cancer. NHL or Non-Hodgkin Lymphoma is characterized by the production of abnormal lymphocytes, a type of white blood cell. The usual symptoms include swollen lymph nodes, fever, stomach aches, night sweats, weight loss, chest pain and a loss of appetite. Brigadier Saini went through the procedures in R & R Hospital, New Delhi. With Guruji's blessings, he did not have any side effects from chemotherapy. The Brigadier was a constant presence in Guruji's abode, rendering sewa to Guruji. Nobody could notice any trace of the debilitating effects of the disease and the aftermath of the therapies and treatments. In 2004, a cancerous lymph node was also removed surgically. The doctors advised him to go for a bone marrow examination. With

Guruji's blessings, this examination showed negative results and he was saved from another round of chemotherapy. Brigadier Saini survived the cancer without much problem and without the cancerous growth regenerating till his last years.

Sumeet Jethra, Software Engineer, Delhi

In 1998, Sumeet, at the young age of 24, was diagnosed with neuroblastoma, a malignant cancer. Such a type of cancer is found in young children when they are three or four years old. But Sumeet got it when he was 24. Post the operation, there was all probability of the cancer recurring and the young adult was in the darkest hour of his life. Depression engulfed him. On the suggestion of a colleague, they went to seek blessings of Guruji. Sumeet mentioned about his sufferings to which Guruji said, '*Kalyan kitta* (I blessed you).' Sumeet felt assured by the divine love and affection of Guruji. He became a regular at Guruji's durbar, savouring the daily dose of the blessed chai prasad and langar prasad. To everyone's surprise, Sumeet's road to recovery was quite fast. After six months of the first operation, CT scans showed that the three suspicious patches on the liver, kidney and stomach had disappeared. After a couple of months, he recovered completely and started leading a normal life. Now, nearly a decade and a half has elapsed, and Sumeet is leading a perfectly normal life—he got married, has twins and has been leading a well settled professional life.

Guruji Knows–No Verbal Rendering: Suo Moto Blessings

The omniscient guru does not need the suffering individual's actual verbal rendering of the accounts of his sufferings. He knows; he understands; he is aware of your sufferings—every knowledge possible! For example, you may have a look into the rendering of the accounts of the sangat like Mr Chhina, Dr Anita, Mrs Sabina Kochhar, Mrs Mathur, Ms Anita Kumar, Mrs Brigadier Saini, Dr Pandove, Mrs Neeru Bhardwaj, Mr Naseer Ahmad, Mrs Nivedita Sahu, Mrs Gayatri Sabharwal, General M.P.S. Sandhu and myself to have a glimpse of such happenings.

Mr Chhina

Mrs Joga's father, Mr Chhina, was a retired civil servant. They were visiting Jalandhar Mandir at regular intervals to have Guruji's darshan. One day, Mr Chhina was ordered to get betel leaves costing ₹51. When the betel leaves were fetched from the market, Mr Chhina was ushered into the 'operation room' and asked to lie down. Guruji put the betel leaves on different parts of Mr Chhina's body and told him that he had operated upon him. They could not understand what the problem was as Mr Chhina was hale and hearty. After a couple of days, Mr Chhina passed blood in his urine and he was diagnosed with bladder cancer. A surgery procedure was done to remove the cancerous part. But he recovered fast and the cancer never came back. Mr Chhina lived a long life without much problems.

Mr Chhina's cancer was pre-diagnosed by Guruji. He was blessed to have a smooth surgery and fast recovery. Though treatment protocols for cancer was not that effective at that time (in the 1990s), by Guruji's blessings, Mr Chhina was able to make a full recovery and lived a normal and healthy life for a long time.

Brigadier Saini

When Brigadier Saini was posted at Jalandhar Cantonment, Mrs Saini developed the problem of cervical spondylitis. Being a doctor himself, the best treatment and physiotherapy were given to her. But there was minimal improvement in her condition. The problem persisted till 1996. By that time, Brigadier Saini has been posted to the military hospital at Chandimandir near Chandigarh. One fine evening, when the Brigadier returned from the hospital to Guruji's abode in the house of Lieutenant General Ahuja, Guruji told him that he had cured Mrs Saini of her ailment. Brigadier Saini learnt that Guruji had treated Mrs Saini by applying his trademark procedure of the kitchen spoon. Guruji had gently run a spoon on Mrs Saini's body, and her pain and discomfort of old-age spondylitis had disappeared instantaneously and never returned.

Gayatri Sabharwal, Gurgaon

Gayatri discovered that a cyst was forming near her eye. Doctors advised a surgical procedure to remove it. The problem was never broached to Guruji. But one day, while she was about to take permission to leave from Empire Estate, Guruji looked at her, intensively focussing on her cyst-affected eye. The communication between Guruji and the devotee was instantaneous. Gayatri understood the intent of the omniscient Guruji for his intense gaze. The cyst disappeared the next morning.

Major General Deepak Malhotra, New Delhi

When, Major General Deepak Malhotra had his first darshan of Guruji, after being in a serious car accident, Guruji could identify the thought process going in his head. It was everything, from family to professional matter in the army. The General was suffering from low back pain for several years. He could not sit down and get up from chairs without undergoing pain and difficulty. The Malhotras never mentioned about this problem to Guruji. One afternoon, the General got a call from Guruji, telling him to come to his abode for he wanted to cure him of his back problem. When he reached Guruji's place, Guruji ordered to get a kitchen spoon and ran it on his spine. After the procedure, he patted his back and told him that he had cured his pain. And, no surprise to the ardent devotees! Thereafter, General Malhotra did not experience any back problem of any kind.

Materialization and Healing

Poonam Sethi, Lecturer, Hindu College, Delhi University

The Sethis were married for seven years and though they were trying to have a baby, they were not able to conceive. After a series of tests and investigations, the fertility experts found the double-layered problem of Poonam's defective fallopian tube and Mr Sethi's low sperm count. They underwent a series of intrauterine insemination (IUI) procedures, but nothing worked.

By that time, they had the opportunity of coming to Guruji's durbar at Empire Estate. They sought the blessings of Guruji before giving the IUI a last try. Guruji blessed them with his usual by-line, '*Kalyan kitta* (Blessed you).' And this time, the IUI worked; Poonam's pregnancy test revealed positive results. In due course, the Sethis had a lovely boy. When they went to Guruji's durbar with the child to thank him and seeking blessings for the new born, Guruji asked Poonam if she wanted one more son. The Sethis did not utter a word. Each time the Sethis went for Guruji's darshan thereafter, he used to implore, 'Do you need one more child?' After a couple of such implorations, Poonam uttered, 'Guruji, as you please.' And this time, she got pregnant without any IUI or IVF. They were blessed with a second son.

Spiritual Healing to Connect People with God

The above are some strange but characteristic methods witnessed by all, including the author. But a mahapurush does not require remedies or a talisman to cure the sufferings and diseases. One day, Sukhmani, from Chandigarh, asked in her innocent way why Guruji was adopting such weird or strange ways of treating people. Guruji replied, 'I do not need to do anything to cure people. The power of divinity is enough to cure people with the right kind of approach—devotion, connection with the divine, *shradha* and positive attitude. The mental frame of the humanity today is such that it needs a remedy to create the positive valence, the right connection to get cured.'[3]

The crucial issue here is the spiritual connection and owning up to the process of undergoing a treatment or catharsis. The methods gradually put the suffering soul in the realm of 'doing something for themself' and they own up on the process. By the time the treatment is over and the ailment is cured or the misery or affliction is lessened, the suffering soul would have established

[3]Sukhmani, *Surcharged With Divine Love*, Unistar Books, Chandigarh, 2012.

a reasonable degree of connectivity with the Supreme Self. That is the ultimate goal of the divine incarnate, to connect people to the Godhead—*Lokanu rab de naal jodna* (To connect people with God).

This connection with the divinity is wrongly interpreted by many as faith. One day, while having some small talk with Guruji in his retiring room in Empire Estate, I mentioned that the people having faith in Guruji were getting cured. I got the rebuke of my life from Guruji. He chastized me by telling, '*Faith ki chiz hunda* (What is faith)?' He went on to elaborate the concept of shradha and connection with the divinity. What I gathered is that faith is an English word, which hardly connotes the all-encompassing shradha. It is a combination of the acceptance of divinity, connection with divinity, surrender to divinity, sincerity of seeking divinity and the absence of doubts in the rational mind—no *kintu-parantu* (ifs and buts), and a positive frame of mind. The word 'faith' fails to denote or express the broad canvas of shradha.

Divine grace is not earned as a matter of right. There are many in the sangat who were distraught that they were not blessed by Guruji towards elimination of their physical, mental and materialistic sufferings. You have to earn the divine grace; not demand it. *Mangde nahi, manande*—never ask for divine grace, earn it by devotion.

If the Godhead is capable of curing the mental and physical ailments with the blink of an eye, the rational mind may be wondering why this standard is not applicable to all suffering individuals. Why are there so many methodologies and so many remedies? We revert back to the karma philosophy of the Indian spiritual tradition. As humans, we are supposed to go through our karmic processes. The guru can lessen our sufferings, and lead us from the morass of darkness (confusion, hopelessness and helplessness) to the path of spiritual awakening. He holds our hand by awakening the latent godliness in each individual to guide the soul to connect with the Supreme Soul. The process may be instantaneous or a lengthy one, depending on the karmic earnings and spiritual levels and moorings of individuals. Asking for instantaneous relief from sufferings would nullify the positivity to be earned through the process of going through or working through the sufferings and developing a connection with the divinity.

Of course, enlightened souls like Guruji are not super doctors to cure people from diseases. From ages, there have been medicine systems in place to take care of that. The human civilization has progressed significantly in various systems of medicine and many diseases are now extinct. Many cures are available and daily new methods, medicines, diagnostic tools are being developed and adopted. The spiritual guru and the divine incarnate are not a substitute for these human efforts and scientific attainments. Their sole purpose is bringing the individual souls closer to the Supreme Soul. The miraculous powers exhibited through compassion and love are only incidental to lead the suffering souls and others to the spiritual high street.

Guruji's mission is not to become a super doctor to cure people of diseases and ailments. He used to say he was neither a super doctor (curing people) nor a super magician (performing miracles) or a *jyotish* (telling the past, present or future of individuals); he was beyond these ascribes. It was through the empathy of the elevated soul with the suffering humans that he invokes the supernatural powers of healing. His love and affection, the umbrella of his blessings, and assurances and the wonderful milieu of the sangat and satsangs worked wonders for the suffering individuals. He was not averse for modern medical treatments. Rather he would advise to get the diagnostics, treatments and surgery done through the modern medical practitioners. But his grace has cured people even without going through the treatments and surgeries. In the present chapter, we have cited a sample of satsangs involving healing of people of their physical, physiological and psychological sufferings. In 18 cases, there is explicit mention of parallel medical procedures. In several cases, there is none. He has diagnosed diseases well before the doctors could, and he had assured people when they got negative diagnostic results.

Guruji (1997)

Guruji's birthplace in Dugri (2004)

Lane leading to birthplace (2004)

Bada Mandir (2000)

Baisakhi at Chandigarh (1996)
Credit: Rajhans Studio, Sector-35C, Chandigarh

Guruji and Urvashi (1997)
Credit: Rajhans Studio, Sector-35C, Chandigarh

Guruji at author's residence, Chandigarh (1996)

Guruji at author's residence (1996)

Guruji at author's residence (1996)

Guruji at author's residence (1996)

At author's residence, Chandigarh (1997)

At author's residence (1997)

At New Motibagh, New Delhi (2004)

At New Motibagh (2004)

At New Motibagh (2004)

Guruji at his smiley best (1997)

Absorbing the Pain of Suffering Individuals

It has been seen that sometimes Guruji used to fall sick after curing some devotee of a fatal or chronic disease. He used to say that not all sundry sages or saints can cure people of the diseases by taking the diseases upon themselves. Only a highly evolved satguru can attain such powers. He used to say:

> *Mahapurush de level honed ne. Jo loka da marz apne utte le sakda hai o universe vich ek honda hai. Oh sadguru honda hai.*
>
> There are levels of mahapurush. The one who takes the disease on himself is the Sadguru.

Moreover, not all saints are blessed to heal people of ailments and diseases, nor can they take the disease upon themselves. *'Har koi logon ka marz apne upar nahin le sakta, unhe hokum nahi hai.* (Not everybody can take the disease of others upon himself. They are not allowed or graced to do so.)'

We may recollect the lines from the Bible: 'He Himself took our infirmities and bore our sicknesses' (Matthew 8:16–17).

Some sadhaks who might have attained certain powers (like mind reading, limited healing power, etc.) get stuck at that low level of spiritual attainment when they are fixated with the exhibition of such powers. While enjoying the powers, sometimes they become egoistic and forget that they have the powers due to the Grace of the Supreme. They get stuck at that level. That is not the ultimate objective or goal of attaining the supernatural powers. So the question is, 'Why do the enlightened, such as Guruji, not always adapt the golden standard of curing the ailing person with a blink of the eye?' The question itself shows the inadequate appreciation of the spiritual path and its ways.

That reminds us of the absurd question being asked by some rational minds, 'Why do the spiritual gurus not destroy the military might of the enemies of the nation by invoking their supernatural powers?' That begets the idea as to who an enemy is. For a spiritually evolved soul, what is the meaning of the geographical and artificial national and international boundaries between nations? Are they confined to and constrained by the narrow framework of nationalism? What is it about universal humanism, which is the bedrock of the spiritual path?

Many rational minds, products of a society built on the mind and ego, frown upon such healing powers stating that these are quasi, scientifically-misguided, charlatan practices. While there are con artists in every field, the genuinely beneficial aspects of spiritual healing are largely ignored because they can't be quantified or reasoned with. What is it about the experiential learning of thousands who get redeemed from their chronic diseases and sufferings and enjoy the showering of love, compassion, positivity and hope from a realized soul? They might not have seen God, but they realized godliness at every moment. You may put yourself in the shoes of many suffering from cancer, asthma, diabetes, infertility and other debilitating ailments, diseases and accompanying existential crisis of helplessness and hopelessness to realize what divine grace is all about. For a suffering individual, a good and sympathetic doctor, the love and affection of near and dear ones and social support are the divine blessings. Guruji is the embodiment of all these and much more.

There are thousands of instances of the miraculous healing power of the revered Guruji. I myself being witness to some, which are part of the testimonials described in this chapter. The other instances have been heard directly from the beneficiary devotees in satsangs in one-to-one renderings or in the presence of Guruji during institutionalized gatherings of sangat. I had the good fortune of knowing most of these devotees in close quarters. However, it does not imply that only these instances constitute the entire gamut of manifestation of miraculous healing powers of Guruji. There are many such incidences, which I might not have heard from the devotees yet. Moreover, the numerous instances of miraculous healing during the initial days of Guruji's enlightened journey, after his college days till the institutionalization of holding a sangat in Jalandhar, are not known to me nor codified as of yet. There is a need for thorough research and survey to collect and codify such incidences from the early devotees of Guruji from Punjab as well as the adjoining states.

4

The Vibhuti Moments

It would be a beautiful journey—one of a dozen springs. On the way, we met many co-travellers embarking upon the same journey. Many comrades of the cohort had already been there many springs earlier than when we embarked on the journey; some of the others joined afterwards. As the caravan would cruise along, we would overcome many obstacles—doubts, confusions, obfuscation of rationality, and peer and professional pulls and pressures. But Guruji used to be there to steer us onto the right path. Yes, this journey used to be important in itself. Would there be a destination? Neither the co-travellers nor Guruji made it explicit whether there would be one. Guruji would be emphatic on continuing the journey, as he would say, '*Ate raho* (Do continue coming, continue the journey).'

Along the way, Guruji had performed extraordinary and miraculous feats. The performances were not designed or preordained or structured. The performances were an integral part of the journey. The travellers, the barnstormers, the wanderers, the tramps, the expedition-chasers and the explorers in this quest encountered many a difficult terrain. The performances were supposed to shed light on the darker and more difficult path. Guruji was sceptical about the performances; he says that he was not ordained to perform these feats only. But, he has to reveal himself and establish the credibility of the journey for a noble end, which each co-passenger has to realize, define and internalize one day.

INITIATING THE PASSENGER

Along the journey, many new passengers would join. Sometimes, the curiosity of the human mind would propel the newcomer to join the voyage. Others would feel that they have a short-term goal to attain. Such goals may range from overcoming mundane troubles and tribulations of the normal human life, to the esoteric. Sometimes, they would be really in need of external guidance because of the state of despair arising out of helplessness, hopelessness and severe depression.

Guruji had to initiate the newcomers for the expedition. Some were already initiated; their karmic disposition made them ready to embark upon the journey. Such explorers would instantly realize the true nature of Guruji and accept him as the captain of the ship without any hesitation. Their search for an anchor ended when they met Guruji. But for others, Guruji may reveal through subtle hints and performances. He may conduct a performance called 'dossiers' for these newcomers. He would reveal the details of their 'files'—life history, their family, homestead (including the number and type of trees within the premises of the homestead), etc. The initiation may see its culmination with complete bewilderment of the newcomer. Others may harbor wonderings about Guruji: how come he knows our secrets? He might have employed a score of detectives! What is it about the unknown secrets, not known to anybody (not even to detectives) like the number of miscarriages their mother had during her productive years; or the secret girlfriend or concubines kept in far-off places, including foreign lands?

The initiation would also take many other forms. Guruji may call the newcomer by their nickname or formal name, though it might be their first-time interaction with him without any formal introduction. There is no way this information could be given to Guruji, the newcomer knows. Guruji would then also remind the newcomer about a meeting with him in the remote past, which the newcomer has to dig hard to retrieve from their long-term memory. Ages ago, some leading lights of this ancient land had given a name to this knowledge—*trikal darshi*, the ability to know the past, present and future of a person.

THE WOODS AND THE FORESTS ALONG THE ODYSSEY

The journey is not a straightforward and smooth one. It is full of obstacles and uncharted difficult terrain. There is no defined path. Some travellers may adopt shortcuts; others may veer out of the charted path. Other times, there would be extremities of weather—heavy rain, storm and fogginess leading to evanescence of Guruji from sight. The Guiding Spirit, by his inherent nature—*swadharma*, reveals himself to conduct the co-passengers towards light from the morass of such darkness. He reveals himself by utilizing the power of his Third Eye. It is figuratively said the enlightened person is seeing through the sixth sense or the third eye. It is *dura-darshanam*—seeing things/happenings far away. It also extended to macroscopic and microscopic vision.

DURASHRAVANA (HEARING FROM DISTANCE) OR THE THIRD EAR

Guruji as a true leader has to lead the pack knowing the distinct abilities, characteristics and above all the mindset of the co-passengers. He would use his extraordinary power to read their minds. And reading the mind and conveying message from a distance is like telepathy. Almost all passengers have had one or many such experiences with Guruji, when the latter has revealed their thought processes. Such revelation need not be a direct recount of their thoughts. It is the subtle way in which he leads you to realize that he knows what is going on inside the mind. The sages term the power of reading the minds as '*para chita adi abhijnata* (knowing the minds of others)'. Shri Bhavesh Pandey, one co-traveller, beautifully describes such extraordinary phenomenon in the following manner, 'I have often heard in satsangs that he knows all your thoughts, but it is much more than that. All our thoughts are his... We are, because he is.'

NO SPEED TO MATCH THE MASTER: THE LAGHIMA (LEVITATION MOMENTS)

On this beautiful journey, we, the passengers, would try to maintain pace with Guruji. It was a vain effort for the ordinary. There were several occasions when we would find him far ahead of the group. The sprinters of the group, who had proven their athletic prowess, would not be able to match his speed. Sometimes, we had to embark upon a trek on a muddy track. While everybody else's shoes would be full of dirt, Guruji's shoes would have none, as if fresh from a showroom. It would be as if he was not walking on the surface but levitating above it. Sages say, it is the ability of the enlightened master to lighten his body weight to the minimum, like a feather so that he can float in the air, walk or float on the surface of water. The ancient sages also called it the power of *Laghima*—the ability to make the body light as a feather.

The enlightened master and guiding spirit, Guruji, would find the co-passengers splitting into smaller cohorts. The splintering would not be deliberate; there was no command and structure of the journey. It was up to the co-passenger to choose the time and place to rejoin the confederate of co-travellers. It is the magnetic pull of Guruji and His Grace which would precipitate such rejoining. The traveller may take days, months or years to reappear to seek the guidance and rejoin the odyssey. To reinforce the leanings and learning, Guruji, the enlightened master, would have to reveal himself in subtle ways. One of the methodologies adopted was to make the co-passenger know that Guruji knew the backroom confabulations of the co-passengers. Guruji would execute the operation of the 'third ear' and recount the conversation carried out by the co-passengers far away from him. The sages say it is the power of *durashravana* or clairaudience.

The enlightened master never prescribed a regimen of do's and don't's. It was the co-passenger's own will and the application of his intelligence and judgment (his free will) that would determine how they would dress up, what they would eat or drink, and the like. There would be no rigid regimen of any particular ritual or discipline or austerities to be a part of the journey. But, Guruji, the enlightened master, had his simple ways, particularly his food habits. He wore neat, clean and elegant (but not ostentatious) attire—cholas and trousers, T-shirts, walking shorts, etc., befitting the occasion or activity.

Guruji was following a sort of his own austerities. During the journey, there were several retreats for recouping the energies and spreading the message of the journey to new potential travellers. Jalandhar is one such retreat. Legend has it that this retreat was established by Lava, son of Rama, of the Ramayana fame, located between two waters (*jala andar*) Beas and Sutlej. At this resting place, Guruji undertook austerities like fasting continuously for four days, Monday to Thursday. It is said by sages that the enlightened masters, who attain the supernatural power of inedia, live on breathing alone, without food, and in extreme cases, without water. The ancient sages of this land also call it *anurmi-mattvam*—the ability to conquer hunger, thirst and other bodily cravings. During our journey, we have witnessed, on a limited scale, the demonstration of inedia by the Enlightened Master. But he never prescribes any fasts or *vratas* to the co-passengers. He would rather advise them just to focus on the journey.

THE VIBHUTI MOMENTS OF MATERIALIZATION

During the journey, we have enjoyed, rather savoured, many beautiful moments with Guruji. The wavering thoughts due to the arduous nature of the journey and the difficult terrain are often taken care of by the radiating divine energy of the enlightened master. It acts like the path strewn with soft flowers to tread by the passengers. One such divine moment comes when the master, with his sweet will or grace, produces sachkhand prasad out of thin air. There are several co-passengers who are direct beneficiaries as recipients of such a prasad. Of course, at the time of production or materialization of the sachkhand prasad, each of the entire group of co-passengers would be given a chunk of the divine prasad. This takes all the pain and gloominess from the passengers embarking on the journey.

Other times, the enlightened master would reveal himself by materializing other articles out of thin air to reinforce the credibility of the essential nature of the journey. There are many such instances. The co-travellers, including myself, often describe their experiential accounts through a system called satsang—recounting the soulful joys, enchantment and glory of such revelations. Again, it is reiterated that such magical moments are not the core strategy adopted by Guruji to guide the passengers. But sometimes, these are revealed to arrest the waywardness of passengers and remind them about the existence of higher forces.

WARDING OFF THE ROUGH WEATHER

When you are part of a journey of this kind, you are likely to face rough weather. But the enlightened master is there to lighten your sufferings and to face the rough weather with fortitude. Several co-passengers have narrated the hand-holding by the Master while they were undergoing tough times on the journey. The usual divine assurance that everything will be all right, and the journey will see the desired positive results, had encouraged the passengers to face the rough weathers with fortitude and calmness. The passengers, thereafter, never veer from the path and undertake the journey with much more devotion to follow the master. The co-passengers have a long list of such narrations.

CHANGING THE WEATHER

During the journey, it would not only be the divine assurance of Guruji that would make the journey less arduous and lessen the sufferings, but sometimes, Guruji also changes the rough weather, if he desires. When you would face the scorching sun, Guruji would cover the sun with clouds and bring the soothing breeze of the spring.

The ancient sages of this great land say that such enlightened masters attain the power to control fire, sun, water, air, poison (*agni arka ambu viṣa ādīnām pratiṣṭambhaḥ*) and their effects. This ability is also reflected in their power to change the weather and control over natural phenomenon like the rain, sunrise, sunset, etc.

THE OMNIPRESENCE OF GURUJI

During the journey, Guruji would look after many groups of co-passengers at several locations. Every group or individual passenger would get used to his physical presence for one-to-one guidance. But as the passenger train becomes longer and longer, the number increases menacingly and the *kafla* (caravan) becomes too long. Guruji has the unique ability of being physically present simultaneously at more than one location. The ancient sages term such ability as *Manaḥ-javah (manojvitva)*—darting simultaneously to multiple locations at the speed of thought.

The divine guiding light has a unique way of being present at multiple locations by way of his divine fragrance. When the passengers genuinely desire his presence or connect with him with sincere devotion, Guruji makes his presence felt by sending a whiff of his body fragrance. This is a universal experience of many a passenger. Such experiences are so numerous that there is no need of specific mention.

THE CO-TRAVELLER ACCOUNTS

The following section contains the co-traveller accounts of the supernatural fits performed by Guruji during the beautiful journey. Under each category, there are many others who have also shared their experiences and eye-witness accounts described elsewhere.

The Initiations

There are many testimonials or satsang abound with anecdotes (the Third Eye, the Dossiers and the Extra Sensory Vision) describing the extraordinary vision, knowledge about the newcomers and the events that have or would engulf them.

When I Met Guruji

When Guruji was at General Ahuja's place in Panchkula and not allowing an open darshan to the sangat, Urvashi was one of the devotees allowed for such a darshan. She would be dropped at General Ahuja's residence by my driver, but as Guruji usually allowed the sangat to leave late in the evening or at midnight, she had to take the help of other sangat from Chandigarh to drop her to our place. By that time, I had heard a lot of stories describing Guruji's miracles, his divine power, his ability to cure people suffering from chronic and other diseases. I was getting the feeling if Urvashi was getting that much peace of mind and satisfaction by being part of the sangat, why should I not assist her in this process. Initially, since the Hoshiarpur days (later part of 1995), I was sceptical about men proclaiming as god, as stories of fraud and exploitation of the gullible were abound. But I never made it an issue about Urvashi going for a darshan from Hoshiarpur to Jalandhar or from Chandigarh to Panchkula. Guruji was telling Urvashi that her husband is a *changa munda* (good boy) and will one day come to have his darshan. Urvashi was not feeling comfortable that her husband was not coming to Guruji for darshan.

It was Janmashtami and Urvashi wanted to go to the Ahuja's residence to have Guruji's darshan. She was told by Guruji the previous day to come early. Being at odd hours, no other sangat might be going to Panchkula. Since it was a holiday, the driver was not called. She asked if I would like to have a darshan with

Guruji as it was an auspicious day. I readily agreed as it would also solve the problem of the driver.

When we reached the Ahuja's residence, Guruji was sitting on the sofa. In those days, there were no open sangat. So, there was a three-seater sofa. Both Urvashi and I entered the hall simultaneously. Guruji got up from the sofa and extended his hand for a handshake to greet me as he said, '*Rahul Sahib, aao ji. Appa pahale mile hain* (Rahul Sahib, we have met earlier).' To which I said to myself, 'No, I think we have not met earlier.' Then Guruji recounted the place, the date and time when we met for the first time. I could quickly recollect the events of that day and nodded in agreement. It was in 1986, when I was a probationer, undergoing district training in Jalandhar. I used to drop in on one of the senior officer's residence in the evening as I had nothing to do alone in one room of the Zilla Parishad guest house. Being a probationer, you had the unhindered access to the senior officer's homes without any prior intimation. Those were the days when seniors were welcoming newcomers to their fold without hesitation. I had the privilege of having excellent seniors in Jalandhar.

One of the seniors asked me to come during the daytime, the next day being a holiday. He wanted me to meet one important person. I landed up in his house at the designated time. He took me to the drawing room where a gentleman in white trousers, a white shirt and yellow boots was sitting on the sofa. He had a receding hairline, very fair complexion and with an unusual way of giving you a side glance. The officer introduced him as 'Guruji'. We exchanged a polite namaste, and he enquired about my batchmates and other officers. After a few minutes of small talk, I left their place.

I had forgotten this incident completely. Guruji made me recollect then, ten years after the insignificant meeting. Then Guruji asked me, 'Do you know why the gentleman fixed that meeting?' Without waiting for the negative response from me, Guruji said that the gentleman wanted to consult him whether it would have been appropriate to approach me for a marriage proposal of his eldest daughter. It was the biggest surprise of my life. I never imagined the purpose of introducing me to Guruji by this senior officer.

We started coming to Guruji's durbar regularly. Here, under the divine umbrella of Guruji, we had the opportunity of getting the companionship of a beautiful and loving sangat family of the Tricity and Punjab.

Urvashi's First Darshan

In 1995, Guruji came to Hoshiarpur to the house of the Chaudhurys. Dr O.P. Chaudhury was a leading and famous doctor. He ran his own practice in town. His son, Dr Rohit Chaudhury, after finishing his MBBS, also joined the practice. Mrs Chaudhury was a social worker, quite active in the Red Cross welfare activities, where Urvashi, as the wife of the Deputy Commissioner, was ex-officio the chairperson of a couple of NGOs. Urvashi developed quite a good social and professional relationship with Mrs Chaudhury.

The Chaudhurys had been devotees of Guruji for a long time. Urvashi was prompted by Mrs Chaudhury to have darshan of Guruji. When Urvashi had her first darshan, she had a realization that Guruji had an other-worldly persona. In her second darshan at Jalandhar Mandir, Urvashi had the surprise of her life. After she paid her respects, Guruji opened the dossier of Urvashi, about her family and the family home at Cuttack. She was told about the personal characteristics of each member, the details of trees within the boundary of their house, and the ailments suffered by the family members. The most astounding part was the revelation of a miscarriage that her mother had to endure. This was unknown to Urvashi. She later got it confirmed from her mother.

Dossiers of the American Doctor

It was one of those evenings when Guruji was in the sangat hall well before the sangat started pouring in. There were a handful of sangat, at best five to six families. I was sitting beside Guruji's aasan and was immersed in small talks. On the other side, the brother of one devotee, who was a surgeon in the US, was sitting and pressing Guruji's palm. His sister was sent to the kitchen for some purpose. Other sangat were sitting in a dispersed manner, keeping adequate distance, as it was not during the regular sangat hours. After some moments, Guruji took the palm of the doctor and examined it playfully. Suddenly, he said, 'Doc Sahib, you have only one kidney!' The doctor was startled and blurted out, 'Yes, Guruji. But how do you know?' Guruji gave a wry smile. The next bombshell from Guruji was, 'Doc Sahib, your girlfriend's name starts with an "M".' The gentleman fell flat at the feet of Guruji and requested him to stop opening his personal dossier. He was in his mid-forties, unmarried and had the companionship of this person with the initial 'M', unknown to his family members.

Extra Sensory Vision and Trikal Darshi

The Bhatias were facing financial problems due to several factors. They were keen to invest their meager savings into one proposed project. They were regulars at Empire Estate, enjoying the divine presence of the revered Guruji. He knew about their difficulties by the virtue of his omniscience. He advised them not to go for the particular investment, which turned out prophetic. He advised them to use the money prudently than investing in dubious projects.

Later on, the project failed and the partners faced severe financial stringency. During these confabulations, one day, Guruji casually mentioned the exact amount in their bank account and in fixed deposits. The Bhatias themselves did not have the exact knowledge about their savings in their bank accounts. They verified from the bank the next day and the amount matched exactly with what Guruji had mentioned the previous day. They were wondering how Guruji knew about the exact amount they had in their accounts. It dawned on them that Guruji had exercised his third eye vision—extra sensory vision or perception. If he wished, he could, by his supernatural powers, know what is happening beyond what could be visualized by the ordinary sense organs. He could know the details of things, people and events happening far away.

Junior Jethra Gets a Job

The younger son of Mr Sumeet Jethra, despite being an engineering graduate, was not professionally engaged in any appropriate job. He was employed in a company handling financial investments, known to not having a good reputation. The all-knowing Guruji could visualize his bleak future in the investment company and advised him to switch to another company. The younger Jethra made frantic efforts to apply for jobs and went through the motions of sending profiles and references and appearing for interviews. Guruji could visualize the palpable distress that was going through the mind of the youngster. One evening in Empire Estate, he told younger Jethra that his period of agony was going to end and he would get a better and professionally befitting job within 15 days. On the thirteenth day after the utterances of Guruji, younger Jethra got a job offer from a company, and the position and job profile was appropriate for his professional expertise and qualification. Who else could prophesize in this manner, knowing well what was going to happen in the future? This is just one among thousands of instances of precognition (future vision of trikal darshi ability) experienced by the devotees of Guruji.

Ravi Rai's Promotion Foretold

Ravi Rai, who was in the merchant navy, was not being promoted to the rank of captain in his parent company due to a lack of positions and other factors. He was contemplating shifting to another shipping company with a promotion. When he was on leave at Chandigarh, he got a call from another shipping company for a personal interaction. They had promised that the interaction would be for captainship. Before going for the interview, Ravi thought it appropriate to seek Guruji's blessings. When the matter was broached to Guruji, he just said, '*Ghum aa* (Okay, make the trip).' Such a cryptic and laconic reply perplexed Ravi. It was neither positive nor negative about the outcome of the interview.

Ravi went for the interview. To his surprise, the shipping company had changed their stance; they offered him a position below the captain's rank. Ravi refused to accept the offer. So, as Guruji had mentioned, the trip was not professionally fruitful but only a visit to Mumbai.

When Ravi came back to Chandigarh, he found that his old firm has offered him to join back. Guruji advised him to accept the offer. He left for Scotland from where he was to set sail. He had a dream in which Guruji was mentioning 14 July as a date to remember. When the ship arrived, he was taken on a parallel trip to the Caribbean. Ravi was given the charge of the ship and made captain, relieving the charge officer on 14 July.

Precognition about December Weather in the US

Mrs Ahuja and Lieutenant General Ahuja sought Guruji's blessings for the wedding of their eldest son, Manoj, an IAS officer in the Odisha cadre. Guruji attended the wedding at Chandimandir and blessed the couple. He told Mrs Ahuja that the couple would have two sons, which turned out to be true. In due course, Manoj and Aarti (also an IAS officer) were blessed with two sons.

Rahul, the youngest son of the Ahujas, was getting married to an American girl. The Ahujas sought Guruji's blessings and permission for the proposal. Guruji not only agreed to the proposal, he also fixed a date in December for the wedding. He gifted cotton trousers and a silk shirt and advised General Ahuja to wear them to the wedding. General Ahuja was perplexed. How was it possible that the cotton trousers and silk shirt would make him comfortable in December in the US? But, as the will of Guruji would prevail, the weather was sunny and bright. General Ahuja wore the trousers and the shirt for the wedding function in the US.

The Zipper Moment

Mrs Krishna Sethi, wife of Mr Gopal Sethi, was suffering from a number of ailments. Before she was cured by Guruji's blessings, she had undergone several surgeries. One day, Gopal Uncle was joking around with his wife stating that she should get a zipper inserted on her body so the doctors could easily open her up without much difficulty to treat her internal organs. During the process of her recovery from the ailments, Gopal Uncle was asked to hold a satsang. Gopal Uncle was describing how Guruji's divine presence and his blessings in the cocktail of chai prasad, sabads, langar prasad and sweet prasads have impacted positively on Krishna and how she is on the way to a fast recovery from her multiple ailments. Guruji intervened in between and asked Gopal Uncle to also add the joke of the zipper in his satsang. The zipper joke was never mentioned to Guruji by anybody. It was a demonstration of his power to know things and utterances far beyond the limits of the sense organs.

From Colonel to General

General Deepak Malhotra was a colonel in 1994–95. One day, Guruji told Colonel Malhotra that he (Guruji) had made him a general. But first, Colonel Malhotra had to cross a couple of obstacles to reach that milestone. The first one was that he has to become a brigadier, the qualifying rank for a general. For that, a colonel has to undergo the Long Defence Management Course (LDMC). Colonel Malhotra was not nominated for the course despite his bright credentials. The second hurdle was that one has to undergo the National Defense College (NDC) course for being promoted from the rank of brigadier to general. The third was the fierce competition among brigadiers from the artillery. By Guruji's grace, without the LDMC, Colonel Malhotra was promoted to brigadier. He was nominated to undergo the NDC course. Though artillery brigadiers were no favourites for being promoted to generals, Brigadier Malhotra made it to the general rank. Guruji's words bore fruit after years. How prophetic was Guruji!

Vision beyond the Walls

Colonel S.K. Joshi was posted out of Jalandhar and had to pack his household goods in neat boxes, duly numbered for easy identification at the time of reopening the packs. During this period when the packing was going on, Guruji paid a visit to their house one evening. When Guruji was about to settle down, the lights went out. There was a frantic search for the emergency back-up light, but it was nowhere to be found. Suddenly, Guruji told them that the emergency light has been packed in Box No. 13. The box was opened, and to everyone's surprise and delight, the emergency light was there.

Water after 100 Years

Sukhi Aunty's father bought a piece of land in Dabkauri Village near Chandigarh. Guruji advised them to dig a tube well and grow vegetables there. They engaged a boring machine to bore a tube well. Even after boring 450 feet, no water could be found. Being distressed, they approached Guruji. He told them to dig the tube well at a particular spot on the piece of land. When they started drilling, water gushed out of the well. The land was initially declared barren, as several attempts to extract groundwater in the past were unsuccessful. The locals say that it has been nearly 100 years since the last instance of a trace of water was found in the locality. There were folklores of dried wells and barren land. It was a miracle to find so much water and that too at such a depth. Guruji advised them and the villagers not to commercially utilize the water from the wells. Now, it is greenery all around and the farmers in the adjoining lands are also getting free water for irrigating their lands.

Reading the Minds

They Were Not Denied Their Party

B.B. Chaudhury, a chartered accountant in Delhi, had his first darshan of Guruji in January 2000. Mr Chaudhury, along with his friend, an income tax (IRS) officer, had planned for a drinks-and-dinner stag party on a Saturday. On Friday evening, when they were taking leave, Guruji told them to come the next day. They were a bit disappointed that they would not get to attend the party.

On Saturday, after the langar was served to the sangat, Guruji asked them to stay back. He took them to the house of a senior customs officer. The officer was celebrating his promotion and when they reached his house, the two of them were offered drinks. They were reluctant to take the drinks in Guruji's presence. Guruji looked into Mr Chaudhury's eye and said that he has been cribbing about the missed party. Guruji directed them to drink to their hearts' content and enjoy the party. Mr Chaudhury fell at the feet of the all-knowing Guiding Spirit.

The Desire to Have Paneer Tikka

One evening, Sukhmani and her mother, Sukhi Aunty, were getting ready to go to Guruji's place. Sukhmani expressed her desire to her mother that she wanted to eat paneer tikka (fried cottage cheese) that evening. They were supposed to reach Guruji's place in time for some sewa, and there was little time left for such preparations. When they reached Guruji's place, they were told to accompany him to a devotee's house. After attending the function there, Guruji asked them to follow his car. Guruji took them to a five-star hotel and went straight to the coffee shop. The disciples ordered some tit-bits along with coffee, but Guruji ordered paneer tikka. Sukhmani had completely forgotten about her utterances to her mother regarding her desire to have paneer tikka in the evening. Now, when the paneer tikka arrived, Guruji pushed the entire plate to Sukhmani and said, 'Our daughter wanted to have paneer tikka, now eat to your heart's content.' Tears rolled down her cheeks realizing the love and affection of Guruji and his omniscient powers.

The Longing of Justice Gill for a Rudraksha Mala

Justice A.S. Gill, while posted in Ropar in 1987, saw a photograph of Indira Gandhi wearing a rudraksha mala. He coveted a similar one and prayed to Guruji for the same. After two months, he went to Jalandhar to have Guruji's darshan. Guruji implored him if he wanted anything. Justice Gill replied that he did not want anything but his blessings. Guruji asked him to stretch his palm and he produced a rudraksha mala out of nowhere and placed it on his stretched palm. Guruji smiled and corroborated what Justice Gill wanted. Justice Gill recollected his prayer to Guruji two months back and how he could read his mind, his desires and blessed him with the rudraksha mala.

Colonel Chatterjee's Request for More Amrit

Guruji used to give a glass of amrit to each devotee who used to come to Jalandhar Mandir. One day, Colonel Chatterjee was sitting close to Guruji's aasan after he had his quota of amrit. But he thought he would be lucky if he got another glass. Guruji suddenly asked Colonel Chatterjee to take another glass of amrit. Again, after 15 minutes, Guruji gave him a third glass of amrit. Guruji, the mahayogi, could read the mind of the devotee and satisfied him with two additional glasses of amrit.

The Third Ear (Clairaudience)

The Party and the Cuisine

One of our batchmates had resigned from service, just after he was posted as a sub-divisional magistrate in one of the remote corners of Odisha. Both the husband and wife were accomplished IT software engineers. That was in 1987 and the career avenues for

IT professionals were just opening up. There were other reasons too for the gentleman's resignation from the Indian Administrative Service. Both of them had joined a reputed multinational and had been posted in Europe. That summer, they had come to Chandigarh to meet their parents. They invited a couple of us for dinner to meet everyone before leaving for Europe. To attend the party implied that we would miss the sangat. The previous evening, we had sought Guruji's permission to attend the party to which Guruji had readily agreed. He further gave a detailed description of the gentleman's father and further furnished the house number where he was staying. We took it casually as Guruji was interacting with so many senior officers (one of whom was the father of the batchmate, a state civil servant).

We attended the party which was uneventful, but the pleasure was in meeting other batchmates and friends. The next day, when we reached the sangat hall, it was almost full. After paying the usual respects to Guruji, we settled comfortably near his aasan. Then he suddenly asked, '*Party kimen raha* (How was the party)?' I kept silent, as there was nothing noteworthy to mention. Then Guruji told about the number of drinks I had, each and every item of food, drink and sweet dish served in the party. We were speechless and kept nodding our heads in agreement. We could realize that Guruji could position himself any time at any place, irrespective of the past, present and future, and as a trikal darshi, would tell the details. No wonder, our heads were bowed in reverence.

Laghima of Guruji

The Sukhna Walks

When Guruji was in Sector 33, Chandigarh, he used to hold sangat regularly. There were no off-sangat days. Every evening, the sangat would be held till 11–11.30 p.m. After giving permission to most of the sangat to leave, he would go for changing his attire to informal trousers and a T-shirt. He would then engage in conversation with the remainder small group of sangat. Sometimes, we would have even a second or even third round of chai prasad or paratha prasad. Sometimes, it extended till 2–3 a.m. in the night. Then Guruji would take the small group for a walk to Sukhna Lake. Everybody, including the author, would try to keep pace with Guruji. But these attempts would result in failure. Guruji would be far ahead. Was he floating in the air? It is a different matter that when Guruji reaches the lake, the peacocks in the golf range or in the lower Kansal hills would welcome him in their characteristic cacophony. In the dead of night, the cacophony of peacocks is not usually heard.

Materialization: Ability to Control the Panchbhutas (the Elements of Nature)

The Divine Prasad

Guruji occasionally, of his own volition, would produce prasad out of nowhere. It would be like he would be in a state of complete contemplation or meditation sitting on his aasan in front of the sangat. For the sangat, his physical presence is immanent, but his real self would be in a different world. This has been noticed by many. During one of those moments of contemplation, he would produce a special kind of prasad out of nowhere. He would just open one palm and a small amount of prasad, a kind of kada prasad, but crystal like mishri, made of suji and piping hot, would materialize. The small amount would grow to a large volume covering Guruji's palm entirely. The sangat knows that whatever Guruji had in his palm is more than what could be accommodated in two palms of any devotee. He would call, immediately after the small amount of prasad was produced, to a chosen sangat and would hand over the prasad when it had attained full volume. Such prasad would always be full of fragrance of a special kind. The devotees reverentially labelled such a special prasad as sachkhand prasad. Guruji would then distribute the sachkhand prasad to the sangat present, and the rest would be given to the chosen individual devotee. After producing the prasad, Guruji would experience a severe headache. He would invariably tie a dupatta or similar cloth around his forehead to overcome the pain. It would remain for nearly half an hour. The occasions of production of sachkhand prasad were very rare.

Urvashi used to go to Panchkula to the Ahujas, where regular sangat was held after restrictions for a month and a half. One day, there were 20–30 odd sangat when suddenly Guruji called Urvashi to come near his aasan. She was sitting nearby and she crawled near his aasan facing Guruji. He produced the sachkhand prasad and handed it over to Urvashi. After distributing to the sangat (in small quantities), he directed Urvashi to share the prasad with her family members and keep the rest as blessings. He said that it would never get spoiled and would retain the fragrance forever. He took Urvashi's dupatta and wrapped it around his forehead.

After Urvashi came home, we shared the sachkhand prasad and kept the rest in a safe place. True to Guruji's word, it never got spoiled, nor did it lose its divine fragrance.

Materialization of Presents

Guruji would call me and Urvashi during the day, well before the usual sangat time. Some other sangat were also being called. He loved to have a small group and would start some discussion or follow up on some matter. On that day, in Sector 33, another senior bureaucrat couple, along with their daughter, was present. The three of them, Urvashi and I were inside Guruji's room. Guruji would be in a reclining position on the carpet or on the bed. He would extend his palm to be pressed. One of the bureaucrat couple was pressing his palm. He got up from the carpet and asked their daughter to come forward. He suddenly stretched his hand and opened his palm. There was a beautiful gold chain. Handing over the chain to the daughter, he said to her, '*Eh blessings hai. Innu paya karo* (These are blessings, keep wearing it).' We were stupefied; Guruji had produced the chain out of nowhere.

That was not all. The next moment, he beckoned me and said '*Lo*'. When I stretched my palm out, there was a gold bracelet in my hand. Again he said, '*Blessed kitta. Innu sambhal ke rakhana*

(I have blessed it. Keep it in safe custody.)' He never asked me to wear it. That was our divine blessing, to be cherished and kept safe.

~

It was Tuesday, the auspicious day earmarked for Lord Hanuman. Guruji was recuperating at Empire Estate. After the langar prasad, Guruji took a limited number of sangat present there for an outing. The destination was not known to the sangat and comprised Sudha Aunty, myself, Urvashi, our daughter Jenny, Jyoti (Guruji's niece), and a couple of others. We had to follow Guruji's car. We stopped in front of Hanuman Mandir on Baba Kharag Singh Marg, Connaught Place. Some of the sangat paid respect to Lord Hanuman at the gate of the temple. Guruji was taking a short walk when suddenly called for Jenny and said, '*Le-take*.' When Jenny approached closer to him and opened her palm, a gold sovereign was sitting on it. All of us were stupefied. The gold sovereign was materialized from nowhere. It was a blessing for an eight-year-old child, who once had expressed (when she was six years old) that she felt Guruji was her heavenly father.

The Mango Bite

Jenny was fond of a variety of candies. She was particularly fond of Mango Bite. Guruji's nieces, Poonam and Jyoti, who were staying with us in Chandigarh, were subsequently allowed to stay in the villa in Empire Estate. Jenny was quite attached to them. So one day, Poonam suggested to Guruji that Jenny could also stay there for some time. Her school vacation had started. Guruji agreed to Poonam's suggestion. During her stay, Jenny would go to Guruji's room and just sit there or sleep on the floor.

One day, Guruji came out of the retiring room and stood in the hall, where the sangat was held. Jenny and one other person were in the hall. Guruji called Jenny and asked to open her palm. Guruji materialized a single Mango Bite from nowhere and handed it over to Jenny. The person present there asked her to pay her respects to Guruji as he had blessed her. She complied with the suggestion. Guruji told her to eat the candy then and there.

In the evening after we came back from the villa, Jenny described the incident. But, being a child, she could not recollect who the other person was.

Car Driven without Petrol

Jagi Grewal and his family (Rimple, his wife and others) are long-time devotees of Guruji. His father-in-law, Dr Chahal, a professor at Punjab Agricultural University, Ludhiana, was one of the earliest devotees of Guruji. One day, Guruji landed up at Dr Chahal's house with a couple of sangat. The devotees and Guruji had langar and by the time it got over, it was quite late. So, Jagi Grewal was asked by Guruji to drop him at Jalandhar Mandir, 70 km away. Jagi drove his car with Guruji. At the outskirts of Ludhiana, he realized that the car was running out of petrol. He needed to refill the tank. Guruji read his mind and told him to keep driving as the car had enough petrol. Jagi Grewal dutifully kept driving at 80 kmph on the national highway. When he reached Goraya, he realized again that the petrol tank was empty. Whatever reserve was there was enough to drive a dozen kilometres, but he had already driven 40 km. He again thought of refilling the tank. Guruji again read his mind and told him to keep driving as there is enough petrol and that he should not lose his confidence in Guruji. Grewal made the drive to Jalandhar and Guruji settled at the mandir in Defence Colony. Guruji told him that he had driven the car without petrol. But the next morning, on his return journey to Ludhiana, he should fill up the tank, as Guruji would not allow him to run the car without petrol all the time.

~

Justice Gill was posted as a district and sessions judge in Patiala in 1989. He sent his personal car for Guruji's use in Jalandhar.

He ensured that the petrol tank was full and also provided extra money to the driver for refill. One day, the petrol tank got almost empty, and the driver had already exhausted the extra money given to him. Guruji asked the driver to drive the car. The driver wanted to refill the petrol tank before embarking on the journey. But Guruji insisted him to go on driving. After a few kilometres, the driver was surprised to find the fuel indicator showing that the tank was full. This happened a couple of times. When the driver was to return to Patiala, Guruji produced three ₹100 notes and told the driver to fill the tank and then embark on the return journey.

Diamonds for Rimple

The Grewals, Rimple and Jagi, are ardent devotees of Guruji. Rimple's parents were among the few devotees who came in contact with him in the early 1980s. Guruji, while undertaking various journeys in Punjab, used to stop at the residence of Rimple's parents in Ludhiana or at the ancestral house of the Grewals. The caravan of Guruji's entourage would invariably stop for a tea break or langar during such tours to various locations in Punjab.

A miraculous event happened during one such tour. Guruji was attending a function in the residence of one of the devotees of Sangrur. The Grewals, along with a couple of other sangat, accompanied Guruji. The function was a grand success. Guruji blessed many new devotees who came to pay their respects to him. After the function was over, Guruji went to retire in one of the rooms. Rimple and Jagi were sitting beside Guruji and rendering sewa. Guruji was in his jovial and wittiest best. He jokingly said that Rimple is fond of diamonds. Suddenly, he asked Rimple to stretch out her palm. He waived his hand and there came, out of nowhere, two diamond studs partially wrapped in a currency note—a British Pound. The diamonds retained the fragrance of Guruji even after 12 years.

Materialization of a Ladoo for Nitin

Nitin Joshi, Colonel Joshi's younger son, had witnessed several occasions when Guruji produced materials, sachkhand prasad, earrings in dollar notes, hot halwa, mishri-lined burfi, chocolate and vanilla burfi and besan ladoos. One day in Jalandhar, Nitin was sitting close to Guruji's aasan. He prayed that Guruji could produce sachkhand prasad. After langar, the sangat were seated around Guruji's aasan. Suddenly, Guruji opened his fist. A ladoo, as big as two cricket balls, appeared and started gaining volume at every passing second. It was a like a sponge that enlarged as you open your fist.

So, Guruji fulfilled the prayers of young Nitin. Not only sachkhand prasad was materialized from thin air, it had also grown in size, as Guruji opened his fist.

Controlling the Elements of Nature

No Rain on a Small Patch

Colonel Joshi was group commander of the National Security Guard (NSG) at Manesar during 1995–8. One day, the Director General (DG) decided to inspect the unit. All preparations were made for the intending visit. As the usual practice in the army and paramilitary forces, there was significant cleaning, putting colourful flags on flag posts enroute and all the places the DG would like to inspect or visit, marking the routes with white powder markers and pulling out the red carpet for reception, banners, etc. The unit roads were swept clean of dust, and even the trees were brushed up.

On the appointed day, Colonel Joshi was travelling from his Delhi residence to Manesar. Unfortunately, the sky opened up and it was raining cats and dogs. The sky was completely overcast with clouds indicating that it could be raining in Manesar too. Colonel Joshi was apprehensive that all the cleaning and markings would get washed away and dirt would cover the roads and the carpets. He prayed to Guruji that the DG should not get disappointed with his preparations.

When Colonel Joshi approached Manesar, it was under heavy torrential rain. But when he approached the vicinity of the NSG unit, he found there was scanty rain and at the gate of the unit, there was practically none. There were a few square kilometres around the unit that did not experience any rain. Colonel Joshi thanked Guruji. The DG visited the unit and was quite satisfied. Colonel Joshi was given a commendation certificate for his excellent management and maintenance of the NSG unit at Manesar.

Rains without Clouds

During his stay at Empire Estate, Guruji would call Colonel Joshi to do sewa at the villa during non-sangat hours or days. One day, the Colonel was pressing Guruji's palms. He had been outside to get some oxygen (his euphemism for a drag of cigarette) a few minutes ago. Guruji asked him, '*Joshi Uncle, ki barish ho rahi hai* (Is it raining outside)?' Joshi Uncle, buttressed by his knowledge of the outside world (no clouds, clear sunshine) from his foray to the lanes of Empire Estate a few minutes earlier, confidently answered in the negative. Guruji told him to go outside and report back after verifying. Colonel Joshi was sure there was no rain. He emphatically told him about his visit to the lanes of Empire Estate a few minutes ago and how there was no rain then. Guruji again insisted he should go outside and check. He trouped outside the villa, and lo and behold, there was a singular cloud hovering over the sky above Empire Estate and there was drizzle. He came back and fell at the feet of the Divine because he doubted his assertion that there was rain outside.

Ability to Locate Himself at Different Places Simultaneously

In 1992, the mother of Justice A.S. Gill fell very sick and went into a coma. She was 95 years old and there was no hope for her survival. Unable to bear the pain, Justice Gill prayed to Guruji to relieve his mother from the pain and agony of the illness, hospitalization, coma and trauma. After a couple of his prayers,

Guruji entered from the front door, which was closed from the inside. Guruji asked Justice Gill to fetch a glass of water, which he blessed. He advised to give two spoons of the blessed water to his mother and told him that her soul will leave the body at 2 a.m. Then, Guruji left the room cautioning them not to come out for 10 minutes.

They came out after 10 minutes. When they enquired from the guard posted outside their residence about the whereabouts of Guruji, the guard informed that nobody had entered or gone out of their house. Justice Gill immediately rang up Jalandhar Mandir to find out about Guruji. The sangat informed that Guruji was very much there entertaining the sangat. Justice Gill's mother passed away exactly at 2 a.m. that night.

Multi-Presence: Fragrance in Oxford and Manhattan

There are numerous instances described by individual devotees of Guruji on how they could actually experience Guruji's presence in the form of his typical fragrance, in locations far away (even in foreign lands) from the place of stay of Guruji. Even after Guruji had left his physical body on 30 May 2007, several devotees have experienced his divine presence by way of a whiff of his fragrance, which lingers for a while (a few minutes) so that the devotees can confirm his presence through their olfactory sensory system, rather than thinking that they are imagining the existence of Guruji's fragrance. Such a sensory experience is not confined to only one individual sangat. If they happen to be in a group, the entire group of devotees experiences such a fragrance—confirming Guruji's cosmic presence. Such a presence is not due to the prayers of the devotees in distress; it is Guruji's own volition as to where and when he would make his presence felt to which individual or group of devotees.

Mr R.L. Sudhir (Retd IAS) has two sons, Sanjay and Shashi. Sanjay was undergoing a course in Oxford when I was pursuing an MBA at Birmingham University. We used to visit Sanjay and engage in impromptu satsangs. After a couple of days, he could smell Guruji's fragrance, signifying Guruji's presence in the proximity of a devotee. Similarly, Sanjay's younger brother was doing a course in New York. He could also sense Guruji's fragrance in Manhattan, making him realize the benign presence of Guruji for blessing the devotee.

Part III

The Leela and Mauz of Guruji

5

Sangat and Satsang

Sangat and satsang are intricately intertwined. Both these words have their origin in Sanskrit. 'Sang' is the common root word to both, and has its origin in the Sanskrit word *sangh,* which means company, fellowship, association or community. The root word *sat* in Sanskrit means true or truth. The word satsang connotes 'association or being with the truth' or 'communion with the truth'. The ultimate truth is the Lord, the Supreme. Hence, the company, the association or the fellowship of seekers of the ultimate truth is called a satsang. In other words, it can be said that satsang refers to associating with good people or being in the company of truth and refers to the act of the gathering of like-minded people on a spiritual pursuit. When satsang is described as an association with the truth, there are two ways it can be interpreted—satsang as an individual activity or satsang as a group activity.

INTERNAL SATSANG (INDIVIDUAL ACTIVITY)

Satsang is associated with the inner quality of *sattva* (goodness or purity), which is one of the three *gunas* (natural attributes), along with *rajas* (passion) and *tamas* (inactivity), the other two. A sattvic person is a natural satsangi in whom sattva manifests as thoughtfulness, wisdom, contemplation and peaceful demeanor. Individual satsang can be practised by cultivating truth within one's inner self (divinity in each individual), remaining centered on thoughts of the Divine. As the great sages have told, the sat is within us. It is the self or *atman* (soul). However, with the rise of false-ego sensibility, individuals identify it with the physical body and the material world (*maya*), which obscures the internal self. This confounding of the self with the body is a duality, and non-confounding, on the other hand, is an identification with the Supreme (divine essence, the homogeneous oneness, etc.). Till the self is not understood to be the sat, we seek external association of those who have experienced and understood it.

In the Indian religious traditions, satsang typically refers to individual spiritual and devotional activities such as meditation or chanting. Satsang, in this sense, is akin to the *niyams* for yogic path to enlightenment as described by Patanjali in his Yoga Sutra. Satsang helps keep people engaged in spiritually centred thoughts and to maintain focus on their spiritual path. The word satsang, in the individual sense, refers to the fellowship with God in meditation.

Osho Satsang Meditation Centre says, 'Satsang meant the company of one's self, of the truth, and that the truth was not to be found outside [...] It is inside you and if you wish to attain it, seek your own company.'[1] In other words, cultivate the truth that you are the divinity and seek the self within you.

SATSANG BY FELLOWSHIP OF LIKE-MINDED PEOPLE (GROUP SATSANG)

Satsang as a group activity refers to the fellowship or congregation of a group of like-minded people seeking the truth. In the olden days, satsang referred only to a gathering in the presence of a true-enlightened being or satguru. However, in recent times, it has evolved to connotate, 'any gathering in which spiritual reflection, discussion, meditation or teaching takes place'.[2] Such spiritual discussions may involve *kirtan,* sabad and/or reflecting upon the mahima of God or guru.

---

[1]'Satsang & Darshan', Satsang-Darshan.com, https://bit.ly/3iRKI2T. Accessed on 19 January 2023.

[2]'Satsang', Yogapedia, 11 August 2020, https://bit.ly/3ifvLHv. Accessed on 4 December 2023.

The satsangs that took place in the presence of Guruji were group satsangs in the presence of an enlightened master. A realized soul like Guruji is always in God-consciousness. He is *Brahmgiani* and self-realized. He is completely established in the highest plane of consciousness, and he has cleansed his heart and conquered his mind. So, he is truthful through and through. Such a great soul also helps other devotees recover from their delusion.

In fact, the Gurbani (SGGS, 140.2) demands such awakened and enlightened beings to help others to get rid of ignorance and illusion.

> *Jan Nanak tisu blihaaranai*
> *jo aapi japai awaraa Naamu japaavai*
>
> Servant Nanak is a sacrifice to one who he understands Naam (Giaan...), and inspires others to understand it as well.

The Gurbani defines satsang or 'true association' in the following manner:

> *Satsangati kaise janio. Jithe eko naam vakhaniao.*
> *Ek naam hokum hai Nanak Satiguru dia bujhai jio.*
>
> How is the satsangat to be known? There, only the name of one Lord is chanted. The one name is the Lord's command. Oh Nanak! the satiguru has given me this understanding.

Satsang or 'true association' is that company where only the *Naam* (knowledge about the Absolute) of the Truth is remembered. Without meeting this definition, any company or congregation is nothing more than a gathering of materialistic beings, in pursuit of materialistic goals—maya or delusion. Meeting of people merely at the physical plane, mental plane, emotional plane or superficial-intelligence plane does not constitute *saadh-sangat*. *Asatsang* (non-satsang) is the greatest hindrance to spirituality. Only in the community of saints and seekers can people aspire to greatness and realization within themselves. With guidance in the form of good company, the seeker may finally reach a place of inner communion with God.

The importance of satsang was beautifully explained by Sant Kabir in the following *doha*:

> *Te din gaye akaarthi, sangat bhai na sant*
> *Prem bina pashu jeevana, Bhakti bina bhagwant*

> I wasted those days when I didn't meet good people.
> A person without love is a beast. There is no divinity without love.[3]

Jagadguru Shankaracharya had also spoken eloquently about the satsang (good and virtuous company):

> *Sat-sangatve nissangatvam nissangatve nirmohatvam*
> *Nirmohatve nishchala-tattvam nishchala-tattve jivanmuktih*
> *Bhaja govindam bhaja govindam bhaja govindam mudha-mate.*

> Good and virtuous company gives rise to non-attachment. From non-attachment comes freedom from delusion. With freedom from delusion, one feels the changeless reality. Experiencing that changeless reality, one attains liberation in this life. I-AM is the ocean of awareness. Realizing this, one feels, 'I am not the body and mind, although I have a body and mind.' Realize Govinda, realize Govinda in your heart, O wise one![4]

One of the important niyams of Patanjali is the practice of *shaucha*, which means cleanliness of the surroundings, the physical body and most importantly, cleanliness of the mind. The mind is like a crystal, which takes the characteristic colour of whatever is near,

---

[3]Abckadwa, 'Sant Kabir Ke Dohe', The Words of Enlightened Masters, 13 August 2011, https://bit.ly/3ItwvU7. Accessed on 4 December 2023.

[4]Gannon, Sharon, 'Satsang', Jivamukti Yoga, December 2012, https://bit.ly/3VKtUZ6. Accessed on 4 December 2023.

and reflects the surrounding environment. Similarly, the mind reflects (colours) according to what you expose it to. Satsang helps cleanse your mind. When so many like-minded people sit together in meditation during satsangs, the vibration is raised to such an extent that it feels like you are transported to a different world (of spirituality).

A satsangi adopts a life of piousness by surrounding themselves with good people engaged in mediation, prayers, reading religious books, biographies of enlightened masters and undertaking sewa for the Lord. Swami Paramhansa Yogananda in his book *Whispers from Eternity* states:

> Fellowship between people strengthens the magnetism of their association. If company is spiritual, such as in the presence of saints and devotees, then the aspirant will be more strongly magnetized along the spiritual path. If the association is material, then the individual will feel the pull of material attachments.[5]

THE RELATIONSHIP BETWEEN INDIVIDUAL (INTERNAL) AND GROUP SATSANGS

The relationship between the individual (internal or within) and the external satsang (in association of sadh sangat or a group of like-minded people sincerely following the spiritual path) is quite intricate. The external satsang provides the true knowledge or atma-gyan to the seeker. The person becomes fit to embark upon seeking the true source through the internal satsang. With the help of the internal satsang, the individual seeker experiences the intuitive understanding of the atman. The seeker feels uplifted and inspired to trudge on the spiritual path and the individual overcomes worries, tensions, doubts, ignorance of one's true nature, mundane thoughts, material consciousness, false ego,

[5]Yogananda, Paramhansa, *Whispers from Eternity,* Crystal Clarity Publishers, USA, 2008. [Audiobook]

tossing or restlessness of the mind. This needs stillness of the mind, which is essential for self-actualization or the realization of God.

There may be an alternative mechanism involved in the relationship between the two types of satsangs. The person, who has attained atma-gyan from the internal satsang, may radiate the divine energy to the rest of the individuals in the sangat. They may be the enlightened one or a highly evolved spiritual being.

These days, a satsang is being loosely interpreted and organized by many religious, semi-spiritual, religious-cum-social-mobilization groups. Organizing kirtan or reading of religious texts followed by some sermonizing by a good speaker is projected as a satsang. This kind of satsang does not strictly qualify as an individual or group satsang. Such satsang may be serving the socio-psychological and political needs of people. But the core or fundamental characteristics of the spiritual quest and the purity of intention of the congregation may be missing.

The other kind of satsang is gathering of the followers of a religious or spiritual guru or elevated soul and listening to the glory of the enlightened spiritual leader, either in the presence of the enlightened person or in the symbolic presence in the form of their swaroop or any other symbolism adopted by the followers.

SANGAT

The word 'sangat' has been in use since the founder guru of Sikhism, Guru Nanak's time. Sangat is an institution, where the devotees gather in the name of the god, Akal, the timeless lord, to pray and sing Guru Nanak's hymns and partake in *Guru Ka Langar*, where all sit together without distinction of caste or status. Since then, it is referred to the Sikh brotherhood. In Sikhism, utmost importance is attached to meeting of the followers in sangat. It is essential for the progress in one's spiritual journey and considered as an ethical training. The opposite of satsang is *kusangat* (undesirable association). In Sikhism, worshiping and praying together by spiritually surcharged seekers (sangat) is considered more rewarding than isolated religious practices. The other associated ethical practices, like engaging in acts of sewa, are highly valued. Sewa can take the form of looking after and dusting of the shoes of the sangat, cleaning the gurudwara, preparing and serving langar to the sangat, and many other acts of service. This inculcates the piousness and egolessness in the spiritual seeker. In these sangat, the disciples mingle together without considerations of birth, profession or worldly position.

SANGAT AND SATSANG IN GURUJI'S SYSTEM

The communion that happens between the sangat and Guruji is ethereal and in total silence. It is not a discussion, nor a discourse or debate or dialogue. Guruji used to say, '*Discussion karan naal rab nahin milda* (God is not realized through discussions).'

The communion between Guruji and the disciple happens when the seeker is completely lost, when he is not there. As the Osho Satsang says, 'At the highest peak it is not even an "I-thou" relationship. It is not a relationship at all. I am not and there comes a moment to you also, when you are not. In that moment two zeroes disappear into each other.'[6]

When you are around Guruji, your thoughts may disappear, you lose your mind. That is the only way to be around a master. Go on losing your mind. That is the reason why Guruji used to ask people to leave everything aside and completely surrender to him. Complete shradha and complete surrender. He used to say, '*Mere naal direct connection jodo* (Have a direct communion with me).'

The human mind is full of wavering thoughts. Each moment you have several thoughts jumping from subject to subject. Once you have rid your mind of thoughts, you are relaxed. There is nothing to say. The ambience of so many people listening to sabad and concentrating on Guruji with love, gratitude, sympathy and

---

[6]'Tantric Transformation: I Am Enough Alone', Osho, https://bit.ly/3iPEvVa. Accessed on 19 January 2023.

rapport enhances the holiness of the place. This place—in the presence of Guruji—is all the *tirthas* put together. The atmosphere in Guruji's mandir or the place where he holds sangat is replete with serenity. The sangat invariably gets charged with positive energy.

Guruji used to say there is no need to go to any gurudwara, temple or church. You need to have purity of the mind ('*mana nirmal hona chahinda*') and then come to Guruji. He used to ask people what is the use of going on pilgrimage when Guruji and purity is here, and what use is going to a temple when your mind is not pure and all you have are negative thoughts. He used to say:

> *Paath kidre v kar sakde ho, ghar de kisi v kamre vich rab nu yaad kar sakde ho, toilet vich v.*
>
> You can have prayer or communion with God everywhere. Your prayer can be in any room, even in the toilet.

There is always a special bonding among the members of Guruji's sangat. Each member feels that they are part of a big family. Guruji used to say that he has made them a member of a bigger family, and Guruji's grace ensured that there was bonhomie among the family members. The love and affection of Guruji for the disciples was the added positive. He used to say, '*Mein apne bhagat nu bahut pyar karda* (I love my bhaktas very much).'

It would be inferred that the congregation of the sangat at places of Guruji's stay during his physical days qualifies as sadh-sang or satsang, as duly described by Sant Kabir and Guru Nanak. Guruji is divinity incarnate and the enlightened spiritual leader. An association with Guruji, when he was in physical form, was the ultimate satsang. The magnetic pull of his divinity has immensely benefited thousands of devotees sincerely seeking the spiritual path. This spiritual seeking might be due to their previous karmic earning. They might have already attained spiritual level to varying degrees. Some might have attained it after coming in association with Guruji due to his divine presence and the blessings showered on them.

During Guruji's physical presence, there were institutional satsangs with his knowledge and permission. There were also informal satsangs, when a group of followers would be discussing Guruji's ways and singing his glory within social or private settings. Those satsangs were impromptu discussions and sharing of experiences relating to Guruji. Of course, that is the way (word-of-mouth) the glory of Guruji spreads far and wide.

Oftentimes, the doubting Thomas's rational mind questions the presence of all kinds of people, sometimes of dubious characters in the sangat of Guruji. They would wonder why such persons were being encouraged by Guruji to be part of the sangat. Such questions beg the basic understanding of spirituality. There are numerous stories in our Puranic and epic literature describing how the worst kind of *jivatma* (individual soul) gets mukti because of the blessings of divinity when such personalities seek the Lord sincerely, after feeling remorse and repentance for their sins or bad deeds.

Moreover, divinity does not distinguish between good and bad personalities. Divine grace is like sunlight, which falls on all surfaces—whether full of fragrances or putrid smell. The sun does not distinguish between good and bad surfaces and elements. Similarly, divine love, compassion and grace are for all. That is perhaps the way divinity pulls the not-so-spiritually inclined jivatma towards spiritualism.

It is the deeds of the individual, being blind with illusion (maya) of the forces of nature, which veils the pure atman in each individual. The atman, which resides in every jivatma, is pure and sacred. It is the veil of maya that leads the individual to profane activities. The deeds may be profane, but the soul is pure. Hence, when you equate individual souls with their deeds, you commit the greatest blunder. The enlightened master is beyond such illusions and for him, everybody, irrespective of the good or bad deeds as per societal norms, is dear to him and he showers his blessings, love and compassion on all such persons.

A friend of mine, Shri Jagmohan Bhasin, an ardent devotee of

Guruji, used to say that Guruji's sangat is like *Shivji ki baarat* (the marriage entourage of Lord Shiva). In *Rudra Samhita* (Chapters 41–50), there is a great description of the composition of the baarat of Lord Shiva when he went to get married to Parvati, the daughter of Himalaya, the king of the mountains. The marriage party consisted of Lord Brahma, Lord Vishnu, Devraj Indra and other gods, the Sureshwar Ganas (celestial army of the gods), the sages and rishis, especially the Saptarishis (seven famous sages), the Yakshayas and other Upadevatas (the demi-gods), the sidhas, the Rudra Ganas (army of Lord Shiva), the Viswavasus, Gandarvas (celestial musicians), the Apsaras (the celestial dancers with divine beauty), the Devakanyas (the daughters of the gods—Saraswati, Lakshmi, Savitri, Ganga, Aditi, Shachi, Lopamudra, Arundhati, Ahalya, Tulsi, Swaha, Rohini, Prithvi, Satrupa, Sanjya, Rati), the demons, the ghosts and spirits and the kinnars (the transgenders). All were Shivji's loved devotees and were part of the baarat. Lord Shiva has no discrimination in choosing his devotees.

There is a beautiful description of the sangat by Maharaj Ishar Singh in one of the sabad kirtans being interpreted by Bhai Harinder Singh, from Jagadhri. The sabad is *'Mere hirday tay Waheguru nam likh de.'* There are four categories of people who come to the satsangs held in gurudwaras and other religious places. These are—*unge, sunge, chunge* and *dunge.*

The first category of sangat is called unge. This category of sangat comes to the satsang after finishing the day's activities. They leave the daily troubles, tribulations and struggles of life back at home. The serene, peaceful and soothing atmosphere at the place of sangat makes them forget all these worldly affairs, making them immediately fall asleep. They get up only when the sewadar is distributing *kaddah prasad* (special prasad usually served in gurudwaras), which helps in waking them up from their deep slumber. They have little connection with spiritualism, the philosophical connotations of sabads or the discourses/preachings of the ongoing satsang.

The second category of sangat is called sunge. They come

to the satsang to observe who is part of the congregation. They have either social needs of interaction or economic agenda (networking) for attending the satsang. They have the least spiritual inclination. They observe the dress, behaviour and interaction of other sangat. For them, gathering the information about these peripheral aspects of the sangat is more important than any spiritual goals.

The third category of sangat is called chunge. This category of sangat is like the first one. The difference is that they keep awake and enjoy the ambience of the satsang. They get peace of mind being part of the sangat. Their home atmosphere is not conducive for a lasting peace of their mind. After finishing the day's work, they rush to the satsang. After settling down at a corner, they cherish the chai prasad and the lyrical sabads. Being part of the sangat fulfils the psychological needs of these individuals. They also take interest in the meanings and philosophies of the satsang and sabads. They are somewhat spiritual but not fully committed.

The fourth category of sangat is called dunge. They are sincerely seeking spiritual goal and have the sincere desire to move forward in their spiritual quest. They try to understand the spiritual connotation of the sabads, the pronouncements of the divinity and all that is offered to them being part of the fellowship of like-minded seekers. They are the real devotees of Guruji, referred to as the ones who pray for the 'real thing' (*asal chiz*) rather than asking for material gains.

The Shiva Puran also describes four kinds of devotees or bhaktas. They are:

(i) *Arta:* A person or individual in distress
(ii) *Jigyanshu:* The curious
(iii) *Artharthi:* A person with the purpose of material gain, and
(iv) *Gyani:* The real wise devotee

Most of the sangat falls into the first three categories and a few belong to the last category—the true followers of Guruji. Of course, some of the sangat, who belong to the first three, subsequently graduate to the fourth category, realizing the divinity of Guruji. It is a dynamic process of evolvement on the spiritual journey.

Guruji, in his characteristic way, would also talk about the sangat. He would jokingly say that the Delhi sangat is fond of allopathic solutions. They do not have patience, which is the hallmark of the spiritual path. Moreover, he described most of the sangat as being after materialistic gains and come to Guruji when they are in distress. They would surrender to Guruji and become fully devoted, but would then ask for material rewards like getting oneself or a near and dear one cured of a disease, getting a promotion, getting a child and resolving the issues of business and profession in their favour. They ultimately fall prey to a more intricate veil of the materialistic world—the veil of nature or maya.

One day in Empire Estate, Guruji asked a lady to do a satsang. She was a regular at Guruji's durbar and quite devoted. She went on describing how her insurmountable troubles got resolved and how her family business prospered due to Guruji's blessings. She described Guruji as *sakshat avatar* of Lord Shiv whose blessings had transformed her and her family's fortunes. After concluding her satsang, she begged leave from Guruji and left for home. After she left, Guruji told the sangat, '*See, kimme maya vich phasi hoi hai* (See, how has she been embroiled in maya of materialistic gains).'

Guruji used to joke about such a sangat by stating '*Na mila maya, na mila Ram* (They never get enough material gains because of their insatiate appetite for such gains, or the real blessings of the Lord).' Then he would, over a hundred times, mention '*Koi asal chiz nahin mangda* (Most of the sangat never seek the real thing), being the ultimate divine realization or blessings of Guruji for further advancement on the spiritual path.

Guruji was also emphatic about the characteristics of a true seeker and devotee. He would say that a true seeker would never ask anything from an enlightened master like him. On the other hand, they were supposed to completely surrender to Guruji with all sincerity to seek God. His bywords in this connection are:

'*Mang de nahin, maan de* (Never ask for anything, just surrender)'; '*Je maang ke litta to ki litta?* (When you ask something from Guruji, what do you get?)' You are supposed to become *rasik vairagi*, a devotee detached of desires. Then what is the point in asking for anything from a true guru, as asking involves attachment—the desire to have the fruits of such asking? A true guru showers his grace automatically.

But there were many who did not go to Guruji with expectations or hopes of solving their worldly problems. It was the magnetic charm of his divinity that pulled them to Guruji and to the fold of the sangat. Guruji would also say that he, as a true guru, tests the disciples to know the sincerity of the spiritual quest. He used to say:

> *Jis tarah mitti da bartan khareedan to pahlan usnu thok kar dekhde ho, ki oh kite kachcha ta nai, usi hi tarah main thok ke poori tasli kar ke bhagat banuanda han.*
>
> Like you test the strength and other characteristics of an earthen pot before purchased, by giving a small knock, similarly I allow a person to become true disciple after testing him through many shocks.[7]

He further says:

> *Jis tarah beri te phal lagey hoae, main pahlan beri nu hila denda haan, jere ta kacche hunde han dig jande han, jere rahe jande una numanu main fir nimbu wangu nichor da haan. in pakanda haan. Pakeyan jade mere kol anda hai, oh hi test pass karda hai. Main fir usdi har ek chhoti to chhoti Zaroorat da khayal rakhda han.*
>
> I treat the sangat like the fruits in the ber tree. First I shake the tree, so weaker ones—weak in intention and sincerity for spiritual attainment—fall down. I further test the remaining seekers from the sangat like squeezing a

[7]Sukhmani, *Surcharged with Divine Love*, Unistar Books, Chandigarh, 1998.

> lemon to get its juice. Some of them fail miserably in this test. Rest becomes ripe to attain a higher level of spiritual attainment. And Guruji takes care of all their spiritual requirements by guiding them, hand-holding them like a true master.[8]

Guruji knew the spiritual intent and level of spiritual attainment of each sangat. He used to say:

> *Meri sangat wich kaun kis class wich hai bhi thok ke oh sirf mainu hi pat ai, eh mahapurushan di secret hundi hai.*
>
> I know which Sangat is at which level of spiritual attainment.
>
> *Main aath paudiyan fata fat chada denda haan. Nauvi paudi te aake main pichlin aath paudiyan kitch denda haan. Jine ahankar na kita oh theek hai warna banda ahankar de mare fir pehli pidi te pahunch jaanda hai.*
>
> I allow the true seeker, the ripened fruit, to attain the first eight levels of spiritual attainment quickly. But, if the seeker becomes egoistic about his spiritual attainment or otherwise, then I pull him down to the first level.[9]

The testing of the disciple has been aptly described in the Shiva Puran. Shlokas 14, 15 and 19 of Chapter 15 of Vayaviya Samhita[10] state:

Shloka 14: Hence, observing the symbols of securing shakti, the preceptor (guru) shall purify and consecrate the disciple either by knowledge or by means of rites.

Shloka 15: Hence, the preceptor (guru) shall test the disciple in every respect.

---

[8]Ibid.

[9]Ibid.

[10]Shastri, J.L., *The Siva Purana: Part I to IV*, Motilal Banarasidass Publishers, Delhi, 1950.

Shloka 19: The test of disciple has in view his worthiness of being taught.

The atmosphere of the sangat in the physical presence of Guruji was always ethereal. Guruji would sit majestically on his aasan and engage in small talk with the sangat sitting close to him or doing sewa; or a devotee would be called from amongst the sangat to sit close to him. Other times, he may contemplate on something giving the impression of being somewhere else. Guruji loved to distribute prasad to the sangat with his own hands, irrespective of the size of the congregation. Most of the time, it would be sweets or dry fruits mixed with mishri or occasionally ber, mangoes and chocolates. The prasad was to be eaten then and there, as they were blessings and medicine for the devotee suffering from various ailments. '*Langar te chai prashad vich meri blessings ne* (Langar and chai prasad are the embodiment of my blessings).' Guruji used to tell that the blessings in the form of prasad gets diluted or even becomes ineffective if it is eaten afterwards. Similarly, chai and langar prasad were to be savoured in the presence of Guruji or in the sangat itself. The time spent in communion with Guruji while partaking langar or chai prasad would spiritually rejuvenate the devotee.

The beautiful rendering of sabads from the Gurubani by famous ragis added to the ambience already radiant with Guruji's divine presence. The sabads were carefully selected by DJ Uncle, Sardar Rajinder Singh. DJ Uncle would source several cassettes from the market and would conduct the preliminary screening of the sabads and the ragis. Then, he would record them in a new blank cassette. Sometimes, he would play it for Guruji who would approve or reject the singer. At other times, DJ uncle would be playing a particular singer and sabad for the sangat when Guruji would direct him to stop playing the cassette. That is an enough indirect hint not to select that particular singer. His logic for the selection and rejection was more specific to the singer than the sabad per se.

Several devotees have described how their doubts and confusion about worldly and spiritual matters got resolved by listening to the sabads. They would have many a query built in their mind before coming to Guruji's sangat. Sometimes, they would pray to Guruji silently to show the right path. Then DJ Uncle would play a particular sabad that would answer their queries, clear their doubts and provide the right path to move forward. They need not bother Guruji for all these clarifications. It was Guruji's way to connect with the sangat through the medium of sabads.

The satsangs being held after Guruji left his mortal body are true to the eclectic and syncretic free will espoused by Guruji. He has not prescribed a fixed method for holding a satsang. The sangat is adopting the practices as they find appropriate. Some try to replicate the ambience and milieu of satsangs held in the presence of Guruji. The absence of the physical presence of Guruji is compensated by his swaroop, chola, jutis, etc., making the atmosphere similar to that when Guruji used to hold sangat in his places of stay or during functions. The simplicity of Guruji's sangat and satsang is of utmost importance. Where is the need for ostentatious showing off of the organizing capability and spending power (like a five-star venue, top-notch event management, multi-cuisine langar)?

In most of the satsangs, the sabad kirtan, chai prasad, langar prasad, etc., are replicated. Guruji used to term the rendering of experiences of a sangat relating to their association with Guruji as satsang. It fitted with the sadh-sang definition of satsang, except that the sadh has himself asked the devotee to narrate their experience in his presence. Now, most of the satsangs fall into this kind of rendering of the devotee's experience during or after Guruji left his physical body. The material gains by the grace and blessings of Guruji are immaterial; the internalization of blessings leading to a higher spiritual path is the essence of such renderings. We can do better by elevating 'the association of good people or the fellowship with truth' by delving into the philosophy, teachings, life history and glory of Guruji, rather than focussing on the material gains obtained because we followed

Guruji. The supernatural powers or the miracles are part and parcel of enlightened masters like Guruji. Those miracles or supernatural powers were occasionally demonstrated to make people realize the existence of higher forces or the Supreme Being. It is possible to attain some of these powers by yogic practices by the sadhaks or devotees themselves. Such attainment is possible for any human being. But Guruji was beyond those miracles and demonstration of supernatural powers.

In God's creation, millions of miracles happen every day. As Paulo Coelho says, 'When you want something, all the universe conspires in helping you to achieve it.'[11] In other words, when you are sincerely motivated to attain something and pursue it, all the universal forces of nature conspire in helping you to achieve it.

Even if people are not followers of Guruji or any god, they experience miracles. Limiting Guruji to the miracles or exhibition of supernatural powers is like straight-jacketing him as an ordinary sadhak, rather than a divine incarnate.

Guruji is ever-present. Today, many of his followers experience his presence by way of his fragrance. But, beyond that, let the materialistic gains be downplayed and his humane, spiritual and philosophical aspects be emphasized.

[11]Coelho, Paulo, *The Alchemist,* HarperOne, New York, 2014, p. 24.

6

The Langar Tattva

THE CONCEPT OF LANGAR

The contemporary practice of institutionalized langar is a Sikh tradition introduced by Guru Nanak. But, the seeds of such a practice have been prevalent in the cultural-religious traditions of India since before the onset of Sikhism.

The religious *mathas* (a sort of monastery or seminary) and temples in various parts of the country provide prasad or cooked meal to the devotees visiting these places. However, it is not universally practised in all temples, monasteries and mathas. Similarly, *bhandaras* (community kitchens) are held on special occasions and festivals. In south India, the *dharamshalas* (modest guest houses) attached with religious places provide meals and provision for stay to the devotees on payment. Sometimes, these are provided without payment depending on the resources of the religious place from land grants or contribution by devotees or rich people.

MAHAPRASAD IN PURI JAGANNATH TEMPLE

The best example of a religious community kitchen is the practice of *mahaprasad* at the Jagannath Temple in Puri, Odisha. Here, prasad is cooked daily, in a special manner, for thousands of devotees. After the prasad is offered to Lord Jagannath and Goddess Bimala, it becomes mahaprasad, which is available for all devotees in Anand Bazaar in the temple premises on a payment basis. The mahaprasad is never wasted. The leftover on your plate may be eaten by other people and the unsold prasad is dried and offered for sale as dried prasad. This practice of community kitchen predates the onset of the institutionalized langar by Guru Nanak.

Even before Sikhism, the concept of langar was introduced as a Sufi tradition. The Chishtiyah Sufis introduced the tradition of sharing food, particularly amid the devotees gathered to pay their obeisance to the Sufi saints. Free public kitchens at Chishti *dargha*s were opened to all visitors and devotees. The concept of public kitchens was brought in to propagate the principle of equality among all. It symbolized the ethical practice of sharing, community service and spreading the feeling of unanimity of all human beings.

Langar is a Persian word, meaning a heavy iron or steel piece, especially made to keep the vessels (ships or boats) in place when they approach the shore. The closest translation in English is 'anchor'. Guru Nanak, after completing his *udasis* (missionary tours), started the practice of institutionalized langar at Kartarpur, in present-day Pakistan. The kitchen was popularly called Guru ka Langar (langar offered by the Guru).

Guru Nanak's famous sayings emphasize the spiritual connotations of langar. His saying, '*Kirat karo, vand ke shako, naam japo* (Do your *niyat karma* and enjoy the fruits of such labor with others with focus on God). He advised the devotees to share one-tenth of their earnings with the community or for its welfare. In this context, one should not forget the great Indian spiritual tradition in which offering food to gods and sharing the food with other living beings have been highlighted.

SHARING AND OFFERING FOOD

The respect for food, sharing of food and eating together are part of our spiritual and civilizational heritage. The Vedas, Upanishads and Bhagavat Gita have described the sacred nature of food and sharing in several shlokas and mantras.

The Bhagavad Gita in Verse 6.16 states, 'Verily this Yoga is not for him who eats too much or sleeps too much, even it is not for him who gives up sleep and food, O Arjuna.'

Food is not for pleasure; it is for sustenance and good health. The Taittiriya Upanishad states that 'From earth herbs, from herbs food, from food seed, from seed man. Man thus consists of the essence of food.' This has been reiterated in the Bhagavad Gita, (Verse 15.14), 'It is I who take the form of the fire of digestion in the stomachs of all living beings, and combined with the incoming and outgoing breaths to digest and assimilate the four kinds of foods.'

Or in other words, 'I having become the flame of life, sustain the physical body of living creatures and united with Prana and Apana, digest the four kinds of food.'

The Brihadaranyaka Upanishad (5.9.1) also states:

> *Ayam agnir vaiśvānaro yo'yam antaḥ puruṣe, yenedam annam pacyate.*
>
> The fire inside the stomach is the Supreme Vaiśvānara Himself. He is the Puruṣha within. By Him the food that is taken is digested.[24]

The importance of food is also inferred from the practice of offering the food first to the gods or God before consuming it by the individual. Offering food signifies gratitude to God and also to ward off the negatives contained in the food or during preparation of the food.

Food is regarded as *Anna Brahma* and *anna* (food) is considered as the first manifestation of Brahman. Rigveda Samhita (10.117.6) states the importance of sharing food with others:

> *Moghamannarh vindate apracetah*
> *satyarh bravimi vadha itsa tasya*
> *naryamanam pusyati no sakhayam*
> *kevalagho bhavati kevaladi.*
>
> Food that comes to the one who does not give is indeed a

> waste. This is the truth. I, the rishi, say it. The food that such a one obtains is not only wasted, it in fact comes as his very death. He feeds neither the devas nor the men who arrive at his door as atithis, abhyagatas and friends. Eating for himself alone, he becomes the partaker of sin alone.

The Vedas urge humans to conduct five daily sacrifices (*panch yajnas*). Cooking food and sharing such food among gods, ascetics, animals, birds, insects and other needy humans is one such yajna. In the Indian spiritual tradition, food is not just a biological substance that sustains and nourishes life, but is equated with Brahman—the Supreme self.

In the Bhagavad Gita, Verse 4.24 states, 'Brahman is the giving, Brahman is the food offering, By Brahman, it is offered into the Brahman-fire, and Brahman is that which is to be attained by Samadhi in Brahman-action.'

Food is called Anna Brahman. Hence, never disrespect food, especially langar, which is blessed by the divine. There is the saying, 'What you eat is what you are.' Eating the right things will put you on the path to not only a healthy and long life, but propel you on the path of spiritual elevation.

The human body is also called the *annamay kosha* (food body). Food contains all the energy you require as both modern and ancient science asserts. The people who cook food and their attitude can have a positive or negative influence upon the person who eats the food. Both Indian and Christian traditions follow the practice of praying to God before eating. In ours, we even offer food to the Almighty before consuming it ourselves. We not only thank God for providing us nourishment but also try to ward off negative influences or toxins in the food by invoking the blessings of God.

Guruji blended the respect for food as described above in spiritual texts—like the Vedas, the Upanishads and the Gita—with the langar concept propagated by the Sufi saints and Guru Nanak. He further elevated the community intake of food by a notch than what has been said in the Vedas and the Gita. It has all the blessings of Guruji as he says:

> *Prashad nu ithe baith ke khao ta davai (blessings), bahar le ke jao te mitthai.*
>
> The sweet prasad served by sewadars or distributed by Guruji with his own hands are blessings of Guruji. If taken away outside for subsequent consumption, these become ordinary sweets.
>
> *Langar te Chai Prasad vich meri blessings ne. Langar tuwhadi dawai hai. Aithe baith ke poora khtam karna chahida. Ainu varata vale dina vich v kha sakde ho. Ainu Prasad di tarah dekho, padarth nahin.*
>
> The chai and langar prasad are embodiments of my blessings. These should be consumed in full while seated in the langar hall itself. These can be eaten on the days of fasting or austerities like vratas. These should be treated like prasad, rather than ordinary food or beverage.
>
> *Langar prashad nu dobara Garam nahin karde*
>
> The langar prasad, if allowed to be taken home for oneself or other near and dear ones, is not supposed to be reheated like ordinary food.

There is no better way of inculcating due regard for food served to the devotees and bringing the spiritual context as ascribed in the Vedas and Vedantic traditions.

The concept of langar fosters community service; it also eliminates the distinction between the rich and the poor, the high or low in society. Irrespective of caste, religion and community, the same food is offered to everybody. In other words, it symbolizes and fosters universal brotherhood.

Guruji elevated langar to a higher pedestal. Langar is not just langar, it is prasad. Guruji's blessings are embedded in the langar and the person who savours it is automatically blessed by Guruji.

Sharing langar with others from the same thali has far-reaching spiritual and social significance. It annihilates your ego. It does not matter who you are—rich, poor, highly accomplished, man of the street, upper or lower caste, Hindu or Muslim, or from any other religious community. You would be sharing the thali with others, irrespective of their social, religious or professional status. The blessings of Guruji obliterate the usual concept of personal hygiene, otherwise observed in typical social settings. One famous industrialist serving langar to his own driver exemplifies the annihilation of the ego. However, this annihilation has to be internalized and practiced all the time, at all places and in respect of all people.

Universal brotherhood was elevated to a higher notch in Guruji's langar system. Guruji's langar not only acquired the divine aura due to the presence of Guruji and his blessings, it was also considered socially much more significant than other institutionalized langars. Each langar thali would be shared by four devotees. The devotees would readjust at their place of sitting on both sides of the langar mat in two rows. The sangat would be sitting in a squatting position, and each devotee would share the thali with three fellow devotees. You might not know who the other three are, and you would not have the freedom of choosing your langar partners. The other three may be strangers just sitting next to you. The feeling of sharing the food and eating from the same plate has a great relevance for fostering fellowship among the devotees. There is no antipathy, only love and affection for the fellow devotee, even a stranger, sitting next to you.

The preparation and serving of langar fosters the ethical concept of sewa to the community. Activities like preparing the langar, serving it and cleaning the utensils also demolish the ego of the devotee engaged in such sewa. In combination to cleaning and taking care of the shoes of the sangat (as a practice in gurudwaras), eating with strangers and consuming food from the same thali brings humility to the devotee and helps annihilate their ego.

There are several satsangs by the sangat regarding the blessings of having Guruji's langar. We have already described how the sufferings of people got alleviated by savouring the cocktail of blessed prasads—chai prasad, sabads, langar prasad, satsangs—and above all, the radiance of Guruji's divine presence.

GURUJI'S MAUZ IN SERVING LANGAR

Serving langar to the sangat was Guruji's mauz. He would give significant importance to the langar, the langar sewa and to the partaking of langar by the sangat. During his days in Jalandhar, Guruji would allow a limited number of sangat for his darshan. As there was no fixed time for sangat, many devotees would pour in throughout the day, making it easier to serve langar to the limited number of devotees. Guruji used to serve the chapatis himself to the devotees. He would take his frugal meal only after everybody present had had their langar, a practice he carried out till he left his mortal body.

Guruji was particular about langar being served to the last man present. He would instruct the sewadars to ensure that the drivers, the security personnel of VIP devotees and the security guards posted at the gate of Empire Estate were served langar. Once he was assured that every person had had their langar, Guruji would give permission to most of the sangat to leave, and then only, in the presence of the remainder sangat, would take his frugal meals.

Ms Bambi Singh has the following to say about Guruji's frugal eating:

> Guruji did not eat much. When some devotee would insist that he should have another roti, he would say, '*Main tuwadi khusi khanda han* (I partake in your enjoyment).' A mahapurush does not need to eat much. Every devotee when he/she prays and eats the first bite, that comes to me.[1]

[1]Quoted in *Jai Guruji*, a booklet circulated privately, written by Ms Bambi Singh.

GURUJI'S LANGAR SEWA

It was a pleasure and privilege for the devotees to perform langar sewa. Groups of sangat or an individual sangat would be given the task of preparing the langar. Places like Jalandhar Mandir, General Ahjuja's residence in Panchkula or even Empire Estate were too small to have facilities to prepare langar for the ever-increasing sangat. Hence, the chosen few would be instructed to prepare langar at their residences. For Empire Estate, langar used to be prepared in the kitchen facility of Bade Mandir. Sometimes a portion of chapati-making would be carried out in the kitchen of the place Guruji was staying, depending on the requirement. In Jalandhar, it was Preeti Aunty or Bhatia Uncle who used to prepare langar at their house and bring it to the mandir at Defence Colony to be served to the sangat. For Panchkula and Sector 33, Chandigarh, it was Vimal Kapoor who would prepare the langar at his house and bring it to the sangat. For Empire Estate, it was R.P. Singla who was given the opportunity of preparing langar in the kitchen of Bade Mandir. All of them would be assisted by other sangat, duly permitted by Guruji.

I had the privilege of serving langar to the sangat at Empire Estate. We had a team consisting of sangat like Colonel Joshi, Mrs Joshi, Sudha Aunty, Vini Kapoor, Satinder Singh (Satty), Dr S.C. Sharma and Singla Uncle, who used to serve the langar brought from Bade Mandir. Chhotto or Chandan and one or two other domestic helps of Sudha Aunty would extend a helping hand in the kitchen in serving the food. Sometimes, due to office engagements or other exigencies, I would be held up and could not reach Empire Estate in time for serving langar. Guruji would innocently ask other members about my arrival. On a couple occasions, he would delay the langar, so that I could reach in time for the langar sewa. After serving langar to all the sangat, the sewadars engaged for langar and the domestic helps would sit together and have their langar. Most of the times, Guruji would take his frugal meals during that time.

It is not that each and every devotee who wants to do langar sewa is allowed to do so. Guruji used to test the sincerity of purpose and good intention of the devotee before allowing them to undertake such a service.

Sukhmani writes in her book:

> One day a lady requested Guruji to allow her to make langar, to which he said, '*Auntie, tenu hale 25 saal hor lagange mere langar wich kam karan nu. Har koi mere langar wich kam nahi kar sakda.* (Auntie, you will wait 25 years to do langar sewa. Not everybody could do langar sewa.)'[2]

NON-WASTAGE OF THE BLESSED LANGAR

Most of the time, the langar prepared would be adequate to cater to the sangat present for that particular day. By Guruji's blessings, the amount would be sufficient to serve the sangat. On many occasions, the langar would be a surplus. There were devotees who would feel privileged to accept the leftover langar to be eaten by other family members or themselves the next day. As such, langar is considered as prasad, and as per the tradition in this land, it is not reheated before eating. Sometimes, Guruji would send langar prasad to some devotee who could not come to the sangat due to illness or other exigencies. Other times, some sangat would request to take langar prasad for their near and dear ones who could not come to the sangat. Their wish would generally get fulfilled after catering to the sangat present in the mandir. Guruji would sometimes direct the sewadars to pack langar, and he would bless it before handing over to the devotee.

Langar served in Guruji's durbar is always frugal and simple—one daal, one vegetable dish, roti, chutney and sometimes raita and something sweet. There was no restriction on spices, garlic

[2]Sukhmani, *Surcharged with Divine Love*, Unistar Books, Chandigarh, 1998.

or onion. The langar served in Guruji's durbar is never lavish. It is at times slightly spicy, but never too oily or spicy. The moderately spicy langar was mostly specific to the langar served at Empire Estate.

After Guruji left his physical body, the devotees sometimes hold satsangs on occasion of their birthdays, anniversaries, etc., to express gratitude to Guruji. But care should be taken to avoid expensive or garish decorations and lavish multiple-dishes langar. There is no need for competition among sangat to showcase their organizing capability and spending power. The essence of simplicity of Guru ka Langar should not be drowned in the one-upmanship shows.

It has always been emphasized that there should not be wasting of langar served to the sangat. Guruji would not directly state that langar should be eaten to the last grain as it embodies his blessings. Sometimes, a few beginners would avoid the langar, fearing it would be too spicy. Some of them would have their supper before coming for sangat and generally would hesitate to take langar at all, or just eat a share of two chapatis. But, Guruji would politely prod them to eat langar properly as it would be full of his blessings.

As said, Guruji never told the devotees to clean up the langar thali by eating till the last grain or licking the last drop of daal. No such rigidity was imposed by Guruji. This practice of cleaning up the last grain of langar or last drop of the chai prasad was a sangat invention by the overenthusiastic ones, overemphasizing the non-wastage of the blessed langar, sometimes driving it to extreme levels. Guruji never insisted on such ritualistic, dogmatic and rigid observance of no-waste practices. His views were simple – respect the langar, treat it as prasad and do not waste it. He used to say, 'I bless everyone through the langar which must be treated as prasad/medicine and not be wasted at all.'

CHAI PRASAD

When the sangat arrives at the mandir at places like Jalandhar, Chandigarh, Panchkula or Empire Estate, they are first greeted with water. It is a tradition in this land that when a guest arrives at your place, the first thing you do after making them comfortable is to offer a glass of water. It quenches their thirst in this humid and hot land and puts the person at ease. After getting settled in this manner, the sangat would sit in the sangat hall listening to the soothing sabads; then comes the time for chai prasad to be served to each and every sangat. This process goes on till the last sangat arrives.

The chai served to the sangat is called chai prasad. Guruji used to say to the reluctant sangat to drink the chai prasad as it would be full of his blessings. The discerning sangat would then learn to cherish and covet for a glass of chai prasad that is served in those small glasses, which you usually find at the corner (nukad) tea shops.

One day, after most of the sangat had been given permission to leave, Guruji called me and asked, '*Rahul, sangat nnu chai pilao, khud bana ke* (Serve tea to the sangat by preparing it yourself).' I had never, till then, ventured into preparing tea—the reason being that none in my family is a tea-drinker. We occasionally would take tea in social gatherings or with friends at tea shops in the nukads or dhabbas while travelling or during morning walks or strolls with friends. But the preparation of tea by the tea-seller was never observed with an intent of learning how to; and the chai prasad at Guruji's place was not prepared as it is prepared in these shops.

Without hesitation, I dashed to the kitchen adjacent to the sangat hall. Colonel Joshi, realizing my predicament, followed me to the kitchen. Then the Colonel, who was regularly preparing and serving chai prasad to the sangat, acted like a master chef and guided me step-by-step in preparing chai prasad using the special method. The number of sangat left was around 15. When the chai prasad was served to them, everybody liked it. Thereafter, Guruji allowed me the privilege of preparing and serving tea to the small remnant group of sangat after the majority was allowed to take leave. It was the most satisfying moment—preparing and serving tea for Guruji's sangat during these beautiful moments.

The sangat would always love to have more servings of the chai prasad. Ms Bambi has the following to say regarding this craving by some sangat, 'We considered ourselves very blessed if we get chai prasad twice. Guruji made sure that every devotee gets at least one glass.'[3]

HOW MANY HAD ENJOYED LANGAR?

After the conclusion of one of those special functions at Bade Mandir, Guruji came back to Empire Estate along with a few of the devotees. Dr S.C. Sharma was one of the devotees who accompanied Guruji back to Empire Estate. While Dr Sharma was doing sewa in the retiring room, Guruji asked him about the number of people who had langar at Bade Mandir on that day. Dr Sharma applied his intelligence and stated that it could be around 10,000. Guruji retorted saying, 'No, it is two and a half lakhs.' Dr Sharma could not understand the utterance and kept quiet. After some time, Guruji could read what was going on in Dr Sharma's mind and stated that it was not only the devotees alone who ate the langar, there were several other living beings, gods, demigods, and others from the cosmos who ate the langar offerings. On another occasion, Guruji had to also clarify Sukhmani in a similar fashion. Guruji told Sukhmani:

> *Thaanu ki lagada hai sirf tusi uthe langar kha ke jande ho? Thaanu ki pata tohade naal kau kaun langar kha ke jande hain. Utte ta muni rishi tarasade han is langar da ek niwala khan waste. Mere hokum naal oh bhi langar chak ke jaande*

[3]Quoted in *Jai Guruji*, a booklet circulated privately, written by Ms Bambi Singh.

> *han. Jadon main kehnda ki inne log ne langar chakia hai, us de wich oh hi ginnati kar ke kehnda haan.*
>
> You think that you are the only fellows who ate langar. You do not know who else are sitting alongside you to have langar there. The celestial Muni (sage), rishis and the like are desperate to have a portion of the langar. They also eat langar with my permission. When I say so many people had langar, which includes all these who have the langar along with you mortals.[4]

Guruji's langar epitomizes spiritual progress by incorporating the divine blessings of the enlightened Guru, annihilating the ego of individual devotees. Simultaneously, it fosters social equity, cohesion, fellowship, sense of sewa and universal brotherhood among the devotees and others who are blessed to have Guruji ka Langar.

[4]Sukhmani, *Surcharged with Divine Love*, Unistar Books, Chandigarh, 1998.

7

The Humane Facets

UNIVERSAL LOVE AND COMPASSION FOR EVERYBODY

The extraordinary display of universal love and compassion, and the supernatural power of alleviating the sufferings (physiological, material and psychological) of mankind were amply evident from the numerous satsangs by those in the sangat who had come in contact with Guruji through his divine grace.

Because of this enlightened state, Guruji remains in a relaxed, heartfelt and authentic communication with everyone he meets, in a way that is grounded in compassion and a state of emotional liberation. In this enlightened state, he feels, sees and experiences a divine quality in everything and everyone because he is living in deep spiritual connection with the divine universal intelligence.

In Patanjali's Yoga Sutra (Vibhuti Pad III.23), it is said that the enlightened persons, through their yogic attainments, get unique qualities like friendliness, compassion or sympathetic joy and that they also imbibe the same feeling in others. The compassion and empathy of Guruji manifested in alleviating the physiological (ailments, disease) and psychological sufferings of people. There are innumerable accounts by sangat on how they have been blessed by Guruji and recovered from or worked through their physiological, physical and psychological sufferings.

Guruji's blessings are non-discriminatory; the universal divine love was for everybody. This had resulted in the beautiful phenomenon of each and everybody feeling that Guruji was really close with them. His universal love and blessings are like the rays of the sun that reaches everywhere, without discrimination. His blessings are for all the children of God—the sinners, the powerful, the weak, the rich and the poor, the man of the street, the yogi and the like. It was like the saying in the Gurubani (SGGS 485.13), '*Kahaa kara-o jaatee kah kara-o paatee*? (What do I have to do with social status? What do I have to with ancestry?)'

Guruji's love and affection for the sangat manifested in his address to each and every sangat as uncle and aunty, barring the young ones. This age-old Indian tradition of addressing elders as uncle and aunty brings the person and the addressee closer. Guruji elevated this practice to a higher level by even addressing persons younger to him as uncle or aunty. He had the uncanny trait of transposing to that of a child, addressing someone as maami (paternal aunt) or maasi (maternal aunt), stating that such relationships span for several births.

HUMILITY IS HIS FORTE

Whoever comes to Guruji and pays his respect, he would do a namaste in return. Namaste is the recognition of the divine in the person to whom you are addressing. God resides in everybody. When you do a namaste, it is as if you are uttering, 'I honor the divine in you. I see that you are a unique expression of God and that we are one.'

Humility is an outward expression of an appropriate inner humbleness, or self-regard, and is contrasted with humiliation, which is an imposition, often external, of shame upon a person. Humility is widely seen as a virtue and opposed to arrogance. Many a saint and sadhaks have fallen aside their spiritual attainment or path due to arrogance. The epics (Mahabharat and Ramayana), the Puranic literature and many other fables are full of such fallen sages due to their arrogance. Hence, the path to higher spiritual attainment should be strewn with the blossoms of humility.

Humility is one of the five virtues highly valued in Sikhism too. In the Guru Granth Sahib, Ang 470 says, '*Mithat neeve naanakaa gun changiaaieeaa tat.* (Sweetness and humility, Oh Naanak, are the essence of virtue and goodness).'

Further, it has been said in Ang 273, '*Braham giaanee kai gareebee samaahaa.* (The God conscious being is steeped in humility).'

Guruji used to say, '*Ham to murkhon ka daas* (I am servant of or I do surrender to the fools).' In other words, 'I do not argue or take position with the fools and accept my position without low self-esteem).' True humility is strength, not a weakness. It disarms antagonism and ultimately conquers it.

THE THREE MUSKETEERS OF DELHI

Guruji was staying in the house of Lieutenant General (Retd) Ahuja in the late 1990s. One day, a group of three youths came from Delhi. They had some issue regarding their transaction with Guruji ka Ashram. The exact nature of the transaction was not known to the two or three sangat present during that time (midday) at the residence. Perhaps the managers of the affairs in Delhi could not settle their matter satisfactorily, and so the group landed in Panchkula to directly talk to Guruji, who was at his modest best with humility. But the youths could not control their own arrogance and emotion. They started berating Guruji with all the foul language they could muster. Guruji did not respond to their berating and was his usual self—calm and composed. After the group had their heart's content of railing and berating, Guruji summoned some sangat present there to offer langar and chai prasad to the three Delhites. The youths were won over witnessing the humility of Guruji, and they had no option but to comply with the offerings. When they were leaving for Delhi, Guruji told them that their grievances would be taken care of.

Guruji was the embodiment of humility. Being an enlightened master, he knew what could be done and what would happen. But he would give the impression as if he was an ordinary human being, full of innocence like Bholanath or a child. His mother passed away while she was with us in Chandigarh. After the bhog ceremony at Dugri, he left for Delhi. After a week or so, we made a trip to Delhi to have Guruji's darshan. When I found a moment alone with Guruji in his room, Guruji talked about Maataji. He said, '*Rahul, Maataji bade jaldi chal base, nahin?* (Maataji left this world too early? Is not it?).' Who is asking innocently and to whom?

Guruji always abjured publicity. In the age of the high-octane electronics and social media, not to mention print media, Guruji never ever allowed any sangat or himself to engage in any activity remotely connected with publicity and media. He never used the platform of organized pravachan, which is one of the modes of publicity. His method was to always spread the message of God through word of mouth and satsangs in informal settings. He could have gathered thousands of devotees, called the media, inserted advertisements, brought out publications, etc., to propagate his philosophy, ideas and spiritual attainments. He had the resources, the manpower and access to many who held weight in such matters. During his lifetime, there was only one instance of media coverage in a fortnightly, where the reporter who featured Guruji was asked by the editor to project one of his supposed professional colleagues, who was an ardent follower of Guruji, in a disreputable manner, ostensibly to settle a score. The intention was to project the colleague in bad light labelling him as a blind follower of a guru; the focus was not on Guruji at all.

The childlike innocence and humility of Guruji was evident from his acceptance of suggestions (however absurd that may be) from the so-called experts in various fields. There were a couple of traditional vaids, naturopaths and the like among the sangat. As usual, Indians are known to extend unsolicited advice on matters in which they have little knowledge in and sometimes even no knowledge at all. Guruji would take them on the long path of realization of the futility of their suggestions and remedies. For example, there was an ayurvedic doctor specializing in traditional medicines who would prescribe a host of tablets, powders and liquids for Guruji, so that he would get healthier. Guruji would not say no and gulp the entire lot like an obedient child. In one of those rare and exclusive moments in his retiring room in Empire Estate, he was asked by someone as to why he complied with remedies of dubious nature. He answered, 'I am blessing the doctor and I do not want to dissatisfy my ardent devotee. Nothing would happen to me; no adverse effect from any of the medicines.'

STHITAPRAJNA

The characteristics of a sthitaprajna, as described by Lord Krishna, in the second chapter of the Bhagavad Gita, were truly reflected in our revered Guruji. The most important characteristics of a sthitaprajna are twofold—equanimity and the complete control of the sense organs and the sensory system, including the mind-space.

Sthitaprajna has been literally translated from the Sanskrit words—*sthita* meaning 'being', 'existing' or 'firmly resolved to' and *prajna* meaning 'wise' or 'intelligent'. Hence, a sthitaprajna is a person of steady wisdom who has renounced all desires (attachments and aversions) (Bhagavad Gita, 2.55); whose mind remains undisturbed amidst misery, who does not crave for happiness or pleasure, and who is free from attachment, fear, and anger (Bhagavad Gita, 2.56); who remains unattached under all conditions, and is neither delighted by good fortune nor dejected by tribulation, (Bhagavad Gita, 2.57); who is able to withdraw his senses from the sense objects, just as a tortoise withdraws its limbs into its shell (Bhagavad Gita, 2.58); and who is firmly fixed in perfect knowledge and firmly established in perfect consciousness (*paramatan*) (Bhagavad Gita, 2.56,58). Thus, a sthitaprajna is called a sage, a man of unwavering wisdom.

The calmness and eternal peacefulness of Guruji has been observed by all sangat who had come in association with him. He had renounced all desires, materialistic acquisition, family, property, name and fame—everything that one can imagine.

EQUANIMITY

Equanimity refers to the feeling of contentment, neither being delighted by good fortune nor dejected by tribulation. It was in 2004 that a news article came out in one of the English fortnightly. During the same period, there was the issue of a high-profile murder case of a model in a posh liquor bar in South Delhi owned by a socialite. The socialite and her daughter were questioned by the law enforcement authorities for suspected elimination of crucial forensic evidence. The socialite also frequented Empire Estate for Guruji's darshan and blessings to ward off the troubles she was encountering. Some devotees, who claimed close proximity with Guruji, with their own analysis, painted an alarmist picture or situation that the crime investigating agencies may question Guruji because the socialite was frequenting Guruji's durbar. They advised Guruji to suspend the daily sangat and go to Punjab for a few days. They became the advisors to Guruji, taking him as a simpleton and one who did not know anything of the worldly affairs. Guruji did not offend these great advisors. He continued his activities as usual and the investigating agencies had no reason to approach him. The nonchalant calmness demonstrated by Guruji was worth observing.

Guruji, on his personal front, suffered the loss of his elder brother at an early age of 52. His elder brother, Shri Bahadur Singh, died in a freak accident. Guruji was at ease the entire time and joined the cremation and bhog ceremony like an ordinary householder. It was the first time after he left his ancestral house in 1976 that he went back to Dugri. For such an enlightened person, the bonds of family ties are immaterial. It was like Guruji condoling the loss of a near and dear one of any sangat attending the last rites. When Maataji was inconsolable and distraught fearing that there was nobody to take care of the two teenage daughters of Bahadur Singh, Guruji assured that he would take care of them. Maataji berated Guruji that he had renounced his family and home, and hence nothing was expected of him. Guruji assured Maataji and promised that he would take the responsibility of settling his two nieces. Guruji was completely calm and never got perturbed by the untimely demise of his elder brother and that he had to take the responsibilities of two nieces like an ordinary householder.

Similar was the situation when Maataji passed away. Guruji found that Maataji was suffering in their ancestral village on account of many factors, including health issues at an advanced age. He advised Maataji to shift to Chandigarh to our house for a change of place, people and for her treatment. She suffered a stroke attack on 5 May 2004 and was admitted to PGI, Chandigarh. Guruji came to visit Maataji and spent considerable time by her bedside. And, as usual, he was calmness personified.

NON-ATTACHMENT AND RENUNCIATION OF DESIRES

Guruji had no attachment to anything. He loved to bless his devotees by giving his spiritual guidance, blessings and temporal things, like items gifted to him or even his personal belongings—his chola, his shoes, his sneakers, his shorts. And it was his way of blessing the lucky devotees.

When Guruji was in Sector 33, Dr M.P. Singh used to render sewa for Guruji, mostly during the daytime on holidays or after duty hours. That day, it was a holiday. Around 3 p.m., I got a call from him. He said, 'Rahul, could you believe that there are no clothes today for Guruji to wear when he attends the sangat. Can anything be done?' Urvashi and I were dumbfounded. We did not know what to do. We never ever managed anything like that for Guruji. There were some chosen devotees who used to get the cholas and kurta-pyjama stitched for Guruji. When we were discussing whom to approach and what to do, we got the call from Dr M.P. Singh. He informed that the issue had been resolved as a particular devotee had then arrived with a chola for Guruji.

After this incident, Urvashi suggested that we should gift a pair of kurta-pyjama to Guruji for his informal wear prior to meeting the sangat. We went to the Sector 22 market and chose the kurta-pyjama with our estimation of the appropriate size. In the afternoon, Dr M.P. Singh called to inform us that Guruji tried the kurta-pyjama and it was a bit tight for him. We informed that we would get the next size to which Guruji messaged not to do that. And he gifted away that pair to some blessed devotee.

After seven years of that incident, Guruji gifted five pairs of kurta-pyjama to me, specially stitched and brought all the way from Malerkotla through Gaurav. All of them fitted me properly!

BADE MANDIR FOR SANGAT, NOT FOR MAHAPURUSH

Guruji took keen interest in design and construction of the Bade Mandir. But he never shifted to the mandir for residing and holding sangat there. He would politely tell the inquisitive sangat that the mandir and its facilities are for the sangat, not for him. A mahapurush like him has no fixed place of residence or an attachment for a particular place. It was only for the large gatherings during functions that he used to have sangat at Bade Mandir. He sacrificed his time, energy and offerings for construction of the Bade Mandir only for the sangat.

AUSTERITIES AND CONTROL OF THE SENSES

Guruji's habits were befitting a highly spiritual and evolved person. His food, whenever he was not fasting, was quite simple—daal (lentil soup) and one vegetable dish. He would take, at best, two chapatis. Many a time, he would take some of the sangat to five-star hotels, and other times to the dhabas of Murthal, near Sonipat. He would order soup or tea, while the sangat were given the freedom of choice. But the sangat would also follow the master and would not order any lavish meals.

Guruji used to observe fast for four days every week, while he was in Jalandhar. He used to take regular meals during rest of the three days. The langar served to the sangat would also bear the austerities of Guruji, consisting of simple daal (lentil soup), a frugal portion of a vegetable dish and a dash of chutney.

Guruji used to wear elegant cholas for formal sangat darshans and functions. But, these cholas were not gaudy or too costly, and mostly designed and stitched by one of the devotees. He used to wear some shorts and T-shirts for walking purposes. Generally, these were brought by devotees from stores of popular brands in India and from foreign stores during their vacations to a foreign land. Nevertheless, he would only selectively use some elegant, matching pairs and the rest would just be given away as blessings to the sangat. And he would not have any attachment to a chosen chola or walking gear. After a couple of weeks, he would give them away.

CONTROL OVER THE SENSES

A couple of days after I met Guruji at Panchkula for the first time, Guruji would entreat us to be present at the Ahuja's residence during the daytime on holidays. On one such occasion, we landed up at the Ahuja's at around 3.00 p.m. and found Guruji walking briskly in the small front lawn. When he saw us, he said that he was waiting for us. Then, we went inside, where he told Mrs Ahuja to pack up the snacks and proceed to the Army Golf Club in Chandimandir. By that time, a young couple, a handsome Sikh gentleman with his beautiful wife, landed up there in their brand new Mercedes. They had driven from Delhi to get Guruji's blessings for the new car. Guruji ordered that all of us would go in this car. There were six of us (General Ahuja, Mrs Ahuja, myself, Urvashi and the couple), in addition to Guruji. There was no question of any hesitation. We know how we all squeezed into the car, both on the front and back seats. We drove to the golf club. While we enjoyed the serene, natural green environment, Guruji ordered the frugal snacks to be opened. Perhaps it was his lunch. First, he distributed the snacks (slightly fried sprouted moong) to the six of us and then took the rest. Chai prasad was also served. After an hour and a half, we drove back. Guruji asked the gentleman to get down and come to the other side. He took the wheels and the roles were reversed. He drove the Mercedes for a kilometre and a half like an expert driver and handed over the keys to the gentleman stating '*bless kitta*'.

Guruji himself had adopted a life of celibacy. But he would not advise his devotees to follow suit as a matter of strict fellowship. It is up to the devotee to choose a particular path. Rather, he would bless married couples to have children; many childless couples have been blessed with children after several years of their marriage. He would also advise parents of some sangat to get their daughters and sons married at the appropriate time. But he would say, after the age of 45, the couples should treat each other as good friends, indirectly hinting at bringing down the sexual quotient in their relationships.

The epics and Puranic literature are full of stories of how highly acclaimed sages, rishis, gods and demigods have fallen for the beauty of apsaras (cosmic dancers and singers) and other earthly beauties. There were hundreds of beautiful ladies and young girls among the followers of Guruji. But being the saint he was, he never ever evinced any interest in them. Unlike the stories agog with many escapades of renowned saints from contemporary times, there was no scope for tarnishing his image. He was a leading beacon showing how a saintly person would have full control (physically and mentally) over the senses.

One day, Guruji, realizing that the sewadars and Sudha Aunty were not venturing out for any entertainment, proposed to watch a movie in Gurgaon. Urvashi was one of the fortunate ones to accompany Guruji to the hall. When the movie started, Guruji closed his eyes and relaxed. After 45 minutes, he got up and left the hall, telling the others to enjoy the movie. He does not need external stimulation (sensory inputs) to get contentment. When a master has control over his sense organs and mind, he does not need such stimuli for entertainment. The sabads, Sufi songs and the folk songs were his way of connecting with the Supreme Self and being in eternal contentment.

THE WITTICISM OF GURUJI

Guruji had an uncanny sense of humour and witticism. He would beautifully construct acronyms for many government services. The following are his acronyms:

IAS: I am Superior; Indira and Sanjay; I Agree Sir.
IPS: Indian Patni (wife) Service
ASC: Atta Subzi Chore Service
PWD: Pant Wale Dacoits
CBI: Corrupt Bureau of India
Wife: Worry Invited for Ever
Husband: Horse Under Severe Burden, and No Diversion
PhD: Paagal Hone ka Dar

He would joke about some sangat. He would invariably address couples having love marriage as '*Aao, love marriage aao.*' A gentleman from Delhi went for a European vacation for the summer. Every year, he would go for such vacations a couple of times. Guruji jokingly would say that the gentleman has gone for a honeymoon without his wife. He would talk about an industrialist who had flats in major cities for his concubines. For the merchant navy guys, he would say they have a wife at every port of call.

THE MAUZ OR LEELA OF GURUJI

The dances, the folk songs, his impromptu and sudden flurry of activities—intuitive or impulsive, the kaflas, the forays into five-star hotels and dhabas or a chosen sangat's house, the drives to Murthal, resorts, the annual functions—all constitute the mauz of Guruji satisfying the psychosocial needs of the sangat aligning with the high street of spiritualism. It was for the discerning devotee to take the spiritual essence of such activities; others to get an upbeat of their moods and get their doses of dopamine, serotonin, endorphins and oxytocin.

Guruji loved the folk songs of Punjab. He used to listen to the famous folk renderings of Surinder Kaur (mother of Dolly Guleria), Dolly Guleria, Sukhi Brar, Gurdas Mann, Hans Raj Hans and others. He was equally fond of the Sufi songs of Nusrat Fateh Ali Khan and Hans Raj Hans. He would invariably ask for folk music to be played when he would be travelling long distances. He was fond of the Dhadi-Tumbi folk songs by Yamla Jat and Surinder Kaur.

Guruji used to love the dance and one-act performances by late Harpal Tiwana and Gulab Kaur. When the duo would come to Guruji's darshan, they would invariably be asked to enact a small one-act play. Mr Tiwana would be asked to perform a dance programme to the song 'Tu Cheez Badi Hai Mast Mast'. Similarly, when the Kuchipudi dancers, Radha Reddy and Raja Reddy, and their daughter would come for darshan, they would be asked to perform a Kuchipudi dance. In one of the functions in Bade Mandir, they performed in full dance regalia in front of the thousands of sangat present in Bade Mandir.

Guruji loved the dance performances of Jyoti (his niece) to the song, 'Dupatta Tera Sat Rang Da'. Similarly, when Rinku of Malerkotla would come for Guruji's darshan, he would invariably be asked to perform a bhangra to the Punjabi tunes. During functions or on special occasions, Guruji would ask DJ Uncle to put dance numbers, and the sangat would be asked to dance to the beats.

The aforementioned activities were at the pleasure of Guruji, best termed as his mauz. But these were not regular phenomena for each satsang or special function. Some followers, after Guruji left this world, make it a point that such dance programmes should be part and parcel of satsangs. There was nothing like that which had been prescribed by Guruji as a routine or ritual to be followed.

Mr Joshi, an IPS officer of Punjab cadre, was an ardent follower of Guruji, who loved his repartee of jokes. He would be asked to crack jokes whenever he would come to pay his respect to Guruji at Sector 33, Chandigarh or Empire Estate. Ankur, his nephew and son of Krishna was good at imitating the mannerisms of people. Guruji would ask him to perform his imitations in front of the sangat at Empire Estate.

MASTER STRATEGIST

Guruji was a master strategist in breaking the egos of individuals. He would show people their places very subtly. The followers who grew bigger than their shoes were shown the door. He knew the limits, the aspirations, the hunger for power and everything about the exploiters among his sewadars and would show them the door. There are umpteen instances of such kind. He would take care of the sewadars (employed ones, not from the sangat), of their personal and family needs and treat them with utmost regard, love and affection. The earlier ones became his staunch devotees. Sagan (the driver from the Jalandhar days), Sudama (the caretaker of Jalandhar Mandir and occasional sewadar at Empire Estate), Chhotto, Chandan, and Amma (the domestic helpers of Sudha Aunty at Empire Estate), Ram Avatar, the gardener and his wife, the two other gardeners and caretakers of Bade Mandir, all testify the beautiful relationship they were sharing with the finest human being, the revered Guruji. They were also blessed from time to time for having children and other gains in life. Guruji would treat the sewadars with utmost regard, love and affection. Sagan and Sudama have a repartee of anecdotes about Guruji from the time when he was staying in Jalandhar.

One day, Guruji directed to Urvashi to come to the Ahuja's residence at 3 p.m. so that we could accompany him to the residence of the then Chief Justice, Punjab and Haryana High Court. A satsang was organized by Hon'ble Chief Justice K. Sreedharan at his official residence. For some reason or sheer negligence, we got delayed and by the time we reached the Ahuja's, Guruji had left for Chandigarh. Maamiji, who was there for Guruji's sewa, informed us that Guruji was waiting for us and left after some delay. We rushed back to Chandigarh to the residence of the Chief Justice. The limited number of invitees, keeping the protocol of the Chief Justice, mostly from the judiciary, were taking their leave. We paid our respects to Guruji and we were ushered to the designated place where snacks were being served. Guruji neither uttered a word to us nor looked at us. While we were having snacks, he left the place. We hurriedly finished the snack and also took leave from the Hon'ble Chief Justice. We learnt our lesson. Never be negligent in the matters of punctuality with Guruji. He expected complete surrender of the disciple. You should leave aside everything and comply with his orders. It was a lesson we learnt quite early in our initiation to his fold.

CLEANLINESS (PHYSICAL AND MENTAL)

Guruji would give utmost importance to the cleanliness of the premises and their surrounding areas, houses, including bathrooms and kitchens. He would politely refuse food cooked by a devotee or a cook lacking sincerity and the right frame of mind. In addition, he would avoid taking food cooked in a kitchen not properly cleaned. One time, he commented to an aunty to go and find a ton of dirt in the nooks and corners of her kitchen and in the cupboards.

Guruji would prefer the sangat to put on clean clothes. On one and two occasions, he had politely pointed out respectable ladies in the sangat to take a bath and put on freshly washed and clean clothes before coming to Guruji's durbar.

The idea of mental cleanliness was emphasized in the sayings, '*Mann saaf hona chahinda* (The mind should be cleaned of the cobwebs of wavering thoughts),' and '*Positive sochiya karo* (Adopt positive thinking).'

ORGANIZATION AND MANAGEMENT SKILLS

Guruji had the uncanny ability and skills of managing the competitiveness among the sangat, control of the numbers of sangat to be present on a particular day, managing large functions single-handedly with suitable delegation of authority with adequate supervision and superb follow-up. The modern-day management gurus could learn a thing or two from his management style and functioning.

Control of the Number of Sangat on a Particular Day

Guruji would direct some sangat to come after a week or 15 days to have his darshan. Some were completely banned to come to the sangat, for reasons best known to Guruji. Others would be called on a particular day of the week. This would ensure that the sangat place at the villa in Empire Estate, the Sector 33 house in Chandigarh or General Ahuja's place in Panchkula was not flooded with sangat creating nuisance for the neighbours and problems for the sewadars. There was not a single day when the sewadars would face a problem with the quantity of langar to be served to the sangat.

Managing Large Functions

Guruji used to manage all the arrangements for the large gathering of sangat on special occasions. He would delegate various tasks to different chosen sangat with his personal touch in broad planning. He would meticulously and scrupulously follow up on the progress at intermittent intervals. So, proper delegation with adequate supervision and information about the progress of activities resulted in excellent and trouble-free functions in which thousands of devotees would throng. He would sit through the functions to give personal and physical darshan to the sangat. There were initially no barriers, and each and everybody could touch his feet. But as the crowds swelled to several thousands, the devotees would be allowed to pay their respects by bowing their head from a distance and subsequently to do pranaam in a standing position. There was no stampede, ruffling of tempers and shortage of chai prasad, langar prasad or ber/sweet/mango prasad to the ever-increasing number of devotees who thronged during special functions. There were no complaints of eve-teasing, theft or misdemeanour in the crowd of devotees.

CONCERN FOR MARGINALIZED PEOPLE

The rich, the powerful and the famous thronged Guruji's durbar. Guruji was courteous to them as an ordinary human being. Nobody felt slighted or disrespected. They would be led to the garden path of Guruji's ways in a subtle way. Some of them would realize the spirituality of the master and become part of the general sangat. Others would continue with their sense of superiority and enlarged egos, and keep a distance from the ordinary folk.

It is the ordinary folk who were never away from the love, affection and blessings of Guruji. When chai prasad or langar would be served, Guruji ensured that the drivers, the security personnel of VVIPs, the guards and other sewadars were served timely and properly. He would invariably enquire about their well-being. Even the security guards at the hotels are blessed with his pleasantries.

Guruji was more at ease and frank with the sewadars like Sudama, Vimal, Sagan, Masterji, Masterani, Amma, Chandan Navaraj, Dharamraj, Kishorie and others. These were the people with least expectations who served the spiritual master with complete devotion. Sagan was the chauffer during the Jalandhar days for the Contessa fondly called 'Choimoi' by Guruji because of its registration number CH01M001. Navaraj would suffer from motion sickness, particularly while travelling in buses or trains. He would ride his scooter all the way from Chandigarh, not boarding a bus or train, to Empire Estate and stay there till Guruji allowed him to return. He would be oblivious of his sanction of leaves from the Punjab Water Supply and Sewerage Board, where he was a permanent employee. Similarly, Masterji would spend his vacations and other leave periods (he was a secondary school teacher in Himachal) in service/sewa of Guruji. Dharamraj, from the Delhi Police, would be available at his beck and call to drive him in and around Delhi. Kishorie was there to perform the duties of the traditional barber in Jalandhar and Chandigarh, and for some time at Empire Estate. When Kishorie was not around, Guruji used to visit a salon in Kishangarh in Vasant Kunj for his daily shaves.

He would lovingly interact with the three gardeners, their better halves and children when he visited Bade Mandir. He would enquire about the life of the gardeners, their family staying near Bade Mandir and the relations in their ancestral village. Mali Ram Swarup acted like the caretaker of Bade Mandir.

These are the people who testify the finest humane aspects of Guruji's personality. They revered him as a friend, philosopher and guide and less as a spiritual master. They testify the love, regard and compassion that Guruji bestowed on them, not the material gains for which most people clamour for.

Part IV

The Great Indian Universal Spiritualism

8

The Great Indian Spiritual Tradition

Our thought process is guided by spiritualism in almost all walks of life. Spiritualism for us is not merely an obsession of the mind but also an inner quest. It is a pathway for reaching the higher truth in life and a composite thinking for enlightening the realities of life. It also considers the challenges of life, and gives integral space for human values and its evaluation.

Indian spiritual texts and spiritual leaders, from time immemorial, have covered a gamut of human emotions and aspirations, making sublime contributions to Indian spiritualism. It has been nurtured by great spiritual thinkers like Yajnavalkya, Maitreyi, Gargi and Nachiketas. The Vedic rishis can be claimed as the earliest spiritual masters on earth, and their mantras resound in all corners of this land and beyond.

THE LIMITATIONS OF HUMAN INTELLIGENCE

The limitations of the human mind to comprehend the Supreme Soul and to objectify and conceptualize it in any intelligible manner have created difficulties even for realized souls to express their experiential wisdom to others. The course of attaining this higher knowledge has been imparted to individuals from time to time by souls that have attained the divine role within their physical being. It is often difficult to explain the essence of such divine beings. The Kena Upanishad (Shloka 1.3) highlights the difficulty in explaining or transmitting the essence of the

Supreme Self realized through such a divine vision:

> *Na tatra cakṣurgacchati na vāggacchati no mano na vidmo na vijānīmo yathaitadanuśiṣyādanyadeva tadviditādatho aviditādadhi.*
> *Iti śuśruma pūrveṣāṃ ye nastadvyācacakṣire.*
>
> The eye does not go there, nor speech, nor mind. We do not know That. We do not know how to instruct one about It. It is distinct from the known and above the unknown. We have heard it so stated by preceptors who taught us that.[1]

Adi Shankaracharya in his commentary of this Shloka states:

> A thing is cognized by the senses and the mind. We do not, therefore, know the Brahman because it cannot be an object of perception to these; and we do not, therefore, know what the Brahman is like, so as to allow us to enlighten the disciple about the Brahman.
>
> Whatever can be perceived by the senses, it is possible to explain to others by epithets denoting its class, its attributes and modes of activity; but the Brahman has no attributes of class, etc. It, therefore, follows that it is not possible to make the disciple believe in the Brahman by instruction.[2]

A WORLD THAT IS JUST, INTEGRAL AND BEAUTIFUL

Spiritualism for Indians is a philosophy of values that aims to usher in a world that is socially just—the state of *satyam*; emotionally integral—the state of *shivam;* and aesthetically beautiful—the state of *sundaram*. All paths discussed in the Indian spiritual traditions lead to this ultimate state of being.

---

[1]Vasu, Srisa Chandra, *The Principal Upanishads,* Panini Office, Bhuvaneswari Asrama, 1909, https://bit.ly/3IDEePG. Accessed on 9 January 2023.
[2]Sastri, S. Sitarama, *Kena Upanishad with Shankara's Commentary,* 1905, https://bit.ly/3WfAAhO.

It is a state where the creation is full and so is the creator. Every individual has the quality to be equally full as the Absolute, who is our teacher, is full. The fullness hence turns out as the highest watermark of man's spiritual speculations about the Supreme Power.

The Indian spiritual tradition suggests many pathways to realize God, or enlightenment, the ultimate purpose of all human beings. The Shiva Mahimna Stotram (Shloka 7) says:

> *Trayi sankhyam yogah pasupati matam vaishnavamiti*
> *prabhinne prasthane paramidamadah pathyamiti ca,*
> *rucinam vaicitryad riju kutila nana pathajusham*
> *nrinameko gamyas tvamsasi payasa marnava iva.*
>
> Different paths to realization are enjoined by the three doctrines of *Sankhya Yoga*, *Pashupata Shaiva* and *Vaishnava Shastras*. People follow different paths, straight or crooked, according to their temperament, depending on which they consider best, or most appropriate, and reach You alone just as rivers enter the ocean.

The Unity and Harmony of the Creation

What is that unifying soul of the varied and rich Indian culture and harmonious living? The credit must go the spiritual thoughts and practices of this great land that has harnessed the spirit of the Indian masses through the ages. The Indian scriptures also cover a gamut of every human emotion and aspiration, irrespective of the state and belief of the individual. The Indian systems of spiritualism is nourished by various philosophical thoughts such as Nyaya, Vaisheshika, Yoga and Vedanta. The Vedas provide spiritual orientation to the Indians giving them the basics of a spiritual and moral life.

Many realized souls, as their realizations are specific to them, have described the Absolute in different ways. It is famously said in the Rigveda (Verse 1.164.46), '*Ekam satyam, viprah bahudha vadanti* (One truth is being told variously by sages—realized souls).'

The beauty of this spiritual tradition is that it promotes acceptance and tolerance of all religions being true, providing different paths for God-realization, liberation or enlightenment.

THE MARVELS OF THE CREATIONS OF THE LORD

When we sit calmly on a sea shore and watch the magnificent spectacle of the fireball that is the sun (*surya*) rising above the horizon; when we are on the mountain-top savouring the panoramic view of the lower hills, forests, valleys, rivers and habitations; or when we are blessed to have a bird's eye view of the snow-clad continent or the vast North Pole from the window of a nonstop transatlantic flight, we could feel, in a miniscule scale, the vastness, beauty and miracle of the Lord's creation within our limited sensory perceptions.

The wonder of the Lord is all-pervasive. The cosmic trinity of the manifestation of the Lord as the creator, benefactor and also the constructive destroyer is universally present. We, the ordinary mortals, blind in vision, physically and otherwise, miss it. Do we not realize the beauty, marvel and wonders of the Lord's creations when we watch the miniscule particles, the quark or virus, in the powerful electron microscope, which is invisible to the naked eye, or the vast expanse of the Milky Way and nebulas through the Hubble telescope.

We witness only a miniscule part, within limitations of human intelligence and scientific achievement, of the vast manifestation of the Lord. It is only Arjun of the Mahabharat fame, blessed with divine vision, who could witness the entire creation of the Lord in its all-pervasive manifestations (the *Vishwarupa*). In the Bhagavad Gita, Lord Krishna says:

> *Ihaikasthatham Jagatkrrutsnam Pashyadi sachraachar.*
> *Mam dehe Gukdakesh Jachanyaddrastamichhasi.*

> Here, today, behold the whole universe with all that is moving and unmoving, unified at one place in My body—

> cosmic body, O Gudakesha, and whatever else thou willest to see. (The Gita, 11.7)
>
> *Tatraikasthamn Jagatkrsnam prabibhaktamankadha Apashyaddwebbedasya Sharire pandavstada.*
>
> The whole world, in multitudes divided and yet unified, is visible in the body of the God of Gods. (The Gita, 11.13)

Arjuna witnesses the splendour of the Lord of souls manifested in the glory and greatness of His spirit in all forms—magnificent, beautiful, terrible, wild, monstrous, orderly and wonderful.

Creation is Inexhaustible and Eternal, Like the Creator

Within the purview of spiritualism are also included the queries regarding the nature of God, about the creation of the world—essential values of a human being and his ethics. The last constituent of spiritualism is ethics reflecting the fine side of the Indian culture, which emphasizes unity in diversity, treating the entire universe as pervaded by the one Almighty.

The first verse of the Isha Upanishad says:

> *Īśāvāsyamidaṃ sarvaṃ yatkiñca jagatyāṃ jagat.*
> *Tena tyaktena bhuñjīthā mā gṛdhaḥ kasya sviddhanam.*
>
> All this, whatever moves in this universe—and those that move not—is covered, indwelt, pervaded or enveloped by the Lord. That renounced—and realizing that—enjoy. Do not covet for anybody's wealth; or, Do not covet, for whose wealth is it?

The rishis and sages of this great land were (so were the sages belonging to other traditions and geographies) visionaries and realized souls, who got the divine vision and were revealed the Absolute Truth; and there were several of them. The Vedic mantras came out spontaneously off the poetic bliss of such realized souls. Through the oral traditions of Shruti,[3] these have been made available for the benefit of the humankind.

This divine realization of cosmic vastness (the infinite) has been beautifully described in the Shanti Mantra (the hymn for peace) in the Isavasyopaniṣad. The Shanti Mantra describes the infinite, eternal nature of the Supreme Soul (the *Param Brahma*), and the infinite and complete state of the universe in the following manner:

> *Oṁ pūrṇam-adaḥ pūrṇam-idaṁ pūrṇātpūrṇamudacyate.*
> *Pūrṇasya pūrṇamādāya pūrṇamevāvaśiṣyate.*
> *Oṁ śāntiḥ śāntiḥ śāntiḥ II*
>
> 'That'—the absolute—is full/complete/whole/all-pervasive/infinite, 'This'—the life-force and non-living beings—is full/complete /whole/all-pervasive/infinite. From 'That', 'This' rises and manifests itself. From 'That', when 'This' is separated/inherited /presented, what especially remains is 'That'.[4]

In other words, only the Param Brahma, the Supreme Lord, is complete in all aspects, and He is complete without the need for anything else. Swami Sukhabodhananda gives the finest example of this scared spread, 'Infinite exists in a finite seed. A seed planted becomes a tree. From a tree again there is a fruit, from a fruit there is a seed, from a seed a tree, so in a finite seed there is the infinite capacity to grow.'[5]

---

[3]Shruti is a Sanskrit word meaning 'that which is heard' and is the tradition of oral rendering and transmitting of authoritative spiritual and religious works. It includes the collection of the four Vedas, along with its four types of embedded texts—the Samhitas, the Upanishads, the Brahmanas and the Aranyakas. This tradition puts utmost importance on the correct pronunciation, utterance and grammar of the Sanskrit texts, memorized through the oral method. This is the medium through which we have received the texts from generation to generation. Still today, in the age of print and electronic media of reproduction, this tradition is maintained in many Vedic schools/muths, as the oral rendering of the Vedic hymns provide correct interpretation and spiritual connotation.

[4]'Om Purnamadah Purnamidam Meaning', Rastra Nirman Trust, 17 November 2019, https://bit.ly/3VZMvAk. Accessed on 9 January 2023.

[5]'Master Swami Sukhabodhananda: Status', Speaking Tree, https://bit.ly/3GTk96p. Accessed on 9 January 2023.

The Supreme Lord (*Satchidananda Parabrahma*) is complete/infinite (*purna*). This world is born out of the infinite Supreme Soul; thus, this world, too, is purna. Even if we remove everything from what is complete/infinite, it still remains as purna. The universe is complete, inexhaustible and eternal.

Man as a Caretaker of the Beautiful Creation

The completeness of the universe exists in us, too. We, too, are born out of this universe and what exists in the universe exists in us. All the components of the universe are from one common source—the universal consciousness of god. Then how can you differentiate and discriminate between human beings based on race, caste, creed, religion, colour, profession, and so on? How can you not become compassionate towards the animals, other living beings and plants? How can you be greedy and destroy the natural environment for your personal need and comfort?

To conclude, while it is true that the thread of Indian spiritual traditions cannot be limited to a period, it is equally true that the tradition is the culmination of the divine visions of many realized souls and such eternal wisdom cannot be confined to a single scared treatise.

THE SPIRITUAL PATHS

Do we need to become an Arjun with a divine vision (*divyachakshu*) to have such a realization (*divyanubhuti*)? The Lord is all-pervading; He is everywhere, in everything. It is the realized souls—the sages, rishis and seers—who were in constant realization of this ultimate reality. They had the yogic integration of such a realization in all stages of consciousness—awakened state (*jagrat*), sleep (*sushupta*), dream (*swapna avastha*), in bliss (*param anand*) and super-consciousness (*karana chitta*). There is no difference in the consciousness of the different stages for the person who has realized 'that' in the true sense.

The pathways to such a realization may be many. But it has

been beautifully summarized in the Bhagavad Gita. For such a realization, the ignorance or illusion (maya) created by the forces of nature (prakriti) has to be cast away. Such an illusion is the result of the inter-generational (genetic) memory, sensory perception and activities, and the application of intellect and the concomitant egoism. When such a veil of illusion is cast away by conquering the desires/attachment and attaining the state of equanimity of joy and grief, the individual is fixed in pure spiritual consciousness.

It has been said in the Bhagavad Gita (Shloka 15.5):

> *NirmanMoha jitsangdosha*
> *Adhatmanitya binibritakamah.*
> *Dwandairbimukta Sukhadukhasanghei*
> *Gachhantyamudha padambyayam tat.*

> To be free from the bewilderment of this lower mayas, without egoism, the great fault of attachment conquered, all desires stilled, the duality of joy and grief cast away, always to be fixed in a pure spiritual consciousness, there are the steps of the way to that supreme infinite.

The annihilation of the ego is the foremost requirement for higher spiritual attainment. Guruji used to say: '*Kis gal da ahankar? Neeme ho jaao. Neeve rukha nu hi phal lagde han, neevi than te jiven paani aap chalk e aanda hai us tarah hi neeve loga kol blessings aap chalk e aandi hai* (What for ego? Be humble, because the lower branches of the tree bear fruit and a humble and ego-less person is graced profusely [by God] like water drains automatically to the lower gradient).'

The methods to attain such fixedness on spiritual consciousness are through the practice of self-mastery by yoga and austerity, the true self-knowledge about the all-pervasiveness of the Brahman, and devotion to the Lord. The Bhagavad Gita has beautifully substantiated this proposition:

> *Kamakrodhaviyuktanam yatinam yatchetsam*
> *Avito brahmnirvana vartate viditatmanam.*

> The spiritual seekers/*yatis* (those who practises self-mastery by Yoga and austerity), who are delivered from desire and wrath and have self-mastery, for them nirvana in Brahman exists all about them, encompasses them, they already live in it because they have knowledge of self. (The Gita, 5.26)

> *Gyanenatutadgyanamyeshamnashitatmanam*
> *Teashamadityavadgyanamprakashayati tat param.*

> Verily, in whom ignorance is destroyed by self-knowledge, in them knowledge lights up like sun, the Supreme Self (within them). (The Gita 5.16)

This is the awakening of the highest, which is even beyond the discerning individuals, engulfed by the forces of nature. The enemy is in the form of desire, which is so hard to assail. One should not get despondent about the forces of nature. Though senses (*indriyani*) are supreme, they are subordinate to the mind, which is, in turn, subordinate to intelligent will, over which is the Purusha (the Lord).

> *Adwastasarvbhutanammaitryahkaruneb cha*
> *Narmamonarahamkharahsamadukhasukha ksyami.*
> *Santusthasantatam yogi tyatatmadridhanischaya*
> *Madhyarpitamanobudhiryomadbhaktahsa me priyah.*

> He who has no egoism, no I-ness, who has friendship and pity for all beings and hate for no living thing, who has tranquil equality to pleasure and pain, and is patient and forgiving, who has a desireless content, the steadfast control of self, and the firm unshakable will and resolution of the Yogin and a love and devotion which gives up the whole mind and reason to Me, he is dear to Me. (The Gita, 12.14)

But God-realization does not require that you leave this world, become a *sanyasi* and undertake rigorous yoga to realize God. It is something you realize, irrespective of the stage of life you are in. Such a realization is not instantaneous and momentary. It is your connectedness with God in every moment of your life. If you truly realize that you are 'that', then you are delivered from the veil of illusion (maya). It is not a realization at the intellect level. It is a realization of the heart, mind and action—the trinity of realization. Guruji used to say: *'Grihast bahut zaroori hai. Grihast wich rahke rab nu yad karna chahida hai* (Leading a life of a householder is karma yoga par excellence and is quite important. You should connect with God while being immersed in worldly affairs as a householder).'

When you realize 'that', then how can you differentiate between you and others? How can you have antipathy for others? If you truly realize this, your perception and understanding (*drishtikon*), and your behaviour towards others (animate and inanimate) would become godly. The basic fundamental is the training of the mind for this trinity of realization. It becomes the life principle, and such constant realization leads to bliss, *gyan samadhi*. This realization has been beautifully described in the Vedas and Upanishads. It echoes in statements/mantras like '*Tat Tvam Asi*—The Brahman is me' or '*Ahaṃ Brahmāsmi*—I am (that) Brahman' in Brihadaranyaka Upanishad of the Yujurveda and in Chandogya Upanishad of the Samaveda. Similarly, the Mandukya Upanishad of the Atharvaveda echoes with mantras like '*Ayam Atma Brahma*—This Atma is Brahman'. Verse 16 of the Isha Upanishad says, '*Puruṣaḥ so'hamasmi*—I am He, the Purusha within thee.'

Here, there is no difference between the person who visualizes/realizes (drastic) and what they see (the objects of their realization). Even when the realized soul leaves the earthly body, their consciousness continues to see/realize 'that'.

As it has been said by Lord Krishna in the Bhagavad Gita, He resides in each and every self. The Supreme Lord is in everybody, and if one has realized this, then it is real knowledge.

Aham ātmā guḍākeśha sarva-bhūtāśhaya-sthitaḥ
aham ādiśh cha madhyaṁ cha bhūtānām anta eva cha.

> I am the Supersoul, O Arjuna, seated in the hearts of all living entities. I am the beginning, the middle and the end of all beings.' (The Gita, 10.20)

Saints, sages and realized souls, over the ages, have provided the guidance for ordinary humans to realize God in the simplest manner—the discovery and realization of the self within oneself.

The Shvetashvatara Upanishad (1.15–16) states:

> *Tileṣu tailaṃ dadhanīva sarpirāpaḥ strotaḥ svaraṇīṣu cāgniḥ.*
> *Evamātmātmani gṛhyate'sau satyenainaṃ tapasā yo'nupaśyati.*
> *Sarvavyāpinamātmānaṃ kṣīre sarpirivānvitam.*
> *Ātmavidyātapomūlaṃ tadbrahmopaniṣatpadaṃ*
> *tadbrahmopaniṣatpadamiti.*

> As oil in sesame seeds, as butter in milk, as water in Srota, as fire in fuel-sticks,
> He finds in his own self that One (Atman), he, who sees him through Satya (truthfulness) and Tapas (austerity).
> He sees the all-pervading Atman, as butter lying dormant in milk,
> Rooted in self-knowledge and self-discipline—which is the final goal of Upanishad.

Sant Kabir, in his dohas, reiterated:

> *Jyon til maahi tel hai jyon chakamak mein aag.*
> *Tera saaim tujh hi mein hai, jaag sake to jag.*

> Like oil is inside the sesame seed, similarly God resides within us. It is up to you to realize this.

Sant Kabir further beautifully described the purity of mind to realize the God within oneself. He says:

> *Maala pherat jug bhaya, phira n man ka phera,*
> *Kar ka manaka d aar de, man ka manaka phera.*

> The person goes on counting the beads in the rosary while his mind is full of disturbances, realizes nothing.

> Unless your mind is pure, you attain nothing.

He further says:

> *Nahaaye dhoye kya hua, jo man mail n jaae.*
> *Min sada jal mein rahe, dhoye baas n jaae.*

> Unless the mind is pure, what is the benefit (in spiritual pursuit)? The person stinks with the spoiled mind, as the fish though stays in clean water still emits the fishy stinks.

Guruji used to say, '*Man saaf hona chahinda* (The mind should be clean/pure).'

With this realization, you need not seek God elsewhere, see Him within yourself. The great Persian poet and philosopher Rumi had asked the whereabouts of God and described his experience as follows:

> I searched for God among the Christians and on the Cross but therein found Him not. I went into the ancient temples of idolatry, no trace of Him was there. I entered the mountain cave of Hira (where Arch-angel Gabriel appeared to the Prophet) and then went as far as Qandhar but God found I not, neither in low nor in high places. With a set purpose I fared to the summit of Mount Caucasus and found there only 'anqa's habitation. Then I directed my search to the Ka'bah, the resort of old and young, God was not there even. Turning to philosophy I inquired about Him from ibn Sina but found Him not within his range. I fared then to the scene of the Prophet's experience of a great divine manifestation only a 'two bow-lengths' distance from him' but God was not there even in that exalted court. Finally, I looked into my heart and there I saw Him, He was nowhere else.[6]

The Sri Guru Granth Sahib resounds with the omnipresence of the Lord and also in everybody's soul:

---

[6]*A History of Muslim Philosophy Volume 2, Book 4*, Pakistan Philosophical Congress, https://bit.ly/3kabdRy. Accessed on 9 January 2023.

Eaek anaek biaapak poorak jath dhaekho thath soee.

Here and there, in each and every heart, and each and every being, You, O Fascinating Lord, you exist. (485.6)

Ghatt ghatt anthar sarab niranthar kaeval eaek muraaree.

In each and every heart, and deep within the very nucleus of all, is the One Lord. (485.4)

Ghatt ghatt mai har joo basai santhan kehiou pukaar.

The Dear Lord abides in each and every heart; the Saints proclaim this as true. (485.12)

Fareedha khaalak khalak meh khalak vasai rab maeh.

Fareed, the Creator is in the Creation, and the Creation abides in God. (138.1)

Eihu parapanch paarabreham kee leelaa bicharath aan n hoee.

In the one and in the many, He is pervading and permeating; wherever I look, there He is. (485.2)

Sabh gobindh hai sabh gobindh hai gobindh bin nehee koee.

God is everything, God is everything. Without God, there is nothing at all. (485.3)

Ih parpanch paarbarahm kee leelaa bichraṯ aan na ho-ee.

This manifested world is the playful game of the Supreme Lord God; reflecting upon it, we find that it is not different from Him. (485.4)

There is no need to go to temples, the church, the mosque or other places of worship to find God. No pilgrimage, no rigours of austerity, no worship and rituals or worshiping with sixteen steps, no fasting and observance of austerities will lead you to God unless those are sincere paths to train you for God-realization. When your mind is full of disturbances and evil thoughts, these peripheral/superficial activities will lead you nowhere.

Intellectualizing that God is everywhere, within everybody and within oneself is not God-realization. Once a person reaches this realization, he attains godliness—eternal bliss, and he is free from the illusion of duality—the distinction between the individual soul (atman) and the supreme Soul (Paramatman). He identifies himself with the Lord.

Jagadguru Adi Shankaracharya succinctly puts it through his composition of Atmashatkam:

Manobuddhyahaṅkāra cittāni nāhaṃ
Na ca śrotrajihve na ca ghrāṇanetre.
Na ca vyoma bhūmirna tejo na vāyuḥ
Cidānandarūpaḥ śivo'ham śivo'ham.

Neither am I the Mind, nor the Intelligence or Ego,
Neither am I the organs of Hearing (Ears), nor that of Tasting (Tongue), Smelling (Nose) or Seeing (Eyes),
Neither am I the Sky, nor the Earth, Neither the Fire nor the Air,
I am the Ever Pure Blissful Consciousness; I am the eternal Shiva, I am the eternal Shiva.

Na ca prāṇasaṃjño na vai pañcavāyuḥ
Na vā saptadhātuḥ na vā pañcakośaḥ.
Na vākpāṇipādaṃ na copasthapāyu
Cidānandarūpaḥ śivo'ham śivo'ham.

Neither am I the Vital Breath, nor the Five Vital Airs,
Neither am I the Seven Ingredients (of the Body), nor the Five Sheaths (of the Body),
Neither am I the organ of Speech, nor the organs for Holding (Hand), Movement (Feet) or Excretion,
I am the Ever Pure Blissful Consciousness; I am the eternal Shiva, I am the eternal Shiva.

Na me dveṣarāgau na me lobhamohau
Mado naiva me naiva mātsaryabhāvaḥ.

Na dharmo na cārtho na kāmo na mokṣaḥ
Cidānandarūpaḥ śivo'ham śivo'ham.

Neither do I have Hatred, nor Attachment, Neither Greed nor Infatuation,
Neither do I have Pride, nor Feelings of Envy and Jealousy,
I am Not within the bounds of *Dharma* (Righteousness), *Artha* (Wealth), *Kama* (Desire) and *Moksha* (Liberation) (the four *Purusarthas* of life),
I am the Ever Pure Blissful Consciousness; I am the eternal Shiva, I am the eternal Shiva.

Na puṇyaṃ na pāpaṃ na saukhyaṃ na duḥkhaṃ
Na mantro na tīrthaṃ na vedā na yajñāḥ.
Ahaṃ bhojanaṃ naiva bhojyaṃ na bhoktā
Cidānandarūpaḥ śivo'ham śivo'ham.

Neither am I bound by Merits nor Sins, neither by Worldly Joys nor by Sorrows,
Neither am I bound by Sacred Hymns nor by Sacred Places, neither by Sacred Scriptures nor by Scarifies,
I am Neither Enjoyment (Experience), nor an object to be Enjoyed (Experienced), nor the Enjoyer (Experiencer),
I am the Ever Pure Blissful Consciousness; I am the eternal l Shiva, I am the eternal Shiva.

Na mṛtyurna śaṅkā na me jātibhedaḥ
Pitā naiva me naiva mātā na janmaḥ.
Na bandhurna mitraṃ gururnaiva śiṣyaṃ
Cidānandarūpaḥ śivo'ham śivo'ham.

Neither am I bound by Death and its Fear, nor by the rules of Caste and its Distinctions,
Neither do I have Father and Mother, nor do I have Birth,
Neither do I have Relations nor Friends, neither Spiritual Teacher nor Disciple,
I am the Ever Pure Blissful Consciousness; I am the eternal Shiva, I am the eternal Shiva.

Ahaṃ nirvikalpo nirākārarūpo
Vibhutvācca sarvatra sarvendriyāṇām.
Na cāsaṅgataṃ naiva muktirna meyaḥ
Cidānandarūpaḥ śivo'ham śivo'ham.

I am Without any Variation, and Without any Form,
I am Present Everywhere as the underlying Substratum of everything, and behind all sense organs,
Neither do I get Attached to anything, nor get Freed from anything,
I am the Ever Pure Blissful Consciousness; I am the eternal Shiva, I am the eternal Shiva.

Such a realization (*divyaanubhuti*) is not easy to come. That is the reason our great sages have advocated the training of the body and mind (yoga, pranayam, meditation) to attain significant control over your senses and the ever-disruptive mind, preferably under a realized Guru. The Bhakti Yoga (the path of devotion) suggests complete surrender to the Lord, constant remembrance of his name and singing in his glory, and engaging in activities with the full knowledge of God's grace. Training to control the disruptive thought process of the mind is a prerequisite, irrespective of the path followed—Kriya Yoga (the path of right action), Bhakti Yoga (the path of devotion) or Jnana Yoga (the path of right knowledge).

It is observed that human beings have approximately 50,000–70,000 thoughts per day. In other words, they have 35–48 thoughts per minute. Such a huge traffic of thoughts prevents us from seeing clearly, listening deeply and feeling our well being and making contact with our own soul and significant others. Hence, the first step in spiritual tradition, whatever path you may follow, is to train one's mind to have stillness, bereft of disruptive thoughts that weaken our superior intelligence. The mind, by instinct, is inclined towards immediate pleasure through the sense organs. The first and foremost step is to put the correct things in one's mind by having positive thoughts and doing positive things. Guruji was always emphasizing positive thinking and positive action. He used to say, '*Positive socho, positive kam kariya karo* (Think positive and do positive work).'

One important part of training oneself is to understand one's own resentments, anxieties, angers and fears. Once a person understands the poison within oneself and trains the mind and associated activities towards positivism, one inches towards calmness or stilling of the mind from disruptive thoughts and the intellect leads you to realize the greater glory of God.

So, as the great sages said, one has a choice of either overcoming one's weaknesses (stilling the mind) or carrying on being a puppet of the mind. Jaggi Vasudev compares our mind and body to that of a vehicle like a car. These are designed to take us to our destination, not the other way around. We should not be driven by our body and mind.

We are blessed to be born as human beings with higher intelligence than other living beings. This higher intelligence should lead us to greater heights than relegating us to the same level as other living beings with lesser intellect.

The universal spiritual tradition of India, [as Sri Aurobindo states],

> ...starts with the Vedic synthesis of psychological man characterised by being in its highest flights and widest ranging of divine knowledge, power, joy, life and glory with the cosmic existence of the gods, pursued behind the symbols of material universe into those superior's planes which are hidden from the physical sense and the material mentality. This is reflection of *divyanubhuti* – God realisation of the Vedic Rishis - something divine, transcendent and blissful in whose unity the increasing soul of man and eternal divine fullness of the cosmic godheads meet perfectly and fulfill them. The Upanishads take up this crowning experience of the earlier seers and make it their starting point for high and profound synthesis of spiritual knowledge. The Gita starts from this Vedantic synthesis and upon the essential ideas builds another harmony of three great means and powers, Love (*Bhakti*),

> knowledge (*gyan*) and works (Karma), through which the soul of man can directly approach and cast itself into the Eternal.
>
> Bhagavat Gita starts from the acceptance of the basic characteristics of Nature (*Prakriti*) – vehement crises and moral degradation. This creates the dilemma and confusion at two levels. At the moral plane, the individual faces the struggle between righteousness and unrighteousness, between self-affirming laws of good and the forces that oppose its progression. At the physical plane, he is also overwhelmed by the vehement physical strife between human beings who represent the antagonistic powers. Arjuna represents the dilemma, due to the interplay of nature, regarding incompatibility with the spiritual state or even with purely ethical ideal of perfection. The nature of crisis which he undergoes (the Kurukshetra within and outside) is an all-embracing inner bankruptcy and he seeks deliverance as a disciple with Krishna.[7]

The Bhagavad Gita advocates the path(s) to higher evolution through the integrated trinity of yogas—karma (action), jnana (knowledge) and bhakti (devotion). Though they look different as paths, they seek the same end. Jnana Yoga consists of the cultivation of the mental attitude that is exclusively riveted on the Supreme Self, the atman. It needs fortification through a long practice of Karma Yoga (right action). Though Jnana Yoga is theoretically possible, in practice, it is nearly impossible for ordinary mortals with body consciousness to follow it. Even if one succeeds partially, there are chances of the mind being blown away by the tendencies (*vasanas*) of the senses—the forces of prakriti or nature. On the other hand, the path of Karma Yoga is suited to all aspirants. It consists of discharging all the works ordained for the individual, while in constant communion with the Lord. To maintain such an attitude in Karma Yoga, one must

[7]Roy, Anibaran, *The Message of the Gita, as Interpreted by Sri Aurobindo*, Sri Aurobindo Ashram Publication Department, Pondicherry, 2017.

have the knowledge of the atman at the core and not the body. This is where Jnana Yoga is needed.

Devotion (bhakti) is also built on the foundation of right knowledge (jnana). It is the understanding that each atman is also a manifestation of the Supreme Soul. A spiritual seeker who has achieved this state gets continuous memory of the Lord. This understanding of one's correct relationship with the Lord is the higher aspect of knowledge that helps devotion to attain the fullest maturity. When an individual gets established in the atman through perfect knowledge, a consciousness towards the Lord starts manifesting. Devotion is generated through the contemplation on the Divine Mystery and Majesty, who manifests Himself as this universe of both the living and non-living and dwells in them as their soul. He pervades everything without being affected by them or limited by them.

Lord Krishna extols Arjun to undertake Karma Yoga, to cleanse the mind of virulent veil or illusion of nature. How does one conduct Karma Yoga? And what is karma or action? He advocates controlling of your senses through austerity, yoga, meditation and sacrifices. The nature forces (prakriti), through our desires, devour all.

The Bhagavad Gita states:

Kāma eṣha krodha eṣha rajo-guṇa-samudbhavaḥ
Mahāśhano mahā-pāpmā viddhyenam iha vairiṇam II

This desire and its companion wrath are children of rajas (passion), all devouring, all polluting; know thou this is the soul's greatest enemy (which has to be slain).

The *Kama* (desire) and *krodha* (anger) are generated from Rajo Guna. They are like the insatiate fire; never satisfied and are the enemies of the *sadatma* (the eternal Soul). (The Gita, 3.37).

Dhūmenāvriyate vahnir yathādarśho malena cha
Yatholbenāvṛito garbhas tathā tenedam āvṛitam II

> The way smoke covers fire, the way the mirror is covered with dirt, and the embryo is wrapped in the amnion, so this (knowledge) is enveloped by it (*Kam—krodh, indriyani*). (The Gita, 3.38)
>
> *Indriyāṇi mano buddhir asyādhiṣhṭhānam uchyate*
> *Etair vimohayatyeṣha jñānam āvṛitya dehinam.*
>
> The senses, mind and intellect are its seat; enveloping knowledge by these it bewilders the embodied soul. (The Gita, 3.40)

The sincere spiritual seeker uplifts themself above the lower labyrinth of Nature—the three *gunas*[8] to the highest principle of the self. At that stage they have attained the peace of soul, and they can become capable of free and divine action.

> *Vaṃ buddheḥ paraṃ buddhvā saṃstabhyātmānamātmanā*
> *Jahi śatruṃ mahābāho kāmarūpaṃ durāsadam II*
>
> It is the purusha way of intelligence; in that we have to fix our will. So holding our lower subjective self in Nature, we can steadily have poised and stilled by means of the greater real self, we can destroy the restless ever-active enemy of our peace and self-mastery, the mind's desire. (The Gita, 3.43)

The *yudha* (fight) in the Kurukshetra is within the individual. Controlling the evil aspects of the senses is the right action. This battle is the karma.

---

[8]Lord Commentary by Swami Muktananda: The material nature constitutes of three gunas. Since the body, mind, and intellect are material in nature, they too possess these three modes, and a combination of these gunas forms the basis of one's character. Peacefulness, morality, well-being, serenity, etc., are the virtues of those in the mode of goodness. Those driven by passion have endless desires and ambitions; they strive to satiate them and work towards worldly enhancement. However, those in the mode of ignorance; are gripped by laziness, excessive sleep, delusion, intoxication, and other vices. A spiritual seeker needs to deal with all these three immensely powerful forces of material nature. Once the soul is able to transcend above these three modes, it attains illumination.

When Lord Krishna implores Arjun to perform the prescribed action (niyat karma), he was referring to the rigours of discipline, austerities (control the nature forces), focussing on the Supreme Soul and sacrificing all desires of action at the altar of Lord. It is the *yajna* (sacrifice) he desired from Arjuna. The Gita proceeds to give elaborate meaning to the yajna, which leaves no doubt about the symbolic use of the word and the psychological character of the sacrifice enjoined in this teaching.

The Bhagavad Gita (3.25) says:

> *Saktāḥ karmaṇyavidvānso yathā kurvanti bhārata*
> *Kuryād vidvāns tathāsaktaśh chikīrṣhur loka-saṅgraham II*

> But those who have knowledge, the simple fact of sacrifice, of the offering whatever work to the Divine itself, of casting all their activities into the unified divine consciousness and energy, in their one means, their own dharma.

The means of sacrifices are various and the offerings are of many kinds. There is a psychological sacrifice of self-control and self-discipline, which leads to higher self-possession and self-knowledge. Senses (indriyani) themselves become the sacrificial fire. The self-control is the sacrifice. All sensory activities and the resultant consciousness (*rupa* or visual sensation, *rasa* or sensation of taste, *gandha* or fragrance/smell or olfactory, *sparsha* or touch and *sabda* or auditory) get reduced asunder to *vasma* (ash) in this sacrificial fire.

The Bhagavad Gita (3.27) says:

> *Prakṛiteḥ kriyamāṇāni guṇaiḥ karmāṇi sarvaśhaḥ*
> *Ahankāra-vimūḍhātmā kartāham iti manyate II*

> Others offer all actions of the senses and all actions of vital forces into the fire of the Yoga of self-control kindled by knowledge.

It may be the austerity of his self-discipline and energy of his soul directed to the higher aim.

There is a misconception that in the knowledge route to the Supreme Soul (Jnana Yoga), there is no need of karma. With this misconception, they say, 'I am pure; I am consciousness; I am Brahman (*Brahmasmi*), and I stop undertaking any karma.' As per Lord Krishna in the Gita, this is not the right knowledge at all. In Jnana Yoga, the spiritual seeker has to perform the same right action as in Nishkama Karma Yoga. The difference between the two is in the application of intelligence/perception and perspective. The follower of right knowledge understands or realizes atman—his own position and performs his actions. The follower of the right actions takes the shelter of the Lord and performs his actions. Performing the right action is the same in both paths—only the perspective for conducting the right action is different.

Is the performance of the various rituals (*karma kanda*) prescribed in the Vedas and other scriptures karma—the right action? Lord Krishna in the Gita says 'no'. These are limited to the three gunas and not beyond that. He asked Arjun to rise above the three gunas. The person, who rises above these three gunas, knows the Brahman, the Supreme Soul. The Vedic rituals have utility for the lesser mortals, though not entirely useless, if performed with all devotion to the Paramatma, the Supreme Soul.

Lord Krishna advises in the Gita (2.47) to perform nishkama karma, an action bereft of desire for its fruits/results:

> *Karmaṇy-evādhikāras te mā phaleṣhu kadāchana*
> *Mā karma-phala-hetur bhūr mā te saṅgo 'stvakarmaṇi II*

> The *Nishkama Karma* advocated in Gita, is sacrificing all desires. The most important desire is the desire for results of your actions. The normal persons, after getting the desired results, and the *Yogis* getting *sidhi (some super natural powers),* become over joyous and happy. But when they do not get the desired results, they become despondent. In the Gita, Krishna extols to abjure desires and be equanimous of results.

Lord Krishna says in the Gita (5.10–12):

> *Brahmaṇyādhāya karmāṇi saṅgaṁ tyaktvā karoti yaḥ*
> *Lipyate na sa pāpena padma-patram ivāmbhasā II*
>
> He who acteth placing all actions in *Brahman*, abandoning all attachment, is unaffected by sin, as a lotus leaf in the waters.
>
> *Kāyena manasā buddhyā kevalair indriyair api*
> *Yoginaḥ karma kurvanti saṅgaṁ tyaktvātma-śhuddhaye II*
>
> Yogis, having abandoned attachment perform action only by the body, by the mind, by the intellect (reason), and even by the senses, for the purification of self.
>
> *Yuktaḥ karma-phalaṁ tyaktvā śhāntim āpnoti naiṣhṭhikīm*
> *Ayuktaḥ kāma-kāreṇa phale sakto nibadhyate II*
>
> The harmonized man, having abandoned the fruit of action, attained to the eternal peace (soul in union with Brahman); the non-harmonized, impelled by desire, attached to fruit, are bound (by action of desire).

But what is nishkama karma? People misinterpret this shloka. They say, 'Whatever you do, never expect results and that is Nishkama Karma Yoga!' On the contrary, an equanimity (*samatya bhava*) of the positive (*sidhi*) and of the negative or no results (*asidhi*) is called Karma Yoga. The person who is not disturbed by the sidhi or asidhi, in which there is no realization of difference between the two, has attained equanimity. He is blessed to get this equanimity from the Lord. He abjures the results, and so it is called Nishkama Karma Yoga. He has to perform his karma; that is why it is called Karma Yoga. The ultimate goal is union with the Supreme Soul, the Paramatma. That is Karma Yoga, when you have the equanimity of sidhi and asidhi, no attachment to the results. Ordinary people hanker after results, and after not getting the expected results, get disinterested in karma. That is not what Karma Yoga, as per the Gita, is about. Some say, 'Do not initiate karma; you become *nishkarmi*.' Lord Krishna says in the Gita (3.2–3), 'If you do not initiate action or karma, no *Nackara bhava* generates. By abandoning karma, such persons have little chance of God-realization and liberation.[9]

In the Gita, Lord Krishna says that you should perform your prescribed (niyat) karma or action. The question arises: what is prescribed karma? In the *Yatharth Geeta*, Swami Adgadanand says, 'The *yojana prakriya* (the process of sacrifice) of your desires through austerities, controlling your senses and thought processes and concentrating on atman with full knowledge of the Absolute is karma.'[10]

Lord Krishna took birth in an avatar to uphold dharma-righteousness, and he motivated Arjun to fight a physical war i.e., his niyat karma. In another plane, he implored Arjun to undergo the yogic process (austerities, controlling your senses and thought processes, and concentrating on atman with full knowledge of the Absolute) and fight the battle of the Kurukshetra raising within him due to disparate tendencies of interplay of various factors of prakriti.

Niyat karma is also what has been prescribed for a person's profession—Brahmin, Kshatriya, Vaishya and Sudra. These are not the so-called *varna* (caste) system characterized and perpetuated by hereditary principles. On the other hand, these are professions adopted by individuals (same family members may adopt different professions from the four categories) depending on their ability, volition and opportunity. Within each category of profession, the individual thrives to excel while graduating from and balancing his *tamasic, rajasic* and *satvik* gunas and ultimately rising above the gunas.

Raja Janak, being a Khastriya, and Tuladhara, being a Vaishya (shopkeeper), could attain God-realization by following the right path. As Tuladhara told Sage Jalali, 'Living in a way which inflicted no harm or inflicting minimum harm, if required; no loan from any one, no quarrels, attraction or aversion he had conquered;

[9]Adgadanand, Swami, *Yatharth Geeta*, Shri Paramhans Swami Adgadanandji Ashram Trust, Mumbai, July 2018.
[10]Ibid.

equal in his book on all, without praising or blaming any; when a man is fearless and is feared by none; when he neither likes or dislikes, when he does no wrong to any, then he reaches Brahman.' (Shanti Parva Book 311–319)

As we proceed further, we will see in Guruji the characteristics of a sthitaprajna, as described in the Gita, and the personification of divine realization as described in the Shatakam by Adi Shankaracharya.

THE LORD LEADS BY EXAMPLE: THE AVATARS

It is not that the Lord just prescribes the righteous path; he takes on avatars, human forms, to lead by example and uphold righteousness. Lord Krishna says in the Gita (4.7-8):

> *Yadā yadā hi dharmasya glānirbhavati bhārata,*
> *Abhyutthānamadharmasya tadātmānaṁ sṛjāmyaham II*
>
> Whenever, oh son of Bharat, there is the fading of righteousness (*dharma*) and the dominant prevalence of unrighteousness (*adharma*), there I take birth.
>
> *Paritrāṇāya sādhūnāṅ vināśāya ca duṣkṛtām.*
> *Dharmasaṅsthāpanārthāya saṅbhavāmi yugē yugē.*
>
> For the deliverance of good, for the destruction of evil-doers, for the enthroning of the Right, I am born from age to age.

This is the normal interpretation. Another spiritual meaning is given by Swami Adgadanand in the Yatharth Gita:

> When the soul of *sadhak (seeker)* is filled with despondency and is pinning for the Supreme Soul, the *Parmatma*, when he is troubled by the internal forces of nature (*adharma*), then I appear before him as self.
>
> In the path of *seeker (sadhak),* to ensure the divine flow of conscience, detachment, etc. and to destroy the negative

> nature forces like desire, anger, attachment, antipathy or malice etc., I appear in the soul of the seeker from time to time. It is my blessings to the true seeker. *Avatar* is not outside, it is inside you.[11]

Each and every individual has a higher goal and purpose of being born as a human being. The ultimate purpose is spiritual—to realize God, the atma gets unionized (merged) with the Paramatma. The methods are many.

Dharma is the path of righteousness and living one's life according to certain positive codes of conduct. As per the Indian spiritual and ethical traditions, dharma is the foundation of the universal moral law of the world, the observance of which enables humans to live a life of contentment, saving from degradation and suffering. Combined with spiritual discipline, this becomes the guiding principle for mankind. Dharma has its etymology in Sanskrit *'dhr'*, which means 'to hold or support'. The older Vedic Sanskrit '*dharman*' has the meaning 'bearer, supporter, sustainer'. The ancient sages of India considered dharma as the very foundation of life, 'that which holds' the people of this world and the whole creation.

The Atharvaveda describes dharma symbolically: *Prithivim-dharmana-dhritam*; that is, 'This world is upheld by dharma—the cosmic norm.' It guides humans to do niyat karma—doing what is right as an individual, whether he is a commoner or a family man or a ruler. Dharma provides a code of conduct for spiritual pursuits, as well as securing worldly joys too. The Indian spiritual tradition suggests various methods for the attainment of the highest ideal and eternal bliss here and now on earth, while simultaneously endorsing the idea that it is one's dharma to lead a normal worldly life in a righteous manner. The normal life may include, for example, study, acquiring skills and knowledge, being engaged in a profession, getting married and raising a family, providing for family in whatever way is necessary, and in pursuing a spiritual

---

[11]Ibid.

path. The practice of dharma gives an experience of peace, joy, strength and tranquility within oneself and makes life disciplined.

The great spiritual and social luminaries of this land, including the Vedic rishis, Lord Buddha, Sant Kabir, Guru Nanak and others have defined the root of dharma as compassion. The Bhagavata Puran has beautifully described the tenets of righteous living, which includes *tap* (austerity), *shauch* (purity), *daya* (compassion) and *satya* (truthfulness). On the other hand, an adharmic or unrighteous life is bedeviled with vices like *ahankar* (pride), *asangh* (bad contact) and *madya* (intoxication). Furthermore, our spiritual tradition emphasizes that a dharmic person should possess certain abilities, power and spiritual strength, which translates into characteristics like *dhriti* (patience), *kshama* (forgiveness), *dama* (piety), *asteya* (honesty), *shauch* (sanctity), *indraiya-nigrah* (control of senses), *dhi* (reason), *vidya* (knowledge or learning), *satya* (truthfulness) and absence of *krodha* (anger), non-violence, non-coveting, and the purity of body and mind. The epics of the Ramayana, the Mahabharat and the Puranic literature provide ample examples of righteous living by various characters, as well as the failings of others.

Dharma should not be confused with organized religion and the rituals associated with religious practices by various religious communities. If the purpose of those practices and austerities is to lead a dharmic life, on the path to spiritual attainment, they coincide with dharma, otherwise these are null.

The life philosophy and practices of an individual should be a righteous one, an integrated whole. A life fragmented by the dogmatic pursuit of religious practices and austerities on one hand and the day-to-day pursuit/adaptation of adharmic ways of thinking and living on the other, does not qualify as righteous.

Though the tenets of righteous living have been so neatly summarized above, the dynamics of leading a life in the real world is fraught with many challenges, turbulences, trials, distractions and allurements, which an individual fights as their own battle of Kurukshetra.

All these battles rage within us and within everybody. You need to cleanse yourself by emerging victorious in this battle of the internal Kurukshetra. There should be an integration of thought, action and soul realization. The dissonance among the three leads us to live a fragmented and hypocritical life. Rabindranath Tagore in *Gitanjali* states, 'Leave this chanting and singing and telling of beads! Whom dost thou worship in this lonely dark corner of a temple with doors all shut? Open thine eyes and see thy God is not before thee!'[12]

It is not only that the Lord takes on an avatar to lead by example and shower his blessings on humankind, He also ordains many sages and realized souls to spread His message and guide humankind, leading by examples, to attain higher spiritual wisdom and enlightenment. These sages are His *ansha* (indivisible part). The rishis, sages and realized souls, like Lord Buddha, Mahavir Tirthankar, Jesus Christ, Prophet Muhammad, Guru Nanak, Sant Kabir, Sai Baba of Shirdi and Guruji, all are His representatives ordained to take human form to spread the message of the Lord and lead humankind towards a better society closer to God. The revered Guruji used to say: *'Ashi light ton aye hain, light nnu chal jawange* (We have come from the Supreme Self; and will go back to Him)'; *Sada kaam lokannu rav de naal jodna* (Our purpose is to bring the humanity closer to God)'; *'Jeh mein ek vi banda rab passe pa dita, mera kaam ho gaya* (If I am able to connect even one person with God, my mission is achieved).'

You can have the God-realization, liberation or enlightenment if you have a sincere desire. It is a matter of your determination, your sincere yearning and the Grace of God. Be positive, love everything God has created and what has been given to you. Empathize with all—jiva (living beings) and *nirjiva* (non-living things)—as manifestation of Almighty. Undergo the discipline of body, mind and perform your day-to-day karma (duty) like Arjun. Then you have the potential to realize the truth of Brahmasmi or *Shivohm.*

---

[12]Tagore, Rabindranath, *Gitanjali*, Rupa, New Delhi, 2002.

The great Indian spiritual tradition promotes positive action for the betterment of society. In addition to promoting self-actualization, it promotes universal love, senstivity to environment, compassion for all living beings, tolerance for all religions, universal brotherhood (all are part of God, and God resides in all). The Indian spiritual tradition enjoins the community/ groups for a positive and decisive action (Niyat Karma) to uphold righteousness. If somebody says, 'I am following karma/gyan/ bhakti yoga,' but closes their eyes to the adharma (the vices, the evils) that is prevailing in the society and their surroundings (stating that God and their own karmas will take care of it), they are failing in their duty to the Lord. It is not a life of karma in pursuit of God; it is selfish abandonment of their niyat karma. Swimming along with the tide of the majority and selfishness is not niyat karma. Even if most people follow this selfish route, the righteous person takes a stand against evil. Guruji used to reiterate the proverb: 'Only dead fish swim with the tide.'

Sri Aurobindo says:

> Arjun is the man of action and not of knowledge, the fighter, never seer or thinker. In Gita he typifies the human soul of action brought face to face through that action in the highest and most violent crisis with the problems of human life and in apparent incompatibility with the spiritual state or even with purely ethical ideal of perfection.[13]

It is a mistake to interpret the Gita from the standpoint of a disinterested performance of duty. The Gita does not teach disinterested performance of duties, the abandonment of dharma or to take refuge in the Supreme alone.

The great Indian spiritual tradition enjoins upon the integration of the life principles at three planes: (i) spiritual self-knowledge and pursuits, (ii) conducting niyat karma, and (iii) compassion to all. The spiritual self-knowledge starts with the realization of the

[13]Roy, Anibaran, *The Message of the Gita, as Interpreted by Sri Aurobindo*, Sri Aurobindo Ashram Publication Department, Pondicherry, 2017.

manifestation of the omnipresent, omniscient, omnipotent Lord who resides everywhere and in everybody, including ourselves, and the earnest desire of seeking the union with God. The second plane is conducting niyat karma, which involves leading a day-to-day life of purity, austerity, discipline, non-coveting, etc., and to be a part of the fight for positive action to assist God in establishing righteousness. The third plane is compassion to all—living and non-living, which results in a life dedicated to the welfare of all of God's creation, sharing the bounties of the Lord with your fellow travellers on the journey, and looking after the welfare of the needy. These three facets of an individual human being are not mutually exclusive; these are part of the integral whole—the core God principle.

The universal spiritual tradition of this great land is expressed in the prayer to the Supreme Lord to ensure peace for everybody.

Om sarve bhavantu sukhinah.
Sarve santu nir-aamayaah.
Sarve bhadraanni pashyantu.
Maa kashcid-duhkha-bhaag-bhavet.
Om shaantih shaantih shaantih.

May all become happy
May none fall ill.
May all see auspiciousness everywhere
May none ever feel sorrow.
Om Shaantih Shaantih Shaantih.[3]

Furthermore, we also pray for universal collective action in Krishna Yajurveda, Taittiriya Upanishad (2.2.2):

Oṃ saha nāvavatu.
Saha nau bhunaktu.
Saha vīryaṁ karavāvahai.
Tējasvi nāvadhītamastu mā vidviṣāvahai.
Oṃ śāntiḥ śāntiḥ śāntiḥ.

Let us together be protected and let us together be nourished by God's blessings.
Let us together join our mental forces in strength for the benefit of humanity.
Let our efforts at learning be luminous and filled with joy, and endowed with the force of purpose.
Let us never be poisoned with the seeds of hatred for anyone. Let there be peace and serenity in all the three universes.

As we traverse through the life history of Guruji and the numerous satsangs by the sangat, we would realize that Guruji belongs to the great legion of realized souls, and his taking the human form is to guide mankind to realize God, leading through examples and his subtle hints and utterances to the discernible disciples.

We seek the grace of the Lord by praying:

Om Asato Maa Sad-Gamaya.
Tamaso Maa Jyotir-Gamaya.
Mrityor-Maa Amrtam Gamaya.
Om Shaantih Shaantih Shaantih.

Oh Lord, lead us from untruth to Truth.
Lead us to light from darkness;
from ignorance to the light of knowledge and wisdom.
Lead us from death (temporary materialistic existence)
to immortality (the eternal super consciousness) through purity of purpose.
Let there be peace, peace and only peace.
(Brihadaranyaka Upanishad, 1.3.28)

9

Guru Tattva

WHY DO WE NEED A GURU?

We have discussed the perpetual battle within each individual. The battle is associated with the tremendous force of nature on the individual—his sensory system, the mind-space and the higher intellect, the disequilibrium due to the imbalances of the three gunas on one hand and the self (atman) on the other. This battle of Kurukshetra within the individual creates significant crisis of moral dilemma and anguish, not to speak of the pursuit of the Absolute. A sadhak like Arjun has his doubts about the meaning of his actions. He seeks the guidance of his friend, his spiritual guru, Lord Krishna. Sri Aurobindo in *The Message of the Gita* comments, 'He (Arjun) is disciple who receives his initiation in the battle field, the type of the struggling human soul who has not yet received the Knowledge, but has grown fit to receive it by action in the world in close companionship and increasing nearness to the higher and divine self.'[1]

There are numerous examples in the Vedas, Upanishads, epics and Puranic literature, on how the Lord himself or the realized souls, such as seers and sages, the chosen ones by the Lord, have all acted as gurus to impart guidance on the path of spiritual quest.

Entering the spiritual path is accompanied by many challenges. The Guru is the true spiritual guide, who shows the way and protects

[1]Roy, Anibaran, *The Message of the Gita: As Interpreted by Sri Aurobindo,* Sri Aurobindo Ashram, Pondicherry, 2010.

the disciple from falling. It is often observed that the spiritual path is more complicated than the difficult tracks of the Amazon. The Guru has already been through the 'forest'.

The Guru matches his high level of spiritualism to the level of the uninitiated. It is the Guru who makes spiritual practice effective. The spiritual wisdom and knowledge of the Guru is the culmination of his experience and/or the combined experience of a lineage of gurus or spiritual masters. Accordingly, such knowledge and wisdom has the transformative effect on the disciple. The advantage of having a guru is that the disciple gets spiritual advice as per his specific spiritual needs. The Guru performs the duty of a friend, philosopher and guide for the disciple by clarifying their doubts, correcting their mistakes, resolving their karma, guiding in the practice of self-discipline and purification. The Guru leads by example, bestows his grace on the disciples, imparts knowledge and clarification, and looks after the soul of the disciple. The Guru–disciple relationship is better than that of parent–child, transcended in birth, and remains eternal spanning various subsequent births.

Lord Krishna says in the Gita (4.34):

> *Tad viddhi praṇipātena paripraśhnena sevayā.*
> *Upadekṣhyanti te jñānaṁ jñāninas tattva-darśhinaḥ.*

> Learn that by worshiping the feet of the teacher, by questioning and by service; the men of knowledge who have seen (not those who know merely by the intellect) the true principle of things, will instruct thee in knowledge.

The etymology of the Guru has been beautifully explained in the Advayataraka Upanishad (Shloka 16):

> *Guśabdastvandhakāraḥ syāt ruśabdastannirodhakaḥ.*
> *Andhakāranirodhitvāt gururityabhidhīyate.*

> The syllable Gu indicates darkness, the syllable Ru means its dispeller,

> Because of the quality of dispelling darkness and the Guru is thus termed.

In the spiritual plane, ignorance about the Supreme Self is symbolized by darkness. Such ignorance can be dissipated by shedding light. The Guru is like a light radiating sun, radiating the light of knowledge. This light of knowledge helps the disciple to understand and see the higher truth. The Guru takes a sincere, devoted disciple off the jungle of intellect and sense-perceptions, and guides him towards God-realization.

The 'Guru Gita' (song of the Guru) believed to be part of the larger Skanda Puran, beautifully describes why you need a guru. Shloka 24 says:

> *Japastapo vrataṁ tīrthaṁ yajño dānaṁ tathaiva ca.*
> *Gurutattvamavijñāya sarvaṁ vyarthaṁ bhavetpriye.*
>
> *Japa*, austerities, observances, pilgrimage, sacrifice, charity—all these become a mere waste without understanding the Guru Tattva.[2]

It further says:

> *Gūḍhāvidyā jaganmāyā dehaścājñānasambhavaḥ.*
> *Vijñānaṁ yatprasādena guruśabdena kathayate.*
>
> The hidden ignorance, absence of the knowledge of self, the world, Maya, the body—are all caused by ignorance. By whose grace one attains direct knowledge of the self—he is known by the name 'Guru'.[3]

The Gurubani (Ang 13) says, '*Guru sakhi Joti pargat hoi.* (Through the Guru's Teachings, the Light shines forth).'

When a disciple is graced to have the association of the true Guru, they are blessed with divine knowledge. The Guru sheds light through his messages. The true Guru reveals the divinity of

---

[2]Tirth, Swami Shivom, *Shri Guru Gita: The Divine Song of the Guru*, Swami Shivom Tirth Ashram, 2006.

[3]Narayanananda, Swami, *Sri Guru Gita*, Divine Society Publication, 2008.

man to the individual. He shows him the way to cross the ocean of life and to reach the kingdom of bliss. Guru Nanak says:

> *Guru sagaru ratani bharpure.*
> *Amrit sant chugahi nahi dure.*
> *Rahi rasu cheg chugai prav bhave.*
> *Sarvar mahi hansu pranpati pave.*

> The Guru is the ocean, filled with pearls. The Saints gather in the Ambrosial Nectar; they do not go far away from there. They taste the subtle essence of the Lord; they are loved by God. Within this pool, the swans find their Lord, the Lord of their souls. (Gurubani Ang 685)

As per the Gurubani, '*Gurehi dhikhaaeiouloeinaa* (The Guru has revealed Him to my eyes. Guru has given me the eyes to see the truth that God resides in everybody).'

'As I received the word from the Lord, so do I deliver it,' says Guru Nanak. (SGGS, 722)

Sant Kabir says that an *atmagyani* (knower of the Soul, self-realized) can be called a *satguru*, for he has experienced the self. He says:

> *Timir gaya ravi dekhate, kumati gayi guru gyan;*
> *Sumati gayi ati lobhate, bhakti gayi abhiman.*

> Darkness disappears when the sun arises, and ignorance goes away by the Guru's wisdom. Good intellect is lost because of greed, and devotion is lost because of ego.

He further says,

> *Guru dhobi sis kapada, sabun sirjanhar;*
> *Surati sila par dhoiye, nikase jyoti apar.*

> Guru is like a washer man and the disciple is like cloth; God Himself is the soap. O Guru! Please wash my thought waves on the stone of meditation, then the unlimited light will appear.

Without a spiritual guide, the likelihood of stagnation or even regression in spiritual growth is high. Using figurative language, it is pointed out that no blind man can find the path without the Guru, as nobody can reach the housetop without the stairs and no one can cross the river without a boat.

At the end of their discourse, Lord Krishna asked Arjun (The Gita, 18.72):

> *Kachchid etach chhrutaṁ pārtha tvayaikāgreṇa chetasā*
> *Kachchid ajñāna-sammohaḥ pranaṣhṭas te dhanañjaya*

> O Arjun, have you heard me with a concentrated mind?
> Have your ignorance and delusion been destroyed?[4]

The true disciple Arjun said (The Gita, 18.73):

> *Naṣhṭo mohaḥ smṛitir labdhā tvat-prasādān mayāchyuta*
> *Sthito 'smi gata-sandehaḥ kariṣhye vachanaṁ tava II*

> O infallible one, by your grace my illusion has been dispelled, and I am situated in knowledge. I am now free from doubts, and I shall act according to your instructions.

At the outset, Arjun was faced with a bewildering situation and was confused about what his duty was. Overwhelmed with sorrow, he had sat down on his chariot, giving up his weapons. He had confessed that he could find no remedy to the grief that had attacked his body and senses. But he now finds himself completely transformed, and announces that he is situated in knowledge and no longer perplexed. However, he adds, '*Tvat prasādān mayāchyuta*', meaning, 'I was not just your (Lord Krishna's) lecture, but your grace that dispelled my ignorance.'

Spiritual knowledge, unlike material knowledge, can neither be purchased nor sold. It is offered through grace and received through faith and humbleness. This is the essence of the *Guru Tattva.*

---

[4]Mukundananda, Swami, *Bhagvat Gita- The Song of God*, Jagadguru Kripaluji Yog, 2013.

SADGURU OR PURAN GURU

The tradition of reverence for the Guru is apparent in the Shvetashvatara Upanishad (6.23) where it equates the spiritually enlightened Guru to that of God, in context of reverence and devotion. It states:

> *Yasya deve parā bhaktir yathā deve tathā gurau.*
> *Tasyaite kathitā hy arthāḥ prakāśante mahātmanaḥ*
> *prakāśante mahātmanaḥ.*
>
> If these truths have been told to a high-minded person who feels the highest devotion for God and for his Guru as for God, and then they will surely shine forth as inner experiences - then, indeed, they will shine forth.

In the spiritual journey, the seeker who internalizes and practises devotion for the Lord and the teacher alike is blessed. It is said in the Upanishads that God teaches the disciple through an illumined human Guru.

According to Sant Kabir, the Guru is greater than God, simply because the knowledge or experience of God is not possible without the Guru. Sant Kabir says:

> *Guru Govind dou khade, kake lagoon paay,*
> *Balihari Guru aapno, Govind diyo batay I*
>
> If both Guru and God appear before me, to whom should I prostate? I bow before Guru as he was instrumental in leading me to God.

Guruji used to say, '*Guruan di gun gaana sav to change ardas* (Singing the glory of Guru is your best prayer).'

Swami Narayanananda, while writing the preface to *Sri Guru Gita* says, 'The Real Nature of *Sadguru*, which is akin to the nature of the Supreme Being unfailingly, serves as a beacon light to all those sincere seekers who are already treading the spiritual path.'[5]

[5]Narayanananda, Swami, *Sri Guru Gita*, Divine Society Publication, 2008.

Iyengar Srinivas's translation of shlokas 5.56–59 of Guru Sikha Upanishad furnishes the beautiful comparison of Guru with God.

The Guru is Brahman, the Guru is Visnu; the Guru is always the Lord Achyuta; greater than the Guru there is no one whatsoever in all the three worlds. One should worship with extreme devotion (the Guru), who imparts divine wisdom, who is the spiritual guide, who is the Supreme Lord (himself) For him, there will be the fruit of knowledge. He should be adored with great devotion. There is no difference between the Guru and Ishvara. One should not engage in debate, on equality of status with the Guru anywhere. With devotion, one should conceive in his mind of the identical character of the Guru, God and the Atman.[6]

The Advayataraka Upanishad (14.15) reverentially narrates that a guru or spiritual teacher is one who knows 'that' (Vedas), a devotee of the Supreme Lord (Vishnu), has no spite, and who knows yoga, has his own views on it. Yoga is part of how he lives his life, is clean, reveres his own guru, if any, and who understands the concept of Purusha (Atman Brahman*)*.

The true Guru or puran guru is equated with God (Lord Shiva). The Guru Gita (Shloka 20) says:

> *Yo guruḥ sa śivaḥ prokto yaḥ śivaḥ sa guruḥ smṛtaḥ.*
> *Vikalpaṁ yastu kurvīta sa naro gurutalpagaḥ.*
>
> He who is the Guru is Shiva Himself, so declares the scriptures and the fact that Shiva is the Guru, and is reminded to us in all the Smritis. He, who makes any distinction between the two, is guilty of the crime of uniting with his own preceptor's wife.

Adi Shankara begins his 'Gurustotram' (verses to the Guru) with the following:

---

[6]Ayyangar, Srinivasa, *The Yoga-Upanisads*, 1938, Internet Archive, https://bit.ly/3iHsroW. Accessed on 16 January 2023.

Guru Brahma Guru Vishnu Guru Devo Maheshwara.
Guru Sakshat Param Brahma Tasmai Shri Gurave Namaha.

The Guru is Brahma, the Guru is Vishnu, the Guru Deva is Maheswara (Shiva),

The Guru is verily the Param Brahma (Supreme Brahman); Salutations to that Guru.

The Gurubani (Ang 759) echoes this:

Satguru mera sada sada na aveina jai.
Ohu abinami purukhu hai sav mahi rahia samai.

My True Guru, forever and ever, does not come and go.
He is the Imperishable Creator Lord; He is permeating and pervading among all.

The Guru occupies the highest status in Sikhism. Guru Nanak says in the Sri Guru Granth Sahib (Ang 462, First Mehla):

Balirahi gur apane diuhadi sad var.
Jini manas te devate kie karat na lagi var.

A hundred times a day, I am a sacrifice to my Guru;
He made angels out of men, without delay.

A satguru or puran guru has distinctive characteristics, not ordinarily found in any other less-accomplished and realized spiritual gurus. Sant Kabir's spiritual philosophy uses the word satguru quite profusely. Kabir says:

Satpurush Ko Jansi, Tiska Satguru Naam.

The enlightened master who has realized the Supreme Lord of truth (Satya Purush) is called Satguru.

He further says:

Devi dewal jagat mein, kotik poojey koye.
Satguru ki pooja kiye, sabb ki pooja hoye.

> There are several deities to whom people go on worshiping. But worship of satguru encompass worship of all deities and God, the Sat Purush.

In one of Kabir's songs, the satguru is described as the real sage (sadhu):

> He is the real Sadhu, who can reveal the form of the Formless to the vision of these eyes;
> Who teaches the simple way of attaining Him, that is other than rites or ceremonies;
> Who does not make you close the doors, and hold the breath, and renounce the world;
> Who makes you perceive the Supreme Spirit wherever the mind attaches itself;
> Who teaches you to be still in the midst of all your activities.
> Ever immersed in bliss, having no fear in his mind, he keeps the spirit of union in the midst of all enjoyments.
> The infinite dwelling of the Infinite Being is everywhere: in earth, water, sky, and air;
> Firm as the thunderbolt, the seat of the seeker is established above the void.
> He who is within is without: I see Him and none else.[7]

Sant Kabir glorifies the satguru in his dohas:

> *Saat Samundra ki masi karun, lekhni karun vanrai*
> *Dharti ka kagaz karun, guru gun likha ne jaaye*

> With the ink as voluminous as the seven oceans, pens made of the entire trees of the world and the writing canvas as big as the earth will not suffice to write the qualities of a true Guru, as these are limitless.

Satguru or Sadguru means the 'true Guru', who is an enlightened master, whose life's purpose is to guide the initiated *shishya*

[7]Tagore, Rabindranath, *Songs of Kabir*, New York, The Macmillan Company, 1915.

(disciple) on the spiritual path, the summation of which is the realization of the Supreme Self. As per the Yogasastra, satguru or sadguru is someone who has returned from *savikalpa samadhi,* the last stage of yoga where the yogi becomes one with the Brahman or Param Brahma.

We have described, based on the Upanishads and the Gita, the dohas of Sant Kabir, the Gurubani and other treatises, as to why a spiritual seeker needs a guru, a realized soul. Nevertheless, attempts have been made to find out some basic characteristics of the true Guru. Amongst the crowd of thousands of fake religious gurus, how should one know who is the true Guru? What are the characteristics of the true Guru, puran guru or satguru?

The true Guru relieves human beings from all sufferings, diseases and sorrows from the life of his devotees. He is the source of ever-lasting happiness in this transient world. The true Guru or satguru provides true spiritual knowledge, which helps the souls attain salvation.

Guruji used to say: '*Main ithe ayah un tuhada antkaran nu saaf karan vaste. Jado tuhada antkaran saaf huve, tuhannu sav kutch mil janda* (I have come here to purify your soul. When your soul is purified; you have attained everything).'

The importance of the true Guru has been beautifully explained in the Yajurveda (19.25):

> *Arddh richae ukthanm roopam padae aapnoti nivid*
> *Prnvae shastranam roopam paysa som aapyate*

> A true Guru has the competence of completing the incomplete sentences or coded words of the Vedas. He is capable of completely understanding and explaining the partial description of *shlokas.* He is such a realized soul equated to the sages (*rishis*) who were initially revealed the Vedas. He should have the capability to expand the Vedas and provide ever evolving dynamic context to the spiritual core of such scriptures.

Sikhism lays down certain qualifications and qualities for a guru. The Sri Guru Granth Sahib (Ang 759.1–2) reads, '*Satguru saagar guna naam mai tisu dekhane ka jau* (The true Guru is the ocean of virtue of Naam, the Name of the Lord. I have such a yearning to see Him!)'

The Guru must be an ideal person who is able to inspire confidence in his disciples. And he should be always accessible to the disciples, who have sincere devotion and yearning. He does not live in an ivory tower. He is the epitome of humility also. He is fearless and without hate. He may come in conflict with hostile social forces, vested interests and evil people out to oppose him, but must deal with them with fortitude.

The Guru immersed in 'the Naam' incessantly acts like a beckoning light leading others to get immersed in it. During the spiritual journey, he holds the hand of the disciple to enable them to reach higher levels of attainment. He is like a boat, ferrying the devotees across the tempestuous ocean of life.

The Upanishads have mentioned five signs of the satguru (true Guru). In the presence of the satguru, (i) knowledge flourishes (*gyana raksha*); (ii) sorrow diminishes (*dukha kshaya*); (iii) joy wells up automatically (*sukha aavirbhav*); (iv) abundance dawns (*samridhi*); and (v) all talent manifests (*sarva samvardhan*).

> Transcending boundaries of race, religion or culture, since time immemorial, the world has always recognised and saluted knowledgeable, insightful, worthy, truthful and creative trendsetters. From early childhood itself, young minds are driven towards seeking knowledge and blessed are those who get the guidance to move away from the darkness of ignorance towards illuminating wisdom.[8]

Humility is the hallmark of the true Guru. Swami Yogananda says that the true Guru should be humble. Swami Vivekananda says:

[8]Chopra, Arti, 'The Guru-Shishya Bond is As Strong As Ever', *The Indian Express*, 26 August 2013, https://bit.ly/3X4BBL8. Accessed on 9 January 2023.

In the teacher we must first see that he knows the secret of the scriptures. The whole world reads scriptures—Bibles, Vedas, Korans, and others; but they are only words, external arrangement, syntax, the etymology, the philology, the dry bones of religion... the teacher must be able to know the *spirit* of the scriptures... That work [taking note, drawing etymology of words, etc.] has its own value in its proper place, but not here in the spiritual realm. Men never become spiritual through such work; you have never once seen a strong spiritual man among these 'leaf-counters'...

The second condition necessary in the teacher is that he must be sinless... For the knowledge that the physical sciences require is simply intellectual and depends on intellectual strength; a man can have in such a case a gigantic intellectual power without the least development of his soul. But in the spiritual sciences it is impossible from first to last that there can be any spiritual light in that soul which is impure. What can such a soul teach? It knows nothing. Spiritual truth is purity. 'Blessed are the pure in heart, for they shall see God'...

The third condition is motive. We should see that he does not teach with any ulterior motive, for name, or fame, or anything else, but simply for love, pure love for you. When spiritual forces are transmitted from the teacher to the taught, they can only be conveyed through the medium of love; there is no other medium that can convey them. Any other motive, such as gain or name, would immediately destroy the conveying medium; therefore, all must be done through love. One who has known God can alone be a teacher. When you see that in the teacher these conditions are fulfilled, you are safe; if they are not fulfilled, it is unwise to accept him be taught by anybody and everybody.[9]

[9]'The Teacher of Spirituality—Swami Vivekananda', VivekaVani, 4 October 2022, https://bit.ly/3is4qSK. Accessed on 9 January 2023.

The spiritual Guru's consciousness leads to greater and greater liberation and freedom of mind. The divine essence emanating from the Guru results in greater dissolution of all structures of material ego whose nature is to contradict the needs arising from the depths of soul. Guruji used to say, '*Tushi jadon mere kol aaunde ho, main tuhade andar baitha nu hi vekhada han.* (When you come to me, I see your soul; I see nothing else.)'

Such masters are not bound by the cannons of scriptures. They are absolutely free and independent in everything they do and teach. Such masters are beyond the realm of jealousy or pride. They are paragons of virtue like great dignity and humility. They don't forbid the disciples from contacting with other spiritual gurus and schools of thought. They constantly indicate that although there are many paths to spiritual attainment, there is only one way and there is only one religion—the Divine Truth.

It is not surprising that there are many vainglorious and fake spiritual teachers, who are narrow-minded to accept the possibility of different methods in spiritual pursuits. They condemn other gurus and other schools of spiritual thought. They have the tendency of possessiveness born out of insecurity for their spirituality and transference to the disciples. That is the reason why they jealously guard their disciples; they want to possess them, not to liberate them. They are too proud to admit that their path represents simply one of the many particular methods. Such gurus hanker after power, influence, publicity and recognition.

Guruji used to say, '*Puran Guru nu kade bhi publicity nai chahidi hundi. Oh kade body guard te gunmen nai rakhu ga.* (A puran guru will never hanker after publicity nor would he be surrounded by bodyguards and gunmen).'

There are several descriptions in the Gurubani (Ang 268) regarding the distinctive characteristics of the true Guru.

Satiguru sikhi ki kare pratipaal

A true Guru takes care of the disciples in all aspects.

Sikh ki Guru dhurmat mal hirai

The Guru washes away the the filth of evil intellect of his disciple.

Satiguru sikh ke bandhan ka tai

The Guru frees the disciple from the illusion of Parkriti and attachments.

Satiguru sikh kau naam dhan dei

The true Guru gives the disciple the wealth of Naam (realization of the Lord).

Furthermore, in the Sri Guru Granth Sahib (Ang 287):

So satigur jis radhai har naau

The True Guru is one whose heart dwells the divine Name.

Nanak aisa Guru baddabhagee paieeaai

Oh Nanak, such a Guru is obtained by the greatest good fortune.

Pooraa gur akhayeo jaa kaa mantra

Puran guru is perfect; his teachings are everlasting.

A(n)mrit dristi pekhai hoi sant

Beholding his ambrosial glance, one becomes saintly.

In Ang 168, it states:

Jis milaai man hoi anand so satiguru kahooaai.
Man ki dividha binas jai param pad laheeaai.

Meeting Him, the mind is filled in bliss. He is called a true Guru.

Duality and confusion depart, and the supreme status of Lord is obtained.

Ang 522 states:

> *Bharam kot maaiaa khaiee kahu kit bidi toreeai.*
> *Guru poora aaraadhi bikham dal fareaai.*
>
> Tell me, how can the fort of doubt and the moat of Maya be overcome.
>
> Worshiping the perfect Guru, this awesome force is subdued.

The true Guru is the epitome of universal love—loving others without any expectation. Such universal love is the all-pervading love of God, extended equally to all His creations right from the non-living beings to the tiniest of living beings, like ants. The true Guru spends most of his time, energy and effort in service of the Supreme Soul.

CHARACTERISTICS OF A DISCIPLE

It is due to the grace of God that one meets the true Guru. The sincere disciple should have the moral discipline and spiritual yearning to obtain the spiritual guidance from the Guru. The Guru is the spiritual and moral beacon, who illuminates the spiritual path for the devotee. The Sikh tradition speaks of the characteristics of a true disciple or devotee in the following manner:

> Just as milk should not be kept in an unclean pot, so in the same way, the Guru will not pour his nectar (Naam) into an uncleaned mind. By practicing goodness and the remembrance of The Naam, an individual prepares his own mind for the Guru's message. After due cleansing, the Guru administers the remedy of the Naam with suitable directions.[10]

The disciple should have cleansed himself of the five cardinal

[10]'Introduction to Sikhism', Sikh Missionary Society UK, https://bit.ly/3XFB8iv. Accessed on 9 January 2023.

vices: *kaam* (lust), *krodh* (anger), *lobh* (greed), *moh* (worldly attachment) and *ahankaar* (ego).

The disciple should be a genuine seeker. As Lord Krishna says, they should have the devotion, service and surrender to the Guru and in addition, they should have an inquisitive mind to get their doubts cleared.

Sant Kabir says:

> *Guru bichara kya kare, sikhahi mahi chuk;*
> *Bhawe tyon parmodhiye, bans bajaye phunk.*
>
> What can the poor Guru do if the disciple is insincere and incapable of receiving? Guru imparts the spiritual, but the net result is ineffective, just as a broken flute does not produce music.

In the contemporary world, many people seek gurus, not for spiritual quest, but for other reasons. Guruji used to tell, '*Asal chiz mangde vaste nahin ande* (People do not come for the real thing [spiritual attainment].' If the individual is a sincere seeker, genuinely driven by an aspiration to achieve liberation, one of the following will happen—either he will find the Guru, or the true Guru will find him.

The Guru transmits the spiritual knowledge by various modes. It can be in person by giving an audience, by initiating through a mantra or by subtle suggestions through hints, symbols, dreams or intuition.

Generally, it is not known to the disciples who their guru would be. Sometimes, the appearance of the Guru may be momentarily for a disciple. Such a guru gives a few instructions and disappears from the life and scene of the disciple. Other times, a disciple may also be initiated by gods or spiritual masters from higher realms.

The true Guru is always in communion with God, and he is the face of God to guide the disciple in their spiritual quest. The Guru is always there for the disciple. It is inappropriate to insist on him for an initiation when the disciple is not ready. That decision should be entirely left to him. The guru, unless he is a satguru, is not your destination, nor should you become attached to his human personality or ego.

In the Bhagavad Gita, Lord Krishna proclaimed, 'I shall dwell as fire in the living beings.' But the devotee would be sufficiently attuned before he acquires perfection in practice to see God who dwells within him. The musk deer would search for the musk in the entire forest, unaware of the fragrance oozing out from its navel. Likewise, the true spiritual seeker would wander in the path of knowledge and devotion in search of God. By God's grace, he comes across a spiritual teacher who lights the lamp of wisdom, and the seeker is able to realize the Supreme Self within his own being.

A person with a spiritual bent of mind would long for a glimpse of God. Swami Vivekananda used to meet a large number of saints and ask, 'Have you seen God? Can you show me God?' The earnest longing and effort of Vivekananda prompted the realized saints to tell him: 'You are the other form of God.'

These days, very few people take up spiritual practice that is universal and beyond the formal and organized religious practices. Even if a few are genuinely seeking spiritual salvation, their spiritual attainment is inadequate to receive subtle and advanced spiritual knowledge. Many disciples lack genuine respect, commitment, devotion and obedience as required from a true seeker to savour the knowledge that the Guru embodies. Many a spiritual seeker do not have the spiritual maturity to be able to discern a spiritual guide. A true seeker develops *sattvik* (pure) intellect and acumen to discern and internalize the true knowledge about the Guru (Guru Gyan). The 'teaching principle of God' keeps a constant watch on all of us. When one achieves the desired spiritual level, the Guru in the human form, comes into one's life. Guruji used to say,

> *Saat janam jadon guru nu paan itchha aur koshish karde*
> *ho tad tuhanu pooran guru milda hai.*

> After making sincere efforts with genuine yearning in seven births, a puran guru appears in your life.

The true Guru or satguru is one with the unmanifested (*nirgun*) form of God. He embodies the divine energy that manifests in the form of bliss and serenity. As the Guru is more one with the nirgun form of God, they do not need to use much manifest energy. However, in order to carry out their mission, the Guru needs to manifest energy given by God. The Guru focuses on his disciple and his spiritual growth, which in turn makes the disciple self-sufficient in overcoming problems where the root cause is spiritual in nature.

The Guru plays a central role in the spiritual pursuit. He is the medium through which his mediation between the soul and the Supreme takes place. Enlightenment, liberation or God-realization, without spiritual mentorship, is difficult, if not impossible, because of the tremendous engulfment of illusion or maya of the forces of nature (prakriti). True devotion or reverence can be shown only in the form of our virtuous thoughts, words and actions. Spiritual pursuit should not be limited to a few minutes or hours in a day. In fact, the whole journey of life should be like a continuous sadhana—spiritual quest and practice. Chanting of mantras, performing certain rituals, practising certain spiritual techniques are not what a spiritual life is about. The whole life journey and activities should form integral part of the spiritual quest. Such a quest should be filled with positive thinking and positive mental attitude, practising humbleness, sharing the wealth and time for making a difference to other living beings on this planet, non violence in thought, serving others in whatever way one can, practising forgiveness, perseverance, dedication, balanced state of mind, living in awareness, detachment, discharging one's responsibilities with utmost sincerity and willingness, etc. Guruji used to say, '*Asli Guru Rasik vairagi hona sikhande hain.* (The true Guru imbibes the genuine detachment in the disciples).'

Dharma is the whole gist of the Bhagavad Gita. It is discharging our niyat karma, understanding our roles and playing those roles to its full extent as a citizen of this planet earth, as mother or father, sister or brother, friend, employee, daughter or son, uncle or aunt, employee of a company, or whatever role we may be playing in our day-to-day life. Hence, as a satguru has his unique and significant characteristics, a true spiritual seeker or disciple should have the ideals and temperament to receive spiritual wisdom from such a realized Guru.

THE GURU–SHISHYA RELATIONSHIP

The Guru–shishya relationship is built on mutual trust and ideals followed by both. As the true Guru, Guruji was the epitome of all the virtues of a puran guru described earlier. His aphorisms relating to the Guru-shishya relationship provide adequate insight into his teachings relating the Guru Tattva. He advised complete surrender and devotion on the part of the disciple. Such a devotion should be bereft of any expectations. The following are some of his characteristic great sayings relating to surrender and devotion without expectations and cultivating the virtue of detachment.

> *Mainu bina kisi itcha de pyaar karo, fir dekho nazaare.*
>
> Love me without any expectations and witness the wonders.
>
> *Guru ko ek mangna hunda hai te ek manana hunda hai.*
>
> There is something called asking from a Guru and another thing as unconditional devotion and acceptance of the Guru.
>
> *Je maang ke litta to ki litta?*
>
> What have you got by asking for? (Material benefits?)

Guruji used to give importance to the sangat. He used to say, '*Sangat tuhada parivar hai* (The sangat is your family).' He would elevate the disciple above the Guru and God. In the Shiva Puran, it has been mentioned that the Guru initiates the disciple to the spiritual path by invoking the Shiva residing within the disciple; and hence, the Guru pays abeyance to the disciple—the Shivohm within him. Guruji used to say, *'Guru pahale than te; sangat duje te rav tije than te hain* (Guru is number one; sangat at number two and rab at number three).'

Within the Guru-shishya system, complete surrender of the devotees is expected. Like Lord Krishna implores Arjuna for unconditional love and regard, similarly, the puran gurus also expected a similar kind of devotion and love from their disciples. The grace of the Guru follows such a devotee automatically. His love and affection are also spontaneous for such devotees. He used to say:

> *Mahapurush pyaar de bhukhe hunde han, saanu bas pyaar te shradha hi chahidi hai.*
>
> The puran guru (mahapurush) is hungry for the love and devotion of the devotee. What we need is love and regard (from the devotees).

The true Guru would test the disciple regarding his sincerity of spiritual purpose and the truthfulness of his mind, heart, intention and activities. After the spiritual seeker passes the test, only then does the Guru accept them to his spiritual fold. Many a disciple fail in such tests of the puran gurus. It is not only during the initial initiation to his fold when the Guru tests the disciple, the testing is a continuous and dynamic process throughout the spiritual journey. Some disciples get carried away because of their so-called proximity to the Guru or even due to intermittent successes along the spiritual journey. However, a puran guru keeps a watch on such failings. For the deliberate and intentionally egoistic, there is hardly any salvation. For others, the Guru holds the hand of the failing disciple and guides him on the safe road to spirituality. Guruji used to say: *'Main aath podiyan fata fat chada denda haan. Nauvi paudi te aake main pichlin aath paudiyan kitch denda haan. Jine ahankar na kita oh theek hai warna banda ahankar de mare fir pehli pidi te pahunch jaanda hai* (I allow the disciple to climb eight spiritual steps quite easily. Then, before they climb the ninth step, I pull them down to the first, if their pride and ego engulfs them).'

Your complete surrender and devotion to the Guru is reflected in unquestioningly accepting the Guru's words and directives. There is no question of doubt and hesitation by applying your ordinary intellect and rationality. This has to be kept in mind when you are a disciple of a real puran guru, not a pretender or ordinary sadhak. Otherwise, you would be exploited by some unscrupulous persons in the garb of sadhus and gurus. The realized souls like Guruji have the wisdom and divine vision beyond reasoning and sensory perceptions. The blessings of the true Guru lie in non-questioning of his utterances and using your rationale mind to analyse the ifs and buts. Guruji used to say: *'Kade mahpurush nu took mat. Main jado bhi kutch keh raha hunda haan, oh meri blessings hai tuhade waste. Mere kahnn naal bhi oh gal ho jaandi hai, je tusi took ge taan blessings othe hi khatam ho jaandi hai* (Never ever contradict a mahapurush or Puran guru. When I say something, that is my blessings for you. When I utter anything, that thing happens. When you question it or apply your rational analysis doubting the possibilities, the blessings end there).'

In summary, every individual, in their daily life, faces significant existential crises of moral dilemma and anguish. The great Indian tradition suggests the pursuit of the Absolute, while discharging one's worldly duties. The spiritual wisdom and knowledge of the Guru has a transformative effect on the disciple. The Guru acts as a spiritual guide who can show the way and protect the disciple from fall. The Guru performs the duty of a friend, philosopher and guide to the disciple by clarifying their doubts, correcting their mistakes, resolving their karma, and guiding in the practice of self-discipline and purification. The Guru leads by example, bestows his grace on the disciples, imparts knowledge and clarification, and looks after the soul of the disciple.

In our day-to-day life, for most individuals, a communion with the Supreme Soul is not easily attainable. When the struggling human soul of the spiritual seeker becomes fit to receive true knowledge through action in the world, in close companionship and increasing nearness to the higher and divine self, the true Guru appears in their life. When a spiritual seeker comes across the Guru, they have to discern the genuineness of the Guru by applying the basic canon of spirituality, the moral and ethical values, the non-exploitive nature of Guru–shishya bond, and the transparency and openness of systems and relationships. On the other hand, the true Guru also tests the disciple regarding their sincerity of purpose, their moral and ethical values and the observance of such values in their day-to-day life.

10

Sadhana, Siddhis and Enlightenment

One important and integral part of the Indian spiritual tradition is attaining enlightenment, God-realization or liberation through adaptation of disciplines and *sadhanas* (austerities) including yoga and meditation. The earliest historical evidence of yogic practices and postures comes from the archaeological findings (seals) from the Indus Valley Civilization.

The ancient spiritual texts, like the Vedas and the Upanishads, have references to yogic and meditative practices in several hymns, verses and descriptions. It is only through enlightenment that the sages could be blessed by the Lord to compose such hymns for the benefit of mankind.

Vedanta, and the other schools of Hinduism accept, adopt and build upon the Vedic foundation of many of the teachings and techniques of yoga. It is mentioned in Katha Upanishad (2.6.10–11):

> *Yadā pañcāvatiṣṭhante jñānāni manasā saha.*
> *Buddhiśca na viceṣṭate tāmāhuḥ paramāṁ gatim.*
> *Tāṁ yogamiti manyante sthirāmindriyadhāraṇām.*
> *Apramattastadā bhavati yogo hi prabhavāpyayau.*

> When the stillness of the mind along with complete control of the five senses attained and when intellect, the power of reason, does not waver, that is called the Supreme State. This Supreme State is called yoga. At this state, the seeker's (yogi) mind is not characterized by thoughtlessness or sluggishness, rather the yogi is quite

> vigilant, lest he/she wavers from the triad of stillness because Yoga is the cause of all creation and dissolution.

The culmination of the Indian spiritual tradition and its core synthesis comes from the Lord's own mouth in the form of the Bhagavad Gita. The Gita describes various forms of yoga—Jnana Yoga, Kriya Yoga and Bhakti Yoga—with beautiful synthesis by stating that all the paths are not independent of each other; rather, they are a part of an integral system for spiritual attainment. It is a matter of perspective and individual choice to adopt any one path, with incorporation of the core principles of the other two. Without perfect knowledge of the Absolute (Jnana Yoga), how can you undertake the right action (Kriya Yoga) or have devotion to the Lord (Bhakti Yoga)?

There are many strands of yogic practices. It is not necessarily meant only for the sanyasis who have renounced the world. As Lord Krishna says in the Gita, there is no need to renounce the world to attain God-realization or liberation. Any householder can follow the right path abjuring the attachment of results and attain enlightenment or get liberated. The Indian tradition is abound with instances of sages to plain householders adopting various professions like soldiering (karma of Kshatriyas such as kings and fighters, example Raja Janak), shop-keeping (Tuladhar) and meat-selling (the famous butcher described in Vyadha Gita, in the Mahabharat), who have attained liberation or enlightenment. In recent times, as Yogi Yogananda states in his book *Autobiography of a Yogi*, Lahiri Mahasaya (a railway accountant) was directed by his guru (guru of many lives) to go back to the hustle bustle of the world from the Himalayan cave to spread the knowledge and impart the methods of Kriya Yoga, to the general population, as expounded in the Bhagavad Gita.

However, the kind of mindfulness and discipline required for higher spiritual attainment is not that easy a task or path. It requires the grace of God through an enlightened Guru, irrespective of the fact that whether you are an ascetic or a householder; and such blessings do not fall upon each and every sundry. It may be your accumulated earnings of spirituality during the previous or current birth (prarabdha karma), and sadhana, sincerity and devotion of the present, which leads you to enlightenment or liberation.

There are many strands of yoga systems prevalent in the Indian spiritual tradition: (i) Kriya Yoga, as per Patanjali's Yoga Sutra, (ii) Hatha Yoga (iii) Tantric Yoga (iv) Kundalini Yoga and (v) Laya Yoga. These traditions are not mutually exclusive; each tradition borrows from or is sharing commonality with the others. There are several variants of these traditions, depending upon the Guru–shishya tradition and the liberalism of the great Indian spiritual tradition. It is up to the spiritual aspirant to follow a particular path, but the ultimate destination is God-realization or liberation, enlightenment, or *nirbikalpa samadhi* or nirvana—whatever name you can give it. The truth is one but told variously by experts. The paths are many, but the destination is the same.[1]

Most of the yoga systems have a lot in common with the basic principles described in Patanjali's Yoga Sutra. At this stage, one should be careful not to confuse with the commercialized yogic postures and meditation practices peddled as yoga by many modern teachers like gym instructors, psychological practitioners, and others. There is another strand of people and community in the villages and towns of India and elsewhere, who demonstrate one singular *siddhi* (supernatural power) acquired at birth, or through sadhana. They are disconnected from the spiritual goal of yoga—the union of the atma with the Paramatma, by design, by default or by negligence.

It is paramount to highlight at this stage that neither are the yogic path and its associated attainments at various stages impossible to attain for individuals nor are they deviant practices only meant for ascetics renouncing the world. The Indian spiritual tradition acknowledges the tremendous power of the individuals when they realize the true self residing in them, and thrives through the control and discipline of senses, mind and intellect to

[1]God-realization or liberation is a core concept in Hinduism; enlightenment or Nirvana is a core concept in Buddhism and/or Jainism.

realize that potential. However, in the name of scientific methods and so-called rationality, there is a lack of appreciation of a world of a different kind. It is nothing but a colonization of the mind-space by the so-called 'superior' thought. The colonization of the Indian mind is evident in the general refrain by educated Indians when they characterize an enlightened soul as a 'tantric' or deprecate the yogic attainments by highlighting only the deviant strands of some yogic practitioners.

The Victorian prudency of the eighteenth and nineteenth century had played a significant role in the purposeful deprecation of the Indian spiritual traditions. The aping of such thought processes have also seeped into the mind-space of many contemporary Indians. The colonization of the Indian mind-space is quite complete by highlighting only the pitfalls and deviant strands of the spiritual tradition by invoking the deterministic and 'absolute certainty' of the so-called modern scientific methods and rationality.

The spiritual world cannot be understood by following a method not meant for it. Rationality is limited by the attainment of intellectual faculty from the current knowledge base. The immense possibilities of the human mind, intellect and intelligence have been explored and demonstrated in the Indian spiritual tradition by several sages throughout the ages, and there are many who are presently living in the world. The spiritual domain is beyond the limitations of the current science and rationality. So, there is no need to judge a system by a method not designed for that. Vivekananda states (in his commentary on Patanjali's Yoga Sutra):

> There are much higher states of existence beyond reasoning. It is really beyond the intellect that the first stage of religious life is to be found. When you step beyond thought and intellect and all reasoning, then you have made the first step towards God.[2]

[2]Vivekananda, Swami, *Patanjali Yoga Sutras*, Shristi Publishers and Distributors, New Delhi, 2021.

THE PATANJALI YOGA SUTRA

Swami Sivananda in 'Light of Yoga' says, 'Yoga is the method by which the finite self or the individual soul is united with the Infinite Self or the Supreme Soul.'[3] Yajnavalkya defines yoga as, '*Samyoga yoga iti ukto jivatma-paramatmano iti* (The conjunction of the individual soul and the supreme soul is called Yoga).'

Patanjali, in the Yoga Sutra, states that the ultimate stage of all yoga sadhanas is to attain absolute liberation or *kaivalyam*. The second aphorism of Patanjali's Yoga Sutra states, '*Yoga shchittavritti nirodhah* (Yoga occurs when the machinations, vacillations, perturbations, whirling, spinning, and agitations of the mind-field dissolve, cease, and become still).' As Swami Vivekananda puts it; 'The organs (*Indriyas*), together with the mind (*Mana*s), the determinative faculty (*Buddhi*) and egoism (*Ahamkara)*, form the group called the *Antahkarana*—the internal instrument. They are but various processes in the mind-stuff, called *Chitta*. The waves of thought in the *Chitta* are called *Vrtti*.'[4]

Thought patterns and its modifications, the activities and the modulations of the mind are synonymous with *vrtti*. The vrittis are wavelike operations or machinations of the ordinary thinking processes, which colour, limit and distort the originality or purity of the pure universal mind (*sat-chitta*).

Robin Sharma, while summarizing his dialogue with Julian Mantle in context of Patanjali's Yoga Sutra, states:

> We each think about 60,000 thoughts on an average day... The human mind is the world's largest filtering device.
>
> ...When you learn to take control of your thoughts and vividly imagine all that you desire from this worldly existence in a state of total expectancy, dormant forces will awaken

[3]'Light of Yoga by Swami Sivananda', Divyajivan, https://bit.ly/3VVuFP0. Accessed on 9 January 2023.

[4]Vivekananda, Swami, *Patanjali Yoga Sutras*, Shristi Publishers and Distributors, New Delhi, 2021.

> inside you. You will begin to unlock the true potential of mind to create the kind of magical life that you deserve.[5]

The yogic processes help annihilate or dissolve (*nirodha*) the fractural and wavelike patterning and conditioning (vrtti) of the perceiver's mind-field (*chitta*). Such an attainment brings unconditioned clarity that shines forth illuminating the darkness, which in turn stills all anxiety and stress. The Yoga Sutra (I.5) further states, '*Vrittayah pangchatayyah klishta aklishtah* (There are five classes of modulations of the mind-field).'

These are *pramana* (right knowledge—knowing correctly), *viparyaya* (indiscrimination—incorrect or false knowledge), *vikalpa* (verbal delusion—fantasy or imagination), *nidra* (sleep—object of voidness attained in deep sleep) and *smritayaha* (memory—recollection).

The mind-space suffers from five types of afflictions or coloured thought patterns, known as *kleshas*. The third shloka of Patanjali's Yoga Sutra states:

> *Avidyāsmitārāgadveṣābhiniveśāḥ pañca kleśāḥ*
>
> The mental and emotional afflictions are spiritual ignorance, misplaced identity, emotional attachment, impulsive emotional disaffection and the strong focus on mundane existence, which is due to an instinctive fear of death.

The five afflictions are *avidya*—ignorance (in the form of a misperception about the true nature of things, which is the condition that reveals the inherent purity of living beings); *asmita*—egoism (in the form of an erroneous identification of the self with the intellect); *raaga*—attachment; *dvesha*—aversion; and *abhinivesaḥ*—fear of death (which is derived from clinging ignorantly to life or the fear of death). Yoga is practised to minimize the kleshas and bring about stillness of the mind and samadhi, the state of bliss.

[5]Sharma, Robin, *The Monk Who Sold His Safari*, Jaico Publishing House, 2003.

Patanjali, in Yoga Sutra 1.12, states that these vrittis can be restrained or controlled through *abhyasa* (practice) and non-attachment or *vairagya* (dispassion). The major part of the Yoga Sutra deals with letting go (releasing) of our attachments for objects, in coarse or even the subtlest way possible.

Patanjali also talks about the *astanga* (eightfold steps or eight limbs) of yoga, ostensibly intended for driving away the impurities in the mind-space and arriving at discriminative wisdom or enlightenment. These eightfold paths to enlightenment are *yamas, Niyamas, Asana, Pranayama, Pratyahara, Dharana, Dhyana* and *Samadhi.*

The yamas are ethical practices—the don'ts that include: (i) *ahimsa*—Non-violence, non-harming other living beings through actions and speech; (ii) *satya*—non-falsehood (truthfulness being the removal of the veil of deceit and falsehood from our lives including that of self-deceit); (iii) *asteya*—non-stealing (honesty, non-exploitation of others); (iv) *brahmacharya*—continence (continuity, centeredness, or one-pointedness to the all-inclusive weave of 'Source'—Brahman—and it is the harmony and union in true integrity while not allowing oneself to be distracted from the spiritual goal); and (v) *aparigraha*—non-possessiveness (non-greed, non-envy, non-attachment, letting go and non-false identification penetrating throughout the mind in meditation as the simplification of our life, so that we are better able to focus on the spiritual goal latent in every moment).

The niyamas (do's) are also fivefold: (i) *shaucha* (purity, cleanliness of mind, speech and body); (ii) *santosha* (contentment); (iii) *tapas* (persistence, perseverance, austerity); (iv) *svadhyaya* (self-study, self-reflection, introspection of one's thoughts, speeches and actions, study of scriptures; and (v) *Ishvarapranidhana* (contemplation of the Ishvara/God/Supreme Being, Brahman, True Self, Unchanging Reality).

Asana is the meditation posture that one can hold for a period of time, staying relaxed, steady, comfortable and motionless. Pranayama is the practice of consciously regulating breath (inhalation and exhalation). Pratyahara implies not taking any input or any information from the sense organs or retracting the sensory experience from external objects. Dharana, which translates to concentration, is attained when the mind holds on to some object, either in the body, or outside the body, and keeps itself in that state. Dhyana is meditation, which is contemplating, reflecting on whatever dharana has focussed on (dhyana is the stilling of the mind). Samadhi is oneness with the subject of meditation when there is no distinction between the actor of meditation, the act of meditation and the subject of meditation. Samadhi is that spiritual state wherein one's mind is so absorbed in whatever it is contemplating on, that the mind loses the sense of its own identity. The thinker, the thought process and the thought fuse with the subject of thought.

All three (dhyana, dharana and samadhi) practised on a particular object or subject is called *samyama* by Patanjali. In other words, samyama can be applied to specific objects (physical and mental) as well as processes. When a sadhak is able to do samyama, he attains extraordinary powers. Patanjali warns that the ultimate objective of yoga should not be attaining these powers. Many sadhaks get carried away with these attainments and that leads to their downfall. These powers may act as impediments and distractions in achieving the ultimate goal. These should not be treated as an end in itself. Patanjali talks about attaining liberation or enlightenment by using samyama, which enables the sadhak to have communion as-it-is without a filter. This leads to true and authentic vision and *prajna* (wisdom) without prejudice or bias, which bathes the sadhak in its *alokah* (effulgence).

THE SIDDHIS: THE ABILITY TO PERFORM MIRACLES

Attainment of siddhis is considered natural in the yogic tradition. But the true spiritual seeker never gets carried away by these powers. They concentrate on the latent innate wisdom in order to realize true happiness and fulfillment. In other words, siddhis are simply intermediate fruits of yogic practice. During the spiritual journey through the yogic path, various levels of perfections and adeptness naturally come forth, evolve and manifest as a result of sustained practice. The seeker or sadhak becomes proficient and able as his horizon upon self deepens and expands. As a result, he becomes more aware and conscious. The true sadhak does not focus on attaining these powers as a goal. He is more focussed on realizing the Supreme Self.

THE SIDDHI POWERS

Approximately twenty-five siddhis are listed in the third book (Vibhuti Pad) of Patanjali's Yoga Sutra. An exact number is difficult to pin down because the abilities may be interpreted in different ways, and there is some overlap. But all the siddhis may be considered as variations of five basic categories, namely (i) clairvoyance (ii) exceptional body-mind control (iii) controlling the five elements of nature (iv) psychokinesis and (v) other non-specific supernatural powers.

i. Clairvoyance

Clairvoyance, which includes precognition and telepathy, is the ability to gain knowledge unbound by the ordinary constraints of space or time and without the use of the ordinary senses. Patanjali's Yoga Sutra (Chapter III) identifies a list of qualities for clairvoyance, depicting supernatural powers attained by yogis or elevated spiritual masters. The list includes:

- The ability to know about the past, present and future; the yogi becomes Trikal Darshi or knower of the past, present and future (Yoga Sutra, III.16).
- Cognition of the sounds produced by all beings, far and near (clairaudience) or *durashravana* (ability to hear from a distance). It is the counterpart of supernatural power of the Third-Eye, and hence it is also called the 'The Third Ear' (Yoga Sutra, III.17).

- The knowledge of the past and of future births (Yoga Sutra, III.18, 39).
- Knowledge of minds (telepathy); (Yoga Sutra, III.19–20).
- Foreknowledge about one's own death (Yoga Sutra, III.23).
- Knowledge of the outer universe, the knowledge about macroscopic objects and systems like the space and the universe (Yoga Sutra, III.27–29).
- Knowledge of the inner universe, a microscopic view of objects and systems and the inner constitution of the body (Yoga Sutra, III.30).
- Celestial Clairaudience—the ability to hear the conversations of the enlightened ones, the subtle mental conversations of others, the celestial music, and receive messages through the ether, both in the awakened or asleep stage. It is the opening of the spiritual ear to allow the yogi for immersion into the divine sound energy (sabda) and the realization of the divine name. It is *devānām saha krīḍā anudarśanam* (witnessing the pastimes of demi-gods) (Yoga Sutra, III.42).
- Refined Clairvoyance—all knowledge, omnipotence and omniscience (Yoga Sutra, III.34,50); and
- Extra sensory perception or sixth sense (or through the Third Eye).

ii. Exceptional Mind-Body Control

There are a group of yogic powers attained by sadhaks that are related to the extraordinary powers of controlling the characteristics of the physical body and mind. These are:

- Liberation from hunger and thirst, the ability to live on breathing alone (breatharianism), without food (inedia), and in extreme cases, without water (Yoga Sutra, III.31).
- Exceptional stability, balance or health—the ability to acquire knowledge of mind-body leads to exceptional health or self-healing (Yoga Sutra, III.37).
- Extraordinary strength (Yoga Sutra, III.24–25).

- Ability to enter another's body (At another level, this ability is called *shaktipat,* when the sadhak acquires the knowledge of the spiritual level of a practitioner and then transmits spiritual energy to the beginner through one's gaze, presence or touch) (Yoga Sutra, III.39); and
- Acquiring blazing radiance, exceptional charisma or aura (Yoga Sutra, III.41).

iii. Control over the Five Elements

• ***The ability to manipulate the characteristics of self-body***

This is the ability to become as small as an atom (*anima*) and similar abilities to change visible appearances *(pradurbhava)* of the body (*kaya*) so that bodily invulnerability or unassailableness (dharma-anabhighatas) is achieved. The perfect body is achieved (*kaya sampat*) from where one remains free from the onslaught of the variegated laws of nature (dharma) such as the five elements, etc. Yogis are able to acquire eight major siddhis out of which four relate to the shape/form of the body of the yogi (*kama-rupam*—attaining/assuming a desired form). These are: (a) *anima*: power to become very small; (b) *laghima*: power to become very light to float in the air, to walk on water, etc., (Yoga Sutra, III.40,43); (c) *mahima:* power to become very large; and (d) *garima*: power to become heavy (Yoga Sutra, III.46,47).

• ***Materialization/Dematerialization***

This power enables the yogi to manipulate matter, including size, appearance, etc. Variation of these abilities include fulfillment of any desire or creation or destruction of material manifestation. The siddhis are: (a) *prapti:* power to obtain anything; (b) *prakamya:* fulfillment of any desire at will (this is attained by the samyama on the characteristics of the gross elements); (c) *vashitva:* control of all the gross elements and their material manifestations; (d) *ishitritva:* power to create (materialize) and destroy the gross and material manifestations (dematerialize); and (e) *Kamavashayitva:* fulfillment of what is determined by the yogi (Yoga Sutra, III.45).

- ***Perfection of the body***

This is the power or ability of welding an exceptional mind-body control, combined with psychokinesis. In extreme cases, it manifests as an indefinite life extension, and non-degeneration of the body after physical death. This is referred to as the 'rainbow body' in Tibetan tradition, in which it is believed that the corpse does not decay but rather slowly fades away and turns into coloured lights (Yoga Sutra, III.47).

- ***Ability to withstand the extremes of weather and elements***

The yogi who has attained control over the elements and the sense and sensory system, can withstand the extremities of weather.

- ***Control of weather***

The yogi attains the power to control fire, the sun, water, air, poison (*agni arka ambu viṣa ādīnām pratiṣṭambhaḥ*) and their effects. This ability is also reflected in their power to change the weather and have a control over natural phenomenon like the rain and sunrise/sunset.

iv. Psychokinesis

Psychokinesis refers to the ability of the mind to directly influence matter. The following kinds of siddhis qualify for psychokinesis.

- ***Levitation: power of weightlessness and lightness***

This is called *udana* and is the ability to become light like a feather, so that the yogi can float in the air, walk on water, etc. This is the ability to rise up or levitate, as a result of which the yogi can walk on thorns and sword blades or stand on fire bed. They can go anywhere through the air (Yoga Sutra, III.40,43).

- ***Love and kindness to all; empathy and compassion to all***

This is the power or ability to love everybody. The yogi becomes the embodiment of love, compassion and empathy, in respect to both living and non-living beings, and remains in a state of permanent bliss and a state of communion with the Supreme Self (Yoga Sutra, III.24).

• ***Disappearance of the body from view: the power of invisibility***

The yogi, with his higher yogic attainment, can suspend the coarse or limited projection of the body. One can become invisible by preventing others' eyes from receiving the light normally reflected from your body.

• ***Telekinesis: ability to move objects in the physical world with the mind***

As one of the most fictionalized forms of psychic power, telekinesis is the ability to move objects in the physical world with your mind.

• ***Bilocation/multi-location and extraordinary physical speed***

This is the ability to simultaneously appear in more than one location. In addition, it is the ability of moving the physical body wherever the yogi wants—by manaḥ-javah (manojvitva)—the speed of thought.

v. Other Non-specific Supernatural Powers

- *Ajna apratihata gatiḥ* (Being unimpeded): The mahayogi's commands are unstoppable and he remains unconquerable.
- *Prakhya siddhi:* This is the ability of the mahayogi to choose the womb in which they would take birth.
- Human morphing: This refers to the ability of the yogi to transform or morph into another human. This morphing can take place regardless of gender, age, appearance, etc.
- Mythic morphing: This is the ability to transform to a mythical entity. With the higher attainment of yogic powers, the mahayogi can transform into mythological entities (persons/creatures), whether partially or completely, as well as use the abilities, traits, appearance and physiology of mythological entities. The mahayogi may be able to transform into mythological personalities (like gods and goddesses) or to alien mythological

creatures and/or mythological creatures that are extinct.

YOGIC POWERS: ATTAINMENT AND RETENTION

In the previous section, we briefly discussed the supernatural or extraordinary powers or siddhis that could be attained through yogic practice. It has also been stated that these powers are concomitant with the progress in the yogic sphere. These are described as intermediate results or perfections of yogic practice. The sadhak should not get carried away by such attainments and should focus on the ultimate goal of enlightenment or liberation. Patanjali states that siddhis are natural outcomes of yogic practices; these come by themselves. It is up to the yogi to deal with them as a benefit or an impediment. The direction of the use of the powers or siddhis will depend on the strength, intent and sincerity of the practice and preparation of the spiritual seeker.

All the siddhis or supernatural powers are not the personal earnings of the sadhak. All these powers come from an intelligent source—the grace of the Great Power. The grace of the Supreme Soul is not bestowed readily on those who may use it for the destruction of others or the self. Power exercised without such knowledge is thus better not possessed at all.

Patanjali, in Kaivalya Pad of Yoga Sutra (Shloka 1) says:

Janm aushadhi mantra tapah samadhijah siddhayah

The siddhis (supernatural powers) are attained by
birth, herbs (chemical means), and the power of words
(mantras), austerity or samadhi.

Siddhis can come as inborn qualities of some blessed persons. Humans are born with their unique karmas, some possessing advanced abilities right from birth. In the initial stage, these siddhis may remain latent, or as in the case of highly evolved souls, it may manifest during infancy too. However, as the individual grows in maturity through childhood and adolescence, these perfections evidently manifest.

The carried-over karmic fruits of yoga from previous births have been succinctly talked about by Lord Krishna in the Bhagavad Gita (Verse 2.40).

> *Nehābhikrama-nāśho 'sti pratyavāyo na vidyate*
> *svalpam apyasya dharmasya trāyate mahato bhayāt.*

> In this endeavor, there is no loss or diminution, and a little advancement on this path can protect one from the most dangerous kind of fear (fear of falling or failing).

Lord Krishna says that no effort in Kriya Yoga goes to waste. Whatever level has been attained remains intact in this birth and even for future births. The spiritual aspirant builds on the existing foundations and attainments; and if well intentioned, again through the yogi's path, they move to the next level.

This is what Patanjali was mentioning about siddhis by birth. Material activities and their results end with the body. But Karma Yoga carries a person again to the super-conscious sphere after the loss of the earthly body. He gets a chance for further elevation in his next birth. Such latent or inherent siddhis

> ...may get enhanced through the wise utilization and communion with nature's medicines and elixirs (*aushadhi*) which in turn trigger/activate the inner evolutionary circuits (including the body's neuro-endocrine system), clear out obstructions in the *nadis*, and in general remove obstructions both in the cellular memory and neuro-psychic pathways. The wise use of certain herbal combinations is known to the tradition of yoga to stimulate/catalyze the production of inner elixirs (*soma, amrita*, etc.) which are also activated by other factors (Yoga Sutra, V.1).

But the use of such *aushadhis* (medicines) alone may not lead to attainment of the siddhis. Moreover, the identification of the herbs and their processes are a mystery to many. Such misconception has led to people to use psychotropic drugs, which is not what

Patanjali referred to as siddhi through aushadhis.

Likewise, the practice of focussing upon the specific dynamic and energetic qualities of specific sound vibrations (mantra) will open up previously dormant pathways that activate heretofore hidden abilities.

Patanjali talks about the enhancement and awakening of latent abilities through the practice of tapas (Yoga Sutra, II.1,43). Tapas eliminates and redirects the outward flowing, misdirected and dissipating energy of a distracted mind to a natural and evolutionary inward flow (kundalini). Tapas, thus, is an important practice in quickening our success. The ultimate goal in yoga is the samadhi, where many a supernatural power are auto-generated along with the path of progress towards Kaivalya Samadhi. After attainment of such a samadhi, these powers become part and parcel of the life of a yogi, during the current birth and subsequent births, if any. Patanjali, in Yoga Sutra (III.33), says: '*Pratibhad va sarvam.* (By the power of Pratibha all knowledge).'

All these powers can come without any *samyama* to the Yogi who has the power of *Pratibha* (enlightenment from purity). This is when a man has risen to a higher state of *Pratibha*, when he has that great light. All things are apparent to him. Everything comes to him naturally, without making *Samyama* on anything. And he carries this attainment to his subsequent births (if any). In this case, they are born as siddhas (enlightened beings) for the betterment of mankind.

THE FALLEN SADHAKS

The spiritual aspirant or sadhak may get fixated with pursuing the siddhis, while ignoring the real source of these powers—the grace of the Supreme Self. With this intoxication and arrogance of power, he gets distracted from the pursuit of the Truth. He gets engulfed in the veil of illusionary benefits. He may misuse the powers and cause himself and/or others harm, becoming oblivious of the negative consequences. In Indian and Tibetan literature, there are many instances and many stories about the misuse of power and the generation of negative consequences (bad karma) for the sadhak. Sometimes, the sadhak's intention may be relatively pure at first, but after realizing a siddhi or two (minor or major), he gets embroiled in pride. He feels and acts as if the supernatural powers are his own, and he acts and feels superior to others. He is covered under the veil of dualism, separating the grace of God from his attainments. This acts as a severe impediment towards the *kaivalya* (final liberation).

Siddhis may appear to be supernormal to ordinary people, but they are a natural concomitant outcome of sincere yogic practices. This is exploiting the tremendous potential of the human mind with the grace of God.

The proverb, 'Power corrupts', is aptly applicable in the case of the misuse of yogic power. The negative consequences of the misuse of yogic powers are profound as the sadhak falls a few notches down from the level of spiritual attainment, achieved with a lot of discipline and practice. The most important aspect in the yogic tradition is maintaining a sustained and disciplined meditation practice. It is observed that many simple siddhis will occasionally happen spontaneously. Through a great deal of yogic sadhana, along with the grace of God, the innate talent flourishes to attain higher levels of siddhis. While the sadhana is under the sadhak's control, the talent and God's grace are not.

Vairagya and *aparigraha* (non-possessiveness and non-attachment) are important disciplines in yoga for attainment of *kaivalyam.* It may be worth pointing out that Patanjali placed extremely high value on vairagya—letting go or non-grasping—as being capable of leading us to kaivalyam. Although it may be implied that Patanjali was referring, in general, to the non-attachment with the siddhis (letting them go), he was also referring to non-attachment to any object in general.

Patanjali gives us a warning that powers do not come from separateness or dualism. The realization of attainment from individual efforts is an illusion; such achievements are rather to be attributed to the process of yoga (integration with the satguru). The trap that Patanjali is warning us to avoid is that, if a practitioner is seduced into attributing siddhi to individual effort, it has the potential to reinforce or increase one's identification to ego, pride and arrogance. This perpetuates degradation of the sadhak and they eventually fall into corruption. Here, one must be clear to avoid reinforcing the insidious ossifications of pride or the ego, while still being able to be instructive to someone who is genuinely seeking the spiritual path. Thus, with the letting go of all that, one then practises samyama upon the self, to reach the stage of union of the atman with the absolute consciousness in sat-chit-ananda.

On the way to superior spiritual attainment with yogic practices, some siddhis may be attained by sadhaks. Such attainments remain with the sadhak across births. But, it all depends on the sadhak to utilize the powers for further spiritual growth or to use and demonstrate it to the world for the sake of showing off or to earn a living—both being materialistic gains, leading to digression from the ultimate spiritual objective. There is nothing despicable about a sadhak adopting a particular yogic practice out of many strands of yoga to attain powers. This includes the so-called tantric yoga practices and attainments. But one should be aware of the narrow-minded, conceited and vainglorious sadhaks who misuse such powers. Sometimes, some practitioners (one should not call them sadhaks) utilize such powers to harm, attain control or influence over others. A discernible spiritual seeker can distinguish a true sadhak from these fallen practitioners.

Part V

The Philosophies

11

The Spiritual Essence of Guruji

The spiritual approach to life, as hinted by Guruji, is best described as syncretic or eclectic. The core or essence of this approach is the individual freedom and choice, which resonates well with the great spiritual tradition of this land. The ultimate goal for each individual is God-realization or enlightenment, and the paths leading to such a realization are many. The Rigveda declares, 'Truth is one; sages call it variously.' The individuals are free to choose their path. It is up to the spiritual seeker to adopt the Kriya Yoga, being part of the world and leading the life of an ordinary householder and seeking the Param Brahma, or to renounce the world and do severe penance to attain enlightenment. They may follow any one prominent path for higher spiritual attainment—Bhakti Yoga, Kriya Yoga or Jnana Yoga, or they may follow an integration of this trinity.

The individual freedom and choice points to the enormous potential of each individual. We are blessed to be born as human beings. The Almighty has blessed us with superior intellect and memory, which is absent in other living beings. The most important aspect of human life is the tremendous potential to master the powers of controlling the mind and attaining enlightenment or God-realization.

A deeper analysis of Guruji's activities (his demonstration of supernatural powers) and his sayings point to distinct philosophical and spiritual connotations. The spiritual essence that is Guruji becomes clear as we take a holistic view of his activities, pronouncements and sayings (aphorisms).

Guruji is part of the great Indian spiritual tradition.

Nevertheless, he is not bound by the strict boundaries of such a tradition. Rather, in his unique way, he has added and enriched this tradition by making the spiritual quest appropriate or harmonious with the contemporary period of the twentieth and twenty-first centuries. He has, in his pronouncements, discarded the ritualistic and dogmatic principles of the spiritual quest, as has been practised and advocated by certain sages and enlightened masters. As Guru Nanak has said:

> Religion lieth not in the patched coat the yogi wears,
> not in the staff he bears,
> Nor in the ashes in his body.
> Religion bob not in rings in the ears,
> Not in a shaven head,
> Not in the blowing of the conch shell.
> If thou must the path of true religion see
> Among the world's impurities, be of impurities free.[1]

These are outward symbolisms followed by certain believers following certain paths. But these should not be the sine qua non of spiritualism. Then, as Guruji said, you will miss the real things. Similarly, idols are the *saguna* form of God, which are anthropomorphic in nature. Guruji was emphatic about the unrealistic nature of these anthropomorphic representations of gods and goddesses, even the sages and gurus.

Guruji used to say that the sculptures, paintings and photos of various avatars and forms of God are the product of the creative imagination of artists, following the descriptions by sages. These are our imaginations or the way we like to represent them. But the masters or maharishis who visualized these figures were not interested in giving you a photographic model or personality of God. They were bothered about the innermost core of God or the God representatives. They are the mystic vision of godliness.

---

[1]Islam, Md Didarul, 'The Philosophy of Guru Nanak: A Critical Analysis', *Arts Faculty Journal,* June 2016, https://bit.ly/402dWN9. Accessed on 27 January 2022.

Guruji, through his deeper message of spiritualism, defied any structure, practices or identity. Again, we may refer back to Sant Kabir, who discouraged the mere practice of parroting the name of God. He was of the view that it is analogous to chanting money and becoming rich. Like Kabir, Guruji disregarded the mechanical reading of religious texts like the Vedas, the Quran, the Bible or the Shiva Puran. Guruji used to say, '*Sirf kitabi paath, paath nahin hunda* (Reading religious texts is not enough for spiritual quest).'

Guruji said that the real bliss is found when one eats, chews and later digests the knowledge that is gradually revealed. In that vein, Guruji de-emphasized ritualistic religious practices, pilgrimages to shrines and religious places, or the necessity of yogic practices for shaven heads, forest-dwelling and leading a life of celibacy.

We have already discussed the multiplicity of paths to reach the ultimate goal—God-realization by the spiritual seeker. Hence, under a syncretic tradition, Guruji advocated for the path suitable to the individual seekers. There are various types of minds and temperaments, as well as spiritual attainments of aspirants. Hence, the paths would be different depending on these factors and based on the individual freedom of choice.

RAV TOWADE ANDAR HAI (GOD IS WITHIN YOU)

Most of the sayings of Guruji point to the *advaita* monism of the Vedanta. This is the essence of the Upanishads and the Bhagavad Gita. God resides in everybody. The spiritual paths may be many; but the ultimate goal is this realization and constant communion with the Param Brahman through your own self. Guruji used to say, '*Rav towade andar hai* (God is within you).' Moreover, we have discussed the concept of Brahmasmi and Shivohm in Adi Shankaracharya's 'Nirvana Shatakam'. It resonates with the advaita philosophy of the Vedanta. This is also the essence of the percepts of Guru Nanak and Sant Kabir.

The word 'advaita' means 'non-dual' (one without a second).

The essence of such a philosophy is that the Brahman alone is ultimately real, the ultimate truth. It denies permanent reality to all others such as the *jagat* (the world) and *jivas* (individual souls). However, this universe consists of many living beings, many physical entities, as well as a multiplicity of our experiences and memories (inter-generational/genetic, as well as the current). The other philosophical schools would say these are multiple manifestations of the Param Brahma, when these are just the multiple names and forms given to the same Param Brahma. But the advaita philosophers say it is an erroneous cognition. The phenomenal transient world is an illusory appearance (maya) of the Brahman, and the true self, atman, is identical with the Brahman. The phenomenal world is the illusory appearance of plurality, experienced through the sense-impressions by ignorance (avidya), an illusion superimposed (*adhyasa*) on the sole reality of the Brahman. It is the avidya that leads to believe that the Param Brahma appears in many jivas and entities. It is the maya of the phenomenal world. Maya is avidya at the cosmic level. The Brahman can be comprehended only through His essential characteristics, which are sat (eternal reality), chit (pure consciousness) and anand (eternal bliss). Sat-chit-anand is not only His characteristic, it is His essence.

The bondage of the atman to the false identification with the body and mind leads to the cycle of births and deaths. In this regard, the sayings of Sant Kabir are appropriate. The importance of the body and its identity is completely shunned by Kabir as he negates the corporeal aspect of being:

> Brother why do you strut about,/ so full of yourself?/ How come you've forgotten/ those ten months/ when you were suspended/ upside down/ inside the womb?/ when the body is cremated/...it is eaten by worms/ the body is a jar of unbaked clay/ containing water/ that is its greatest claim to fame.[2]

[2]Dharwadker, Vinay, *Kabir: The Weaver's Songs,* Penguin India, 2003.

The illusion (maya) and transitory nature of the human body is well put by Guruji:

> *Tusi bande mere ko kide makude lagade.*
>
> I see you like insects and pests.
>
> *Jithe main khada han, mainu tusi log chinti verge nazar aande ho.*
>
> From my perspective, you people are like ants.

Instead of taking a literal view of these sayings, Guruji was emphasizing the transitory nature of human existence and equating the lives of followers, bereft of spiritual quest, to that of insects and pests.

The remedy lies in adopting a life of disciplines, like *viveka* (discrimination between the eternal and non-eternal), vairagya (non-attachment or dispassion), the sincere desire and action for liberation, and *sat sampatti* (cultivation of the six virtues) like *shama* (mind control), *dama* (keeping the body and the senses under control), *uparati* (the state of mind above and beyond all dualities such as joy and grief, liking and disliking, good and bad, and praise and blame, which agitate and affect the common man), *titikshya* (the attitude of forbearance, which refuses to be affected or pained when afflicted with sorrow and loss, and the ingratitude and wickedness of others), shradha (unwavering faith in the atman and the guru) and *samadhana* (single-pointed concentration). Then one has to approach a competent guru and learn the truth and guidance from him for spiritual salvation. This will lead to the realization that the individual herself/himself is atman—the liberation or mukti of the atman from the illusion. This freedom is called *jivamukti*. Such a mukti is not liberation from transmigration from the cycle of births, but recognizing the already existing original state. This is what Guruji was referring to when talking about the realization that God is within you.

THE PATHS TO REALIZATION

Guruji's system comprises a couple of spiritual symbolisms—Lord Shiva, Shiva Puran, Guru Nanak and the traditions of the sabads, langar, sangat and satsangs, and the dohas of Sant Kabir.

The path preferable for spiritual seekers in the Kalyug is through Bhakti Yoga, the devotional way. Guruji used to say, '*Ay kalyug hai, aide vich rab jaldi mil janda ve. Puttha nahin latkana painda* (This is Kalyug; God is realized without much difficulty; you need not do severe penance for that).'

Guruji has, through his practices and sayings, emphasized the superiority of Bhakti Yoga. The concept of the puran guru or satguru has been emphasized by Guruji. He indirectly ascribed himself as a puran guru. The chapter on Guru Tattva has succinctly described the Bhakti Yoga to be followed in the Guru–shishya relationship. Equating puran guru or satguru as God, Guruji has enunciated the Bhakti Yoga in the first stage. It is a complete devotion to the Guru and the Guru leads you, holding your hand, to God-realization.

Guruji was averse to ritualistic prayers and reciting God's name with prayer beads. He used to say, '*Kade v mala nahin jap de, mala japan naal ahankar aa janda ve* (Never get embroiled in ritualistic prayers with the help of prayer beads. The counting itself leads to an ego-trip).'

Similarly, Guruji was against the attempt to connect with God through just from reading written prayers or texts. He used to say, '*Sirf kitabi paath paath nahinhonda* (Just reading written prayers or books is not the real prayer to connect with God).'

There are several aphorisms ascribed to Guruji regarding his percepts of Bhakti Yoga. We have discussed in detail the Guru Tattva in a chapter. Here, we will discuss some sample aphorisms of Guruji to highlight the basic principles of Bhakti Yoga he was espousing. The complete surrender and unwavering devotion to Guruji have been the hallmark tenets of Guruji's espousal of Bhakti Yoga. These are reflected in his sayings:

Complete surrender to Guruji, phir dekha na kaisa maja ayega.

Completely surrender to me and witness the great happenings.

Tusi towhada logic (dimaag) nu bahar rakh ke aya karo.

Leave your logic outside when you come to Guruji's premises.

Jad jutti bahar lande ho taa apni intelligence vi bahr la ke aayo karo, uda aaithe koi kam nahin.

Leave your logic and intelligence outside when you come to Guruji's premises.

Guru vaste aina pyar hona chahinda ki suttee, jagte, lipstick lagande vele vi guru chete hove.

The devotion to Guruji should be that strong so that when a lady is applying makeup, her mind should be concentrated on Guruji.

Shradha inni honi chahindi ki jadon aurat apani marad kol sote hua Guruji nuu unhade wich mehshush karna.

Real shradha is like when the woman sleeps with her husband, she is still connected with Guruji.

THE ULTIMATE ASPIRATION AND PRAYERS

Guruji would guide his disciples to become *rasik vairagi* (lover of detachments). For that reason, he would politely and subtly tell the devotees not to ask anything from Guruji, or in that matter, to God. Asking involves desire, and desire leads to attachment. His utterances make it quite clear.

Asli chij mangamn baste koi nahin aunda. Log to a chiz kar do, o chij kar do, mere kudi da biya ho jai, munda nuakuri

> *lag jabe-is tarah chis mang de Han. Mere kol jo pudiya hai, uno magmgan baste koi nahi aunda.*
>
> Nobody comes for the real thing. People are after Guru for materialistic benefits like daughter's marriage, job and profession. But none of them are asking for the real thing from me.
>
> *Gurua nu manga na nahin chaiya, parntu man na chayia.*
>
> You should not ask things from Guru; just surrender to Guru.

The spiritual path for each devotee is unique to them. There is no standardized path applicable for everybody. The Guru is there to hold your hand and guide you to the garden path of higher spiritual attainment.

> *Har bande vaste mere kol bakhara bakhara injection hai.*
>
> The disciple is guided or advised according to their level of spiritual attainment.
>
> *Jeh koi meri taraf ik kadam badanda hai toh main oddi taraf sau kadam chalkar aanda haa.*
>
> If someone takes one step of surrendering and shradha towards me, I take a hundred steps towards them, bless them profusely.

THE TESTING OF THE REAL AND SINCERE DISCIPLE

The sincerity and devotion of a spiritual aspirant or disciple is tested by the real or puran gurus. You should be worthy of being a true disciple to get the shower of blessings and divine grace of the Lord. Guruji has put it succinctly in his sayings:

> *Main to chele nu pahila nimbu jaise nichod dena. Baad'ch uno phir kol bulauna.*

> I squeeze the disciple like a lemon; once they are able to pass the test, then I accept them as a true disciple.
>
> *Mere kol an da rasta bahut pathreela hai. Main nimbu vakan nichodanga... Jeh zara v ras reh giya phir ki faida?*
>
> The road to reach me is too difficult. I squeeze the disciple like a lemon. If there is still some juice left, then the testing is incomplete!

Guruji would discourage via-media for reaching God. It is in that vein he was discouraging priests and their associated rituals. God or Guruji can be connected directly. He used to say:

> *Mere naal direct connection jodo.*
>
> Connect with me directly.
>
> *Guru an di gal pathar di lakeer.*
>
> The words of Gurus are cast on stone; never question or contradict the pronouncements.
>
> *Sangat nuu satsang karna chahinda. Satsang naal bolan bale nuu te shunan bale nuu blessings hunda hai.*
>
> Devotees should narrate the blessings they have received. Satsang confers blessings on the narrator as well as on the listener.

Guruji gave utmost importance to complete devotion, surrender and *smaran, manan, shravana* and kirtan of the Guru by the devotees. The tenets of Bhakti Yoga were reverberating in the systems of sabads, langars and satsangs adopted in the manner Guru Nanak and other Sikh gurus enriched this sacred land. Similarly, the dohas of Kabir and the Sufi songs were a testimony of the prioritization of Bhakti Yoga in Guruji's spiritual approach. Guru Nanak emphasized on sabads and the recitation of the name of God as a part of the devotion to the *Akal Purakh* (Lord). Reciting the names of God purifies one's soul. The names may be the attributive names of the Lord—his qualities (mercy, power, etc.), or the name may be *satnam* (the eternal or true name). By surrendering to the Lord and reciting his name, one annihilates one's ego that leads to the automatic conquering of the evils like lust, anger, greed, attachments and pride, which are derived from ego. Guru Nanak says,

> When the clothes are soiled and rendered impure,
> They are cleansed with soap.
> When the mind is defiled by the sin
> It is rendered pure by the love of His Nam.[3]

Guruji was also emphasizing the teachings of Sant Kabir. Usually, during congregation of sangat, the dohas of Kabir would be played. As per Sant Kabir, Bhakti should not be confined to the metaphysical sense of the term, i.e. the love of God alone. It has to simultaneously be a part of the human aspect of love. Persons who can love humans and other living beings can express divine love. Though Sant Kabir's philosophy touched many aspects like equality, the dignity of people, non-pharisaic attitude (against ritualism), and purity of the heart and mind, the core of his philosophy was devotion to the Lord. Sant Kabir emphasized the idea that it is within oneself that the salvation is to be attained through loving God.

Like Sant Kabir, Guruji emphasized the path of devotion for the well-being of humanity, not only at the spiritual level but also at the social and cultural level. He did not only teach about the fullness of life through his spiritualism but also the gracefulness of life through love, purity of mind and heart, and the harmony in society. Guruji was advocating a humble, pious and duty-minded worldly life, internalizing God at every moment and in everybody, including oneself.

[3]Singh, Khushwant, *A History of the Sikhs*, Oxford, 2004, p. 40.

THE SHIVA PURAN AND BHAKTI YOGA

The Shiva Puran testifies the Advaita Vedanta philosophy and theist elements of bhakti. Vidyeswar Samhita of the Shiva Puran describes the greatness of Lord Shiva and the devotion to Him through the icon of the lingam. Rudra Samhita talks about the step-by-step yajnas, starting with Karmayajna, graduating to Tapoyajna and culminating into Gyanyajna; and all of them leading to *sajujya* (ultimate union) with Shiva within. The Rudra Samhita emphasizes Bhakti Yoga as the path to salvation.

The Puran also presents the Brahman as sat-chit-anand. The Shiva Puran asserts that love-driven devotion (bhakti) leads to knowledge, and such love, combined with knowledge, leads to attracting saintly people and the Guru, and with them, one attains liberation.

Guruji used to suggest many a sangat to read the Shiva Puran. Basically, he was nudging them to the trinity of smaran, kirtan and manan of the Bhakti Yoga. All the three components are satisfied when a devotee of the Lord reads, internalizes and remembers the qualities, characteristics and glory of the Lord described in the Puranic literature or religious texts of similar kind.

Guruji emphasized that God's manifestation is not to be realized through intellect but by devotion and complete surrender of the mind. It is evident from his sayings:

> *Discussion naal rab nahin milda.*
>
> God is not realized through intellectual discussions.

What was being said by Osho (Osho International Foundation) is apt here:

> All knowledge is borrowed... Knowledge does not liberate you; it is your deepest, subtlest bondage. Through knowledge you are not available to reality. Drop all knowledge, knowing becomes pure; then you are no more clouded. Not knowing

anything borrowed, your purity is intact; then your mirror has no dust on it. Then you start reflecting. Then reality is reflected as it is.

The mind is enclosed in knowledge, in boundaries, in prejudices; the mind that has been cultivated by the environment in which we grew up- the mind that has been programmed by the society. When these barriers are broken, when these obscurities are removed, then you attain the great Mind.[4]

INTERRELIGIOUS HARMONY

One key feature of the philosophies of Sant Kabir and Guru Nanak, which resonates with the great Indian spiritual tradition, is the Universal God. God does not belong to any particular community or religion. He is for all human beings. Guruji's spiritualism reiterates this universal spiritualism. It is up to the individuals or communities to ascribe names and follow paths, suitable to them to reach God, realize God and love God and God's creation.

This spiritual essence of Guruji gets reflected in the diversity of his followers. His devotees or followings are inclusive, not confined to any particular religion or community. As we have discussed in a previous chapter, his followers are from almost all major religious communities. This leads to the furthering of interreligious harmony. The core principle is that all human beings are the embodiment of God (God is within everybody) and they are from the same stock. Sant Kabir says, 'Look within your heart and you will find both Karim and Ram. All the men and women of the world are His living form.'[4] Sant Kabir had a strong faith in the concept of oneness of God. He advocated the notion of '*Koi bole Ram Ram koi khudai*'. It has been beautifully incorporated in the Sri Guru Granth Sahib (Ang 885):

---

[4]'Tantric Transformation: Intelligence is Meditation', Osho, https://bit.ly/3JeydZY. Accessed on 16 January 2023.

Koee bolai Raam Raam koee Khudhaae
Koee saevai Guseeaa koee Alaahi
Kaaran karan Kareem

Some call the Lord 'Ram, Ram', and some 'Khuda'
Some serve Him as 'Gusain', others as 'Allah'.
He is the Cause of causes, and Generous.

The basic idea is to spread the message that whether you chant the name of a Hindu god, Muslim god or a Christian god, the fact is that there is only one God who is the creator of this beautiful world.

Guru Nanak had profound respect for other religions and its followers. According to him, every human being is equal and one must not be judged because of one's difference of religion. Guru Nanak had a deep respect towards the religious texts of other religions like the Vedas or the Bible. He said to the Muslims and the Christians that it not enough to read the Quran and the Bible, and rather they have to own the teachings of the Quran and the Bible in their hearts. Guruji, by assigning Guru Nanak a pivotal place in his spiritualism, reiterated this aspect of universalism of spiritual moorings, which, in turn, fosters inter-religion respect and harmony.

GREAT ADVOCATE OF HUMANISM

When all human beings are of the same lot and from the same source, there is no point in discriminating against anyone. Universal humanism is a logical corollary from this spiritual principle of Guruji, who, like Guru Nanak, was against any sort of divisions amongst people on the basis of religion, birth or lineage, colour, caste, race, nation or wealth. He believed that human beings are one big community, and any kind of discrimination would violate the unity of people. God has created humankind from His love, and to Him, none is superior or inferior.

To establish universal humanism, Guruji adopted the system of langars and sangat, as was established by Guru Nanak. The same food is served to everyone, and everybody partakes in langar sitting together and from shared thalis. This practice fostered universal brotherhood, apart from annihilating the egos of individual sangat. Universal humanism is reflected in his saying, '*Sangat tuwhada parivar hai* (The sangat is your family).'

He showed us the path to loving each other. He also emphasized the dignity of man and the superior intelligence of human beings that can be utilized for a greater goal of self-realization—ultimate God-realization. Human life is a grand opportunity and a great challenge for the goal of self-realization.

KARMA THEORY

Guruji was, as part of the great Indian spiritual tradition, a believer of the karmic principles. Every man is responsible for their own deeds. You cannot blame God, others or the external world for your sufferings or good times. Guru Nanak says:

> Why blame others, blame your own deeds
> For one receives the fruit of what one sows.[5]

The interrelation of the birth cycle of karma and rebirth has been often highlighted by Guruji. The salvation from the karmic cycle and resultant sufferings lie in the spiritual quest. The start of the quest is receiving guidance of a true guru (if you are graced to find one) after surrendering to him. In the alternative, follow the path of surrendering to God and loving Him directly. Man can conquer suffering by attaining salvation that is free from the cycle of rebirth. To purify one's own heart, one must seek the love of God or Guru. As Guruji would say, '*Rab nu pyar karo, ude kolon daro na* (Love God, do not fear him).'

Was Guruji of the view that the followers should renounce the world? Not at all; he would say that a householder needs to lead a normal life, earning from legitimate means and interests, and only then may they enjoy their wealth. He was against the flaunting of wealth and showing off one's spending or money

[5]Singh, Dr Gopal, *A History of the Sikh People,* Allied Publishers, Mumbai, 1998, p. 137.

power. Simultaneously, he was insisting on the principle of sharing your income and wealth with others and contributing to charity. He would also say '*Neema ho jao* (humility is best) and do remember that whatever you have is by God's grace and you should be thankful to Him.'

Guruji used to say, '*Je karam change ne, sab kuchh lavo, koi mania nahin* (There is no bar to enjoy the fruits of legitimate earnings or righteous living).'

A number of devotees pray and seek the blessings of Guruji for many materialistic gains. Some people get distraught that they could not get the intended things for which they sought Guruji's blessings. As we have already discussed, Guruji nudges people to work through their sufferings and despair with fortitude. He invokes the potential of man to overcome the adversity; he lends a helping hand to lessen the sufferings. But some devotees are insistent that they should not suffer and should not encounter any difficulty as Guruji's devotees. It is like praying to Guruji to change their karmic destiny. In this regard, Guruji dissuades them from praying for the impossible, which is against nature. To demand the impossible is unintelligent.

It has been observed that some devotees digress from Guruji's fold because their prayers were not fulfilled. They pray for a secure future, absolute security for tomorrow, a life free from troubles and sufferings. They wonder, 'Why is this happening with me? I am a devotee of Guruji!' No Guru, nor God would guarantee such security as it is not in the nature of things.

The karma theory, as expounded by our ancient sages, has been beautifully depicted by Robin Sharma in his dialogue with Julian Mantle:

> There is no chaos in the Universe. There is a purpose for everything that has happened to you, and everything that will happen to you. Remember, every experience offers lessons. So stop majoring in minor things.[6]

---

[6]Sharma, Robin, *The Monk Who Sold His Safari*, Jaico Publishing House, 2003.

HUMILITY AND ABSENCE OF SPIRITUAL ARROGANCE

Humility was the hallmark of Guruji. Despite his spiritual attainments, devotees or any individual interacting with him or having his darshan would be bowled over by his humility and lack of any arrogance. The Puranic literature is abound with instances of supreme arrogance of sages and others, with some degree of spiritual attainment or being graced by God, to have acquired some supernatural powers.

Spiritual arrogance is the worst form of arrogance; and the spiritual quest is not confined to ascetics who renounced the world. It has been beautifully described in the Vyadha Gita, which is a part of the Mahabharat, 'No duty is ugly, no duty is impure.'

The story goes like this: a *sanyasi* (sadhak or monk), after years of austerities and meditation, acquired yogic powers. One day, while he was in meditation, the fight between a crow and a crane resulted in some dry leaves dropping on the sanyasi. As his meditation was disturbed, he looked in anger at the birds, and his gaze burnt the two creatures to ashes. By realizing the effect of his yogic power, the sanyasi was filled with pride and arrogance. Thereafter, he went for begging alms and reached a household where the house lady was nursing her ailing husband. The lady politely told the sanyasi to wait as she was nursing her husband. The sanyasi felt slighted, as he was not attended to immediately. He was full of rage and said arrogantly that the lady did not know the accomplishment of the yogi. The lady gave a wry smile and told politely that she was not like the two birds that got burnt from his rage. The sanyasi was surprised that the lady knew about events happening far away from her visual boundaries. He realized that the house lady is much more spiritually accomplished than him. He begged pardon of the lady and implored how come she had attained such a level of spirituality. The lady explained that she did not practise any austerities, and by doing her duty with cheerfulness and wholeheartedness, with the Supreme Lord in mind, she became illumined.

The sanyasi requested the lady to impart him spiritual knowledge. However, she redirected him to a vyadha (butcher/hunter) in the town of Mithila who could answer all his queries on dharma and spirituality. After reaching Mithila, the sanyasi met the butcher at his shop. He was full of thoughts like, 'How could a butcher become illumined by doing filthy, ugly work?' The butcher read his mind and told him that the old lady had redirected him to the butcher. Again, the sanyasi was stupefied learning that the vyadha had divine vision. He waited patiently while the vyadha wrapped up for the day. After the butcher finished his routine, he took the sanyasi to his home. There, he also attended to his old parents, making the sanyasi wait further. Ultimately, after treating the sanyasi well, the vyadha explained the principles of karma and swadharma. He said that he was working as per the principles of karma, which placed him in a circumstance into which he was born. The vyadha further advised, 'No duty is ugly, no duty is impure,' and it is only the way in which the work is done that determines its worth. The vyadha advised him that all work must be done by 'dedicating to God' and by a sincere and unattached performance of the allotted duty, one can become illumined. The vyadha taught that not birth but dharma and virtuous conduct makes one a Brahman.

According to the story, a vyadha, who is a butcher or hunter, considered low by birth, but engaged in dharma and doing good to others, is capable of teaching a Brahman, considered higher by birth, who practices austerities for his own good. The attainment of freedom, by the performance of swadharma, is also one of the central teachings of the Bhagavad Gita.

TRANSITORY NATURE OF MATERIALISTIC WORLD

Guruji was of the view that people should not hanker after too much money and wealth. One should have limited requirements. He used to say:

> *Botta paisa change nahin hundu. Sui itneya doojiye ja main kutumb samal.*

> Hankering after too much money and wealth is not good. Pray to the Almighty to give you enough for providing reasonably for your family.

While observing the relentless quest for materialistic gains, he used to say:

> *Pave sadde kol pura ghar hai, par rahna ek bedroom vich hai. Rahne vaste ghar da ek hi kamara kaam aunda haa.*
>
> You may have a mansion, but you will be sleeping in one room. Only the bedroom of a large house is used.

The futility of running after too much money and wealth is beautifully said in the following aphorism:

> *Pal da khabar nahi; saaman sau saal da.*
>
> You never know what is there in store for the next moment. But people go on accumulating wealth and money for a hundred years!

Guruji discouraged ostentatious living and showing off of one's wealth and money. He was against lavish weddings and ceremonies. He used to say:

> *Loki enna faltu kharcha karde ne vyah ute! Vyah simple hona chahinda ne.*
>
> People spend unnecessarily too much on weddings. Weddings should be a simple and austere affair.

UNDERLYING SPIRITUAL ESSENCE OF THE SHIVA PURAN

The Shiva Puran signifies the Advaita Vedanta philosophy, which incorporates theistic elements of bhakti. The Shiva Puraṇ advocates the Shiva-advaita as a system for salvation. The Shiva Puran also presents the Brahman as sat-chit-ananda, with the masculine and feminine binary Shiva–Shakti as a unity.

It is stated that the Purans are supplementary explanations of the Vedas intended for different types of men. All men are not equal and they have different levels of spiritual attainments. The Purans are intended for a different category of men who can make use of it and gradually get out of the hard struggle for existence.

Lord Shiva has been beautifully described by Dr Mrittunjoy Majumdar, based on the state of dissolution (pralaya), during the period when the Lord was alone, there was no creation, no day, no night, no time, etc. Drawing parallel from the modern quantum physics about the composition of the cosmos, he states:

> Regardless, in all this, one of the key ideas that emerges is that at the most fundamental, these fields, when unexcited, compose a quantum vacuum. Unlike our idea of vacuum in day-to-day life, this (quantum) vacuum is a teeming, frothing sea of particles and anti-particles zooming into existence and popping back into an un-manifested state, within the vacuum. Thus, most of physics, from that described by electromagnetism to the weak interaction and strong interaction (quantum chromodynamics), can be conceptualized in terms of everything manifested coming out of an apparent nothingness and going back to it after a while. The basis of existence itself and the fundamental reality of the cosmos seems to be a vast void... It is this void that I believe was thought of as Shiva in times of yore, albeit spiritually and metaphorically rather than empirically or scientifically, given that seers posited that everything comes from Shiva and goes back into Shiva...[7]

The Shiva Puran in Rudra Samhita (Verse 6.4-13) states this beautifully in the following manner:

> At the time of great dissolution when all the mobile and immobile objects of the world are dissolved everything

[7]Majumdar, Mrittunjoy Guha, 'Shiva As the Fundamental Reality Underlying the Diversity of Phenomena in the Universe', *Bengal Chronicle*, 11 March 2021, https://bit.ly/3k9D83G. Accessed on 9 January 2023.

> gets enveloped in darkness, without the sun, planets and stars. There is no moon. The day and night are not demarcated. There is no fire, no earth and no water. There is no unmanifest primordial being. The whole firmament is one complete void, devoid of all *tejas* elements. There is no *dharma* or *adharma,* no sound, no touch. Smell and colour are not manifest ...Thus when there is pitch darkness that cannot be pierced with a needle and what is mentioned in the Vedas as 'The Existent and the Brahman' (Lord Shiva) is alone present. When the present visible world is not in existence, the Sat Brahman alone is present which yogis observe perpetually in the inner soul, the inner firmament. It is incomprehensible to the mind. It cannot at all be expressed by words. It has neither name, nor colour. It is neither thick nor thin. It is neither short nor long. It is neither light nor heavy. There is neither increase or decrease in it. The Vedas says that it envelops whatever is in a surprising way. It is the splendour, the truth, the knowledge, the eternal and the great bliss. It is immeasurable, propless, changeless, formless, attributeless, and perceptible to the yogis, all pervasive and sole cause of the Universe. It is free from alternatives, it has no beginning, and It is free from illusion and its harassment. It has no second. It has neither beginning nor end. It has no development. It is in the form of pure knowledge.

As Satguru Jaggi Vasudev says:

> This vast emptiness that we refer to as Shiva is a boundless non-entity – eternal and always. But since human perception is limited to form, we created many wonderful forms for Shiva in the tradition and culture. The enigmatic, non-perceivable Ishwara- the auspicious Shambho; disarmingly naïve Bhola; Dakshinamurthy, the great master and teacher of the Vedas, Shastras and Tantras; the easily forgiving Ashuthosh; Bhairava, the one tainted with the very blood of the creator; Achaleshwara, the absolute stillness; the most

> dynamic of dancers, Nataraja—as many aspects as there are to life, that many aspects have been offered to him.[8]

In summary, the spiritual essence of Guruji resonates with the Advaita philosophy of the Vedanta, emphasizing the Bhakti Yoga as the proffered path to God-realization. Simultaneously, such an approach also emphasizes the universalization of spiritualism—the Universal God and the syncretic and eclectic choices for individuals to choose the appropriate spiritual path. Guruji's spiritual tenets resonates with the concept of Universal God, Lord Shiva where Universal God principles are akin to the universal principles of modern quantum physics.

Inter-religion harmony and universal brotherhood are the logical corollary of such a spiritual core. This approach comprises positivism and optimism, which is a stark contrast to the despair, helplessness and hopelessness of western existentialists. The spiritual approach of Guruji abjures such negativisms by emphasizing positivism in one's outlook and activities. This is further amplified in highlighting the karma theory of the great Indian spiritual tradition. The human being is the special gift of God with superior intelligence and memory. They can realize the tremendous potential by controlling his wavering mind and senses to work through their karmic journey. In this journey, the grace of Guruji and his handholding leads to the lessening of sufferings and a step towards God-realization—better karmic earnings.

[8]Sadhguru, 'Shiva Puran is All-Encompassing', The Hans India, 9 August 2018, https://bit.ly/3j2D1XM. Accessed on 25 January 2023.

12

The Social Aspects of Spiritualism of Guruji

Social philosophers formulate the rules for ideal social interactions. They try to seek to explain the nature of society in the light of the principle of social solidarity. They show the value on which the social progress of man depends. As British philosopher Bertrand Russell emphasizes, social philosophers seek the conditions in which all the constructive tendencies of man, such as love and sympathy, flourishes. In *Doctrine of Virtue,* Immanuel Kant talks about the obligation to develop friendships and to participate in social intercourse. The social philosophers highlight the individual's 'highest good' in society. Most of the time, they are concerned with general questions concerning the problems of society, such as social cohesion, progress and disintegration. They try to expose the drawbacks of social institutions and the social behaviour of people. They set the higher ideals for the guidance of conduct in human society by defining the social values, such as thinking for the common good, happiness, peace, security, justice, freedom, excellence/beauty, punctuality and discipline. In *Religion within the Boundaries of Mere Reason,* Kant discusses the development of an 'ethical commonwealth' in which human beings strengthen one another's moral resolve through their participation in the moral community of a church.

In the context of spiritual development, ideal human behaviour brings harmony in individual conduct and in society. Such harmonies set the perfect platform for the individual seeker to progress in the spiritual quest. In addition, much of the ideals also relate to the austerities, the good conduct of a seeker, as has been emphasized by great spiritual masters and avatars.

Guruji as an enlightened master has emphasized, through his aphorisms and small talks, on ideal social behaviour by individuals. Though he was neither a social preacher nor a social reformer, he has spoken about the ideal social relations and behaviour through subtle hints and aphorisms. We will discuss some of his aphorisms that exemplify the social aspects of his spiritual teachings.

INDOMITABLE SPIRIT OF MAN

Many a devotee and non-devotee used to pay their respects and seek Guruji's blessings when they were in distress. The distress might be due to health issues, family matters, business affairs, children's education and settlement, professional and official matters, etc. All were welcome with open hands with the sole purpose of instilling confidence in them to overcome such distress. Guruji would provide the assurance (*kalyan kitta*), or through his utterances, that everything would be alright. Even Guruji would invoke the karma principle that the sufferer had to go through his karmic cycle, but the true Guru would show them the light from the darkness of the painful abyss and hold their hand to lessen their sufferings. By all these processes, Guruji would subtly guide the individual to discover the strength of the human spirit in overcoming adversity in life. He would say, that even though he is capable of reversing one's karma, he prefers the individual to overcome the adversity himself with the guidance, love and protection of Guruji. He championed the indomitable spirit of man to work through sufferings and adverse situation with fortitude. This is one of the most important aspects of Guruji's spiritual tenets. By that process, Guruji would subtly de-emphasize the invoking of supernatural powers or divine interventions. Though, sometimes, he used to take recourse to such powers to make the devotees realize the existence of the Supreme Self.

He used to say, '*Mein shristika pher mein kabhi hastakshepa nahin karda* (I do not want to interfere in karmic destiny).'

But it was his pleasure to lessen one's sufferings through his grace, which would amount to rewriting their destiny. He further said, '*Main suli nu sui bana dena* (I help reduce your great sufferings to lesser tolerable ones).'

TREMENDOUS POTENTIAL OF MAN

The individual freedom and choice points to the enormous potential of each individual. We are blessed to be born as human beings. The Almighty has blessed us with superior intellect and memory, which is absent in other living beings. The most important aspect is the tremendous potential to realize the powers of controlling the mind and attaining supernatural powers and God-realization.

Guruji used to say, '*Rav tohade ander baitha hai* (God is inside you).'

This aphorism of Guruji signifies the principle that man has tremendous potential to rise to the level where there is no distinction between the man and God. We have discussed our spiritual traditions expounded in the Vedas, Upanishads, Bhagavad Gita and in Puranic literature, as well as in the preaching of great sages and avatars, like Lord Krishna and Lord Buddha, great saints, like Guru Nanak and Sant Kabir, and others of their stature, in which the core principle is that the individual atma/self is said to be part of the Supreme Self/Paramatma. And all of them have expounded the possibilities of each human being to realize God, if they adopt the right path, and the right principles and practices. At that stage of realization or attainment, man would reach the greatest heights. All material achievements—climbing Mount Everest, reaching the pinnacles of a professional career or political leadership—pale into insignificance in comparison. Patanjali's Yoga Sutra espouses the principles of yogic practices to reach Kaivalya Samadhi. It states, in no uncertain terms, that there is the inherent potential in each person to reach the stage of mahayogi and acquire supernatural powers. It is not only that the avatars or God himself has supernatural powers; it is the man who can attain supernatural powers on the way to Kaivalya Samadhi. And after such an attainment and realization, these supernatural powers remain as the inherent characteristic of man, who, then, typifies the characteristics of God, and godliness manifest in him. So, when the individual discovers and realizes God residing within themselves, they find no distinction between their individuality and God.

Robin Sharma, summarizing his dialogue with Julian Mantle, a follower of Ramana Maharshi states:

> When you are inspired by a great purpose, some extraordinary project, all of your thoughts break their bonds; your mind transcends limitations, your consciousness expands in every direction and you find yourself in a new, great and wonderful world. Dormant forces, faculties and talents become alive and you discover yourself to be greater person than you ever dreamed yourself to be.
>
> Start to revere life again and celebrate all of its wonders. Awaken yourself to the power of your own mind to make things happen. Once you do so, the universe will conspire with you to work magic in your life.[1]

INHERENT GOODNESS OF MAN

Guruji used to say, '*Positive sochiya karo te positive kam karo* (Think positive and do positive).' He would further say, '*Man nirmal/saaf hona chahinda* (Your mind should be clear of wavering thoughts).' By saying so, Guruji was invoking the inherent goodness in each individual. He would not characterize a person as bad and nobody would get scorned. If God resides in everybody *(rav towade andar hai)*, then how can you despise, hate or dislike anybody?

[1]Sharma, Robin, *The Monk Who Sold His Ferrari*, Jaico Publishing House, India, 2003, pp. 49–50.

Guruji was the shining example of leading the way and practising what he used to say to the devotees. His durbar was open to everybody, irrespective of their spiritual attainment, social and religious background, and caste or race affiliation. When Guruji was welcoming everybody, sinner or not, to his fold with open arms, it signified his recognition of inherent goodness in each individual. We have already discussed the composition of sangat—his followers—like Shivji's baarat. There is no place for exclusion under the goodness principle.

Guruji never imposed any method, practice or ritual for greater social and spiritual attainments. As the true Guru, he would treat each individual separately and suggest spiritual or worldly solutions or remedies for the problems or issues brought before him or known to him. He would not compel individual followers to follow a standardized set of guidelines. He would encourage each individual to choose their own path to attain their worldly or spiritual goals. He would tell people not to believe in superstitions, unnecessary rituals like fasting, vrata, etc. He wanted people to be free from ritualistic traditions and exercise their free will and freedom of choice to follow the right path. He would say one should not depend upon astrologers and soothsayers. He discouraged wearing stones for prosperity and good health, thereby freeing the person from the shackles of false gurus and soothsayers and encouraging them to exercise their free will to choose the right path. Similarly, he would say, '*Manglik phazul de beham ne* (The concept of *manglik* is a foolish one).' Nobody is born bad.

Such a freedom of choice and respect for individuality, individual potentialities, the indomitable spirit of human beings, and the inherent goodness of each and every individual are hallmarks of Guruji's spiritual essence.

GENDER EQUITY

Guruji used to say, '*Aurat ne marad nu janam diya, parntu marad ne aurat nu baajar diya* (Woman gives birth to man; but man is ungrateful and throws the woman to the marketplace [as an object or commodity to be enjoyed or devoured]).'

What a profound statement! The contradictions of societal behaviour brought out succinctly. The objectification of women happens every day, starting from advertising, to misogynist comments by youngsters and adults about the dress and body features of women, and worst of all, the trafficking of women and flourishing flesh trade—all testimonies of the degradation heaped on women, who are supposed to bear men and women for society.

Guruji would also talk about the position of women in a husband–wife relationship. He would say, 'After 45–50 years of age, husband and wife should behave like good friends.' Intimate physical relationships should be of secondary importance. He would further say, '*Gharwale gharwali di sewa kare, gharwali gharwale di sewa kare* (Both husband and wife should serve each other).'

It should not be a typical patriarchal and chauvinistic system, where only the wife is supposed to serve the husband and not the other way round. This is how the teachings of Guruji resonates with the modern thinking on the equality of the sexes, which is in contrary to the teachings in some texts where the subservient nature of women in the household has been emphasized. Guruji used to say, '*Husband te wife da relationship best friends di tarah hona chahinda hai.* (The relationship between husband and wife should be like between two best friends).'

Guruji used to say that the greatest *punya* (spiritual attainment or good karma) would be attained if you can bring up a girl, educate her and give her away for marriage or settlement. This saying has a lot of significance for emphasizing a girls' education. One may recollect the saying, 'If you educate a man, it is for only one person; but if you educate a woman, you are educating a generation.' Guruji would reiterate the sanctity of the institution of marriage, and he would advise, guide and help the parents to get their children married at an appropriate age. He would also encourage girls to take up professional jobs to become financially self-reliant.

EGALITARIANISM

Egalitarianism refers to equal treatment in all respects. People should be treated as equals, should treat one another as equals, should relate as equals, or enjoy an equality of social status of some sort. Egalitarian doctrines tend to rest on the idea that all humans are equal in fundamental worth or moral status. This follows from the great Indian spiritual tradition that God loves all human souls equally. This has also its foundation in Christian theology. In modern democratic societies, the term 'egalitarian' is often used to refer to a position that favours a greater degree of equality of income and wealth across the society than what currently exists.

In Guruji's system, all devotees and non-devotees are treated equally. Guruji's has love and affection for each and every person. None is a favourite of Guruji, and people who had shown such arrogance or tendency had been shown the door. Guruji's langar principle of sharing the same food and sharing the same thali by four people also promoted the principle of equality and non-discrimination.

Of course, Guruji was apolitical. He had not pronounced any political ideology espousing egalitarianism. He has not expressed his views directly or indirectly about the connotations of egalitarianism, like a greater degree of equality of income and wealth across persons. However, from his utterances and practice, it is well-inferred that Guruji was placing importance on the concept of equal fundamental human worth—the fundamental premise that all people have the same fundamental worth and dignity, which commands respect.

LOVE AND EMPATHY TO ALL

The compassion and empathy of Guruji manifested in alleviating the physiological (ailments), physical (deformities) and psychological sufferings of people. There are innumerable accounts by sangat on how they have been blessed by Guruji and recovered from their physiological, physical and psychological sufferings.

Because of this enlightened state, he maintained a relaxed, heartfelt and authentic communication with everyone he met, in a way that was grounded in compassion, love and a state of emotional liberation. In this state, he felt, saw and experienced a divine quality in everything and everyone because he was living in deep spiritual connection with the divine universal intelligence.

In Patanjali's Yoga Sutra (Vibhuti Pad, III.23), it is said that the enlightened person, through his yogic attainments, gets unique qualities like friendliness, compassion or sympathetic joy, and he also imbibes the same feeling in others.

Guruji would advise the sangat to show compassion to animals and insects, etc., even serpents. He would often tell, '*Kala kuta ka sewa koro* (Serve the black dog).' This is not to be understood in the literal sense that only black dogs be served. His empathy to all canines comes from the saying, 'Human beings are not that grateful. Rather an animal like a dog is more faithful and *wafadar* (loyal) than any human being.' Furthermore, the futility of human existence, unless the individual utilizes his intelligence for societal good and a higher order of spiritual attainment, has been highlighted by him in the saying:

> *Insaan kis kam da? Janwar mar ke bhi ham ande ne, chamde de bag, joote, belt, khan de kam andene. Lekin insaan te mar ke kis kam da nahin. Jeende ji sirf path kar sakdu ve.*
>
> The human being is useless! The animals are even useful when they are dead—we have leather bags and belts, people and other living beings feast on dead animals. But when the human being dies, he is useless. Hence, when you are alive, do connect with God.

He would empathize with the poor and the deprived. His advice was to treat them with dignity. He used to say, '*Je kis gareeb nu khana dena ve, te party ton pehla ude vaste kadh ke rakho, baad vich left over nahin* (Never give the leftovers of a party to the poor or needy; if you want to give them some food, do keep aside the food for them and then give to them).'

Similarly, he would advise to treat the beggars with dignity. He used to say, '*Je bhikari nu kutch nahi dena, kadi ve dutkaro na. Hath jod kar ditta karo.. Ki pata kaun kide bhesh vich aa jave?* (If you do not want to give anything to the beggar, never mistreat them. Fold your hands and express your inability or unwillingness to give something to them. You never know who might have come in the garb of a beggar).'

THE PRINCIPLE OF SOCIAL SOLIDARITY AND SEWA

Guruji accorded tremendous importance to the concepts of langar, sangat and satsang, all of which promote universal brotherhood. He used to say, '*Asli parivar, guru parivar jeda tohada kam me ayaga.* (The true family is the guru family—the fellow followers of Guruji. These are people who will come to your assistance).' The concept of *gupt daan* was encouraged by Guruji. He would say, '*Gupt daan and gupt path karna chahide* (One should do charity secretly).'

Similarly, the path (*mantra jap* or remembering God) to God should be silent: so that '*naal baithana walianu pata nahin lagada* (the prayer, the communion should be so silent that the man sitting next to you may never know that you are saying your prayers).' Guruji would encourage sharing of your income and wealth with fellow human beings, as it has been enunciated by Guru Nanak in his saying '*Band ke shako* (share your bread).' Social philosophers like Immanuel Kant also advocated that it is the duty of citizens to support those in the society who could not support themselves, and he even supported the State to arrange for this help.

The sewa to others should be rendered without any expectations and reward. Guruji used to say, '*O sewa jide picche mang hai, o asal sewa nahi. Asal sewa niswarth hondi hai* (The sewa [service to others] with expectations is not real sewa, *niswartha* [without any expectations] sewa is the real sewa).'

HEALTH IS WEALTH

Guruji gave a lot of importance to sound physical and mental health. A sound mind and healthy body are the foundations for spiritual attainment. He would also empathize with the suffering individual—devotee or casual visitor—and would bless them to recover from their ailments. Curing people of diseases was one important mission of Guruji. He would even talk about the importance of sound health while sitting with non-suffering individuals and devotees. He gifted five sets of shorts and T-shirts, his walking gear to me and advised to go for morning walks every day, donning the walking ensemble.

He would advise that eating bitter things, like bitter gourd and gooseberry, are good for health. He would source *kodtumba* from the deserts of Rajasthan and get them rubbed on his body. Kodtumba is a bitter fruit from the arid regions of the country. It is not only the sweet things in nature that are good for health, the bitter ones are also beneficial.

Guruji used to say, '*Pani har marz da ilaj hai* (Water is the elixir of life and cure for all diseases).'

For many ailments, he would advise to cleanse the body by taking adequate quantity of water. He would jokingly say, '*Pite jao, sushu karate jao* (Go on drinking water and urinate to cleanse the body).'

He further used to say, '*Ghar da langar saboton changa honda hai* (The food cooked at home is the best).' The tendency of youngsters to binge on fast food and the tendency among adults to take food in unhygienic dhabas and eating joints need a course correction to develop good eating habits. He used to say that the house in which you live, particularly the kitchen, should be spick and span. You should maintain utmost personal hygiene yourself, and also in your surroundings.

SOCIAL INSTITUTIONS AND RELATIONSHIPS

Guruji was in favour of the social institution of marriage and strong family ties. We have already mentioned about him encouraging equality of husband and wife in the institution of marriage by stating that both husband and wife should treat each other as best friends, and they should render sewa to each other. Similarly, Guruji would emphasize on this when he would say, 'Husband and wife should look after each other; together, they should look after their children and keep their house happy and worry-free.'

Guruji used to tell us to treat our children as our friends and never go for corporal punishment for any mistake committed by them. He would always support the professional and independent choices made by youngsters. He used to say, 'When your children turn out well, that becomes your real earning.' To children, he used to say, '*Maa baap di sewa karani chahidi hai. Is de bina kutch nai milega* (You should serve your parents. Without that, there is nothing).'

SOCIAL VALUES

Guruji was promoting positive action amongst his followers. He would say, '*Banda da bhalla karana chahinda.* (Do good to others as much as you can. Never harm anybody).' Similarly, he would say, '*Positive sochiya karo te positive kam karo* (Think positive and do positive).' His positive attitude permeates all around with positive vibration. He would say, '*Tohada man change to nal ke pani Ganga* (If your mind is positive, the tap water will be like water of scared Ganga).'

He would also suggest, '*Chugli nain karna chahinda* (Never gossip about other persons).' Backbiting and talking behind the back of people promotes negativism. He would say, '*Kadi kis di rees nahin karani chahindi* (Never be zealous of others. Never try to keep up with the Joneses).'

He would further advise, '*Negative ganna nahin sunne chahide, har negative serial, picture nahin dekhni* (One should not listen to negative songs, watch negative movies and serials).' They create negativism in you. He would add, '*Changa character hona bahuta zaroori hai. Rab sab kutch maaf kar sakda hai, par bad character di maafi nai hai. Is di maafi sirf ek mahapurush hi de sakde han* (A person should have a good character. God forgives everything but not bad character. Only a mahapurush can forgive such a person).'

He would advise not to engage in futile arguments with foolish people. He used to say, '*Ham to murkh ki dass* (We bow before foolish people).'

Robin Sharma, in his book *The Monk Who Sold His Ferrari* has beautifully expounded the concept of positive thinking in the following manner:

> To live life to the fullest, you must stand guard at the gate of your garden and let only the very best information to enter. You cannot afford the luxury of a negative thought- not even one. We all come from the same universal source. However, the ones who do more than just exist, the ones who fan the flames of their human potential and truly savour the magical dance of life do different things than those lives are ordinary. Foremost amongst the things tjhat they do is adopt a positive paradigm about their world and all that is in it.[2]

---

[2]Ibid.

13

Maladies of Interpretation

Guruji was the epitome of universal love. He abjured preaching. It was only through subtle hints and small utterances that he spoke of profound things to the discernible sangat. He perfectly fit into the image of the great sage described by Swami Vivekananda in his discourses in California.

> There is a sage in India, a great Yogi, one of the most wonderful men I have ever seen in my life. He is a peculiar man; he will not teach any one; if you ask him a question he will not answer. It is too much for him to take up the position of a teacher, he will not do it. If you ask a question, and wait for some days, in the course of conversation he will bring up the subject, and wonderful light will he throw on it.[1]

Guruji was also a true master who would lead by his own example. He was not at all in favour of dogmas, rigidities of organized religion, and he emphasized the positives of the self. He implored one's own godliness (Lord Shiva within) to cleanse oneself. It echoes with the great invocations of the ancient sages of this land in their famous shlokas like Shivoahm or Brahmasmi of the Upanishads, the Vedas, and satgurus like Guru Nanak and Sant Kabir.

There are five narratives about Guruji, which are gaining traction among his followers. Unless these narratives are put in proper perspective and some misconceptions are dispelled, the

[1]Vivekananda, Swami, *The Complete Works of Swami Vivekananda: Volume 1*, Advaita Ashrama, 2005.

spiritual essence of Guruji will remain highly distorted. The first narrative relates to the sayings of Guruji that one should read the Shiva Puran. The second is the so-called telepathy of Guruji, after he left his physical body, which the followers are describing through their satsangs. The third kind of narrative relates to the *mahavakyas* or great sayings of Guruji when he was in his physical form and the associated literal meaning assigned to them. The fourth category of narrative relates to the unintended or intended adaptation of rigid ritualistic practices wrongly ascribing as being prescribed by Guruji. The fifth narrative relates to, again, intended or unintended, the relegating of Guruji to a narrow confine of family, village and community, thereby completely distorting the universalism of Guruji and his principles.

WHAT IS AN APHORISM?

As we have mentioned earlier, Guruji was not known as voluble or loquacious. Generally, he used to speak a few words or sentences—full of witticism and deeper meanings. These taciturn, reticent and laconic aphorisms may be a terse statement of the truth or an idea. Aphorisms are the forte of spiritually evolved sages or gurus, leading to the commonly expressed statement that they are mystics.

The short and terse aphorisms of spiritual masters have different connotations for individuals at different levels of spiritual attainment and moorings. There are three different levels of spiritual context of individuals that furnish meanings of the sayings of such masters. The first group is the ordinary householders who are not immersed in too much of spirituality and for who the aphorisms provide literal meaning to guide better action and thought. The next group is for the true spiritual seekers who are hungry seekers of God. Here, the same sayings take the individual from a mundane level to the higher level, in terms of implications. The third kind of meaning is intended for the individual or the soul that has attained or is nearly ready to attain liberation or enlightenment. For such kind of individuals, the aphorisms lead to the correct and crystal-clear meanings. There are many esoteric and intrinsic meanings of spiritual aphorisms that unravel to enlightened souls and not necessarily to linguistic scholars, academic thinkers or even intellectual giants.

This runs parallel to the analogy generally ascribed to the interpretation of the Vedic Sanskrit mantras. It is said that every Vedic mantra has meanings at three levels—*adhibhautika*, *adhidaivika* and *adhyatmika*.

Adhibhautika refers to the meaning derived at the physical plane/phenomenal world level, loosely for our objective understanding. It is akin to the *Nirukta* (etymological) school of interpretation of the Vedic mantras.

Adhidaivika refers to the subjective understanding in relation to invoking the celestial forces. This can be loosely described as akin to the *Yajnik* (ritualistic) school of interpretation.

The adhyatmika interpretation is akin to the *Parivrajika* (mystical) school of interpretation of the Vedic mantras. Here, the true meaning of the aphorisms is revealed to the true spiritually enlightened individual. Adhyatmika is the truest and deepest meaning of the mantra or aphorism at the spiritual state or level for contemplation and meditation.

To give an example on how aphorisms uttered by sages and evolved souls have deeper meanings, we may take the example of Patanjali's Yoga Sutra. It consists of 195 sutras or aphorisms. Sutra 34 of the Vibhuti Pad, the third chapter, is one of the shortest phrases: *Pratibhad va sarvam.*

The literal translations of the three Sanskrit words are as follows:

Pratibhad: By pratibha (enlightenment)
Va: Knowledge
Sarvam: All

So the literal meaning is, 'By the power of pratibha all knowledge.'

What do we get through the literal translation? Unless the

context in which these words are strewn together to form a sutra is known, the literal translation will not lead us to any meaningful understanding. These sutras can be read in context of one's own meditation experience, because the very context which it tries to elucidate lies outside of the individual intellect and conceptual reality.

The ultimate goal in yoga is the samadhi, when many a supernatural powers get naturally manifested, along with the path of progress towards kaivalya samadhi. And after the attainment of kaivalya samadhi, they become part and parcel of the life of the yogi during the current birth, as well as in subsequent births. All these powers manifest with the individual who has the power of pratibha (enlightenment from purity) without any samyama. This is when a man has risen to a high state of pratibha. At that stage, he has that great light. All things are apparent to him. And he carries this attainment to his next birth. In this case, they are born as enlightened beings for the betterment of mankind.

In other words, the shortest sutra of Patanjali's Yoga Sutra has deep spiritual meaning and connotation. Similarly, the aphorisms uttered by Guruji have deeper connotations than their literal meanings.

Sant Kabir says:

Eke shabda guru dev ka, taka anant bichar;
Thake muni jan pandita, veda na pawe par.

The one word of *Satguru* gives limitless meanings. *Munis* (sages) and pandits became exhausted trying to find its meaning. Vedas cannot fathom its depth.

THE MAHAVAKYAS OF GURUJI

The revered Guruji was most reticent in his spiritual utterances. He was not known to indulge in *pravachans* (preaching or delivering sermons and lectures). He used to say:

> *Jo pravachan karde ne, bolde ne, o asal nahin... asal guru hamesha apne aap nu lukaayega.*
>
> The persons who are fond of pravachans (sermonizing) or lecturing are not the real gurus. The real Guru is reticent and self-effacing.
>
> *Eho jiha guru milega kidre? Mein koi pravachan nahin karda, practical karke vikhana hai.*
>
> I do not indulge in sermonizing and lecturing. I adopt the experiential (practical) approach to spiritualism.

The experiential approach to spiritualism is the hallmark of the Indian (and in that matter, the eastern) philosophical approach in contrast to western spiritual traditions.

> The fundamental difference between Western philosophy and Indian Philosophy is that while Western philosophy tries to uncover the real with the use of the intellect, Indian philosophy is basically an attempt to logically reconcile the world of experience, with the spiritual experience of the sages. The sages, such as Yajnavalkya had in fact experienced reality. Unlike Western philosophers they were not speculating, analyzing with the help of reason what reality might be. They know what it is because they have experienced it.[2]

Guruji would be in his wittiest best when he would be with a small group of devotees or, in some instances, in a one-on-one situation with a beloved individual devotee. These aphorisms are to be analysed in respect of proper context. This is the caveat with which one should approach to understand the aphorisms of our revered Guruji. These have come out, most of the time, suo-motto, from Guruji. These aphorisms have deeper meaning. But many a time, the devotees interpret them literally, which has resulted in creating a narrow spiritual space of the enlightened

[2]Srinivasan, Kadambi, *Roots*, Tirumala Tirupati Devasthanams, 2016.

master. There is a need to find the context (spiritual and otherwise) of these aphorisms to infer about the spiritual and social philosophy of Guruji.

LITERAL AND CONTEXTUAL MEANINGS

In the context of interpreting the aphorisms of Guruji, we may delve into the interpretation of ancient philosophical texts of this great land. In this context, the analysis of Shashi Tharoor is quite apt:

> Many hold the view that literally all academic translations of the Vedas may be faithful initial rendition but mostly the deeper and contextually correct meaning elude them. The beauty of the Indian spiritual tradition is that there is no firm belief that religious texts as claiming to embody absolute truth. Instead, a work of scriptures is a means of self-realization; the words, and the insights they contain, are devices through which a diligent person approaches into cosmos, and its self-transformation. A religious text is a breach in the fog of ignorance that enshrouds the human mind. Allow its insights, the magic of its words, the music of its mantras, to penetrate through the fog, and a transformation might follow. The transformation does not merely understand the words of the text, but it helps you understand your true self, if it opens your minds and eyes to the ultimate truth of creation and helps merge your soul into the cosmos, it will have served its purpose.[3]

Spiritualism is considered *para vidya*, the higher kind of knowledge by which the imperishable, *Akshara Brahman*, is known. So when we say that we have heard the words of Guruji and we interpret the words literally through the method by which *apara vidya* (worldly knowledge) is understood, we may miss the real essence of those words. It is like the sophomore complex. It refers to

[3]Tharoor, Shashi, *Why I am a Hindu*, Aleph Book Company, New Delhi, 2018.

the undergraduate medical students, particularly majoring in psychiatrics. When they learn the series of symptoms pertaining to abnormal psychological problems like depression, schizophrenia, anxiety disorder and psychosis, they promptly diagnose mental states as psychological problems, even if many of the symptoms are absent; and the few present have seen consistency for only a short duration. Moreover, they self-diagnose themselves as persons suffering from the mental disorder. The problem is that to diagnose a mental state as a psychological problem, it requires a holistic view and an integration of a series of symptoms consistently for a considerable period.

Various methods are used in ancient and modern times to interpret Vedic texts and Puranic literature. The Nirkuta school refers to the etymological method of interpretation of words and phrases occurring in the Vedas. It is akin to the literal meaning, bereft of any spiritual connotations. The Mimamsa school believes that all the Vedas should be treated as a harmonious whole. The correct meaning of the hymns can be understood if we consider the context, the relationship of various sentences and words in those sentences. The Parivrajika school is of the view that the Vedas convey the spiritual ideas and that the hymns be explained in a spiritualistic way.

Drawing parallel with the wisdom of the Vedic ages, the words and phrases, or aphorisms uttered by spiritually evolved souls like Guruji should not be understood on a standalone basis, or through a literal translation by analysing its etymology. These need to be interpreted in a holistic manner, in the context of Guruji's spiritual essence.

Mein Mahashiva Hun (I am Mahashiva)

Most of the time, Guruji would address himself in the third person. He would say, in his casual manner, '*Tuhannu ki patta, mahapurush ki hunde hai?* (What do you know what is a mahapurush?)' But a few (one or two) devotees had heard him saying that he is 'Mahashiva'. The word Mahashiva has not been used in any of the spiritual texts or in the spiritual discourses of this great land. The equivalent of that is 'Mahadev'—one of the eight fundamental names of Lord Shiva in Vayviya Samhita of the Shiva Puran. Even if we find it acceptable on particular occasions for that place and time, how do we interpret Guruji telling a particular devotee in another instance that he is Lord Shiva himself?

Satarudra Samhita of the Shiva Puran describes various forms and incarnations of Lord Shiva in Verse 1.4:

> The incarnations of omnipresent Lord Shiva are countless in different eons.
>
> A Kalpa is a day of Brahma or one thousand Yugas equal to a period of four hundred thirty-two million years of mortals. Each Kalpa is presided over for instance, the Svetalohita Kalpa has Sadyojata as presiding deity, Rakta has Vamdeva, Pitavasas hass Tapurusa, Siva has Aghora and Visvarupa has Ishan.[4]

In Verse 1.39, it states:

> The five famous forms of Mahesha are thus named Ishan, Purusa, Aghora, Vama and Brahman. They are symbolical scheme of creation evolved out of 25 constituents, five gross elements, five subtle elements, five organs and five of knowledge, besides mind, ego, intellect, nature and the individual soul.

Chapter 2 talks about the eight forms of Lord Shiva. These are Sharva, Bhava, Rudra, Ugra, Bheema, Pashupati, Ishan and Mahadeva. Chapter 3 talks about the Ardhanarisvara form of Shiva. Chapter 5 talks about 19 incarnations of Lord Shiva. Satarudra Samhita and Kotirudra Samhita describes the countless forms of Lord Shiva. However, Lord Shiva is not known for taking famous and well-known incarnations (avatars) like Lord Vishnu. In the spiritual tradition of this great land, many devotees of

[4]Gita Press Gorakhpur, *Sankshipta Shiva Puran*, Generic, 2018.

enlightened masters impute the lordship of their presiding deities to such masters.

There are many Vedic hymns describing the enlightened individual who has attained God-realization and has the understanding of being part of the Param Brahma. Such a realization is not temporary; it is permanent with the enlightened master. Hence, they state, '*Brahmasmi* (I am Param Brahman).' The mahavakyas quoted in the Shiva Puran (Kailash Samhita, Chapter 16–190) are from various Vedas and Upanishads, which can be corroborated in the statement, '*Aham Brahmasmi* (I am Brahman).' (Brihadaranyaka Upanishad, 1.4.10). Kotirudra Samhita (Verse 43.20) states that, 'Everything is Siva. Siva is everything. There is no difference at all.'

Kotirudra Samhita states that the realization of the Param Brahma and the non-duality of the individual and the Param Brahma is the pinnacle of yogic attainment. It describes:

> In the first instance find a Sadguru. Worship him, regard him and remember him, when you impose your faith in Guru, your body and soul get cleaned up of all toxins (of life). The devotee becomes real *gyani*-wiseman. He becomes ego-less. In the state of ego-less, the man of pure wisdom realizes Shiva, the Lord. He becomes Shiva roop. Like you see your reflection in the mirror, similarly such a realized person sees Shiva all around. He becomes Jivamukta. After leaving the earthly body, the jivamukta atma merges with Shiva, the Parambrahman.[5]

The yogi, with the attainment of Kaivalya Samadhi, does not distinguish between his self and Param Brahma. In that stage, the yogi realizes and, utters that he is Brahman himself. This is the ultimate stage of yogic attainment with the Lord's grace.

Can we interpret the sayings of Guruji from that angle? It is left to the individual reader/devotee/spiritual seeker to internalize

---

[5]Shastri, J.L. (ed.), *The Siva-Purana: Part I to IV*, Motilal Banarsidass Publishers, Delhi, 2014.

the saying in that manner.

The Shiva Puran is replete with the concept of the puran guru and the equivalency of it with Lord Shiva.

The Kailash Samhita states:

> The preceptor (Guru) is the Shiva and Shiva is the preceptor (Guru). The ascetic, after deciding this in mind shall express his intention (to acquire spiritual wisdom). (Verse 12.34)
>
> Oh Sage, the sruti says, 'Think that everything is Brahman, everything is Rudra.' Thus Sadasiva is the Atman of the universe. (Verse 14.34)
>
> Due to the thirty-eight Kalas the concept of duality is ever present but he who has purified the Atman by the concept 'I am Sadasiva' becomes the preceptor Siva. (Verse 14.35)
>
> Such a disciple becomes the preceptor Siva himself. He attains the form of the yantras, mantras and the cosmic deity (Lord) itself. (Verse 14.36)

The Guru teaches the disciple—the shishya—that he (the disciple) should be able to realize that he is Shiva (*Main Shiva hun.*) In the initiation of the disciple, the Guru bows to the disciple as he is considered as Shiva. But before imparting or bestowing such spiritual wisdom, the Guru tests the disciple whether he is ready and capable of such an initiation.[6]

Shiva, who is beyond the three gunas imparts Shiva Tattva to the shishya. That is the reason Shiva is called the Guru (beyond the gunas). Worshiping the Guru is worshiping Lord Shiva.

We also have the famous Gurustotram (verses to the Guru) by Adi Shankaracharya:

> *Guru Brahma Guru Vishnu Guru Devo Maheshwara.*
> *Guru Sakshyat Param Brahma Tasmai Shri Gurave Namaha.*

---

[6]Ibid.

> Prayers to you, Oh my Guru who is the Brahma
> (The Creator),
> Who is the Vishnu (The Preserver),
> Who is the Maheshwara (The Destroyer),
> With this knowledge, Guru you are the Parabrahma
> (Supreme God or the Absolute Truth),
> My Salutations and obeisance to you Shri Guru.

So, can we interpret the aphorism of Guruji's 'I am Shiva' in the above sense of a puran guru who is equated with the Lord Shiva?

Reading the Shiva Puran

The revered Guruji had, during his physical days, told some of the sangat to read the Shiva Puran regularly. Other times, some sangat have heard him uttering the phrase, '*Shiva Puran padhana chahinda* (You should read Shiva Puran).' It has been observed that many a sangat have taken this aphorism in the literal sense, without going into its deeper spiritual connotations.

The revered Guruji was a paragon of virtues. He was beyond dogmatism. He was not known to prescribe a rigid code of conduct to the sangat. Hence, when he uttered the aphorism that 'one should read the Shiva Puran', that should not be construed as a commandment, as done by some sangat trying to interpret the statement in the literal sense. Guruji has, among his followers or devotees, people from all sections of society and many of them belong to religious communities other than Hinduism. A lot of his followers belong to the Sikh community. I had witnessed the presence of many Muslims, Christians, Jains and Buddhists in the sangat. A prominent Muslim family from Kashmir was frequently coming to Guruji's durbar at Empire Estate. Similarly, there were the famous Christian expatriates; one of them was a famous musician, who was an ardent follower of Guruji. A devotee's husband, who was also an ardent follower of Guruji, was from Ireland and a practicing Catholic. Guruji would never dissuade his followers from respecting other religions, religious teachings and other highly evolved gurus. How can such a cosmopolitan and highly evolved Guru be confined to the narrow tenets of reading only the Shiva Puran? However, there should be no doubt about the universal appeal of the lucid and sacred Shiva Puran.

From this, it is imperative that the aphorism 'you should read Shiva Puran' should be interpreted and understood in the broader context of Guruji's spiritualism than narrowly prescribing each and every individual to read the physical text. The aphorisms are context- and time-specific in their interpretations.

Guruji used to say that God is revealed to man easily in the age of the Kalyug. But people are reluctant to spend even 10 minutes a day for a spiritual quest. Under such circumstances, the long path of austerity, yoga and meditation (Yoga Marg) becomes difficult for the ever-busy modern man. The better alternative is the Bhakti Yoga—to God's doors. Bhakti Yoga involves shravan (listening to satsangs about Lord Shiva), kirtan (singing or talking about the glory of Lord Shiva) and manan (remembering or meditating on Lord Shiva, remembering His qualities, forms, names and leela with a pure mind). This Bhakti Yoga can be extended to any form of God (Lord Vishnu, Lord Krishna, Lord Shiva, or any other Hindu deity, Guru, the enlightened Buddha or Lord Mahavir, Jesus Christ—all saguna forms of the Lord); and if you are a spiritually evolved soul, the nirguna, *nirvikar* (without form and beyond the three gunas), the Supreme Self—Param Brahma, Allah, Akal Pusrush, God—whichever name you love to ascribe Him, worship Him.

The Purans open up wide windows and doors to the spiritual world. They help destroy ignorance, illuminate vistas of knowledge, provide guidance for the present and caution about the pitfalls to be avoided in the future. The trinity of shravana, kirtan and manan is an integral part of enlightening the human psyche. The triumph of good over evil, the standards of character set by the sages and devotees, and the exemplary actions of the incarnations, all prove the existence of the Supreme Self.

Reading the Shiva Puran or any other spiritual text or scripture of any religious community embodies the three functions of shravana, kirtan and manan, and it is a journey on the path of spiritualism. It is, in this context, the aphorism of Guruji that 'one should read the Shiva Puran' should be understood.

The second contextual content of the aphorism comes from the purity of purpose and concentration it provides for attaining the stillness of mind for higher spiritual attainment. As we have discussed earlier, the human mind is full of wavering thoughts and the mind, with its past memory, including inter-generational memory and perceptual veils (nature forces), acts as an impediment for self-realization and super-consciousness. Hence, the sages advocate gradual training of the mind through yoga, satsangs and reading of scriptures to prevent the mind from getting embroiled in furtive thoughts. Reading the Shiva Puran may serve this purpose to some extent. The time spent in listening, reading and discussing scriptures like the Shiva Puran, Bible, Sri Guru Grantha Sahib, etc., puts the mind in a positive groove, which ultimately leads to a better spiritual journey.

The third contextual domain of the aphorism 'one should read the Shiva Puran' could be Guruji's way to initiate the uninitiated to the great Indian spiritual tradition. It is generally accepted that the universal spiritual tradition of India is embodied in three categories of ancient texts—the Vedas, the Upanishads and the Bhagavad Gita. The Purans are aimed at mediating the profound and complex spiritual contents or truths of the Vedas, Upanishads and Bhagavad Gita for the understanding of the common man, not versed with the Vedic Sanskrit and abstract spiritual tenets.

The Purans are meant for the common people and describe the times, tribulations and triumphs of their heroes. Most use the abundance of religious and philosophical concepts in their narration from Bhakti to Sankhya. The Purans, composed between CE 250 and CE 1000, convey the philosophies of higher texts like the Vedas, Upanishads and Gita in the form of short stories. Almost all Purans have these higher texts as their fountain head of the philosophy, with a little emphasis here and there. The Purans revolve around the essence of these texts, popularizing through concrete examples, myths, stories, legends, lives of saints, kings and great men, allegories, and chronicles of great historical events. The Purans are not meant for scholars, but for ordinary persons who can hardly fathom the high philosophy of the Vedas and other higher spiritual texts.

The fourth context of the aphorism may be the deepening of knowledge by the devotees about Lord Shiva. Guruji is a mahayogi and Lord Shiva symbolizes the perfect yogic personality. Guruji's Jalandhar and Bade Mandir contain the saguna swaroop of Lord Shiva along with the swaroop of Guru Nanak. It symbolizes the path he wants the devotees to follow for spiritual growth. As it has been told by many a sangat, Guruji used to tell that the Bade Mandir contains the divine energy of the twelve Jyotirlingas. Moreover, the Bade Mandir architecturally (approved and conceptualized by Guruji himself) symbolizes the nirguna—formlessness of Shiva in the form a huge Shiva Linga, projecting to the sky. There is also the Shiva swaroop installed in the middle of the fountain in the front side of the mandir.

The importance given to Lord Shiva in all his utterance, the practices of having Shiva swaroop in the mandir, the conceptualization and execution of the architectural design of the Bade Mandir in the form a huge Shiva Linga, lead us to the inference that Guruji, through the above aphorism, also inspires the devotees to know the essence of Lord Shiva—the Shiva Tattva, the fountainhead of universal spiritualism—in more depth. The devotees are subtly guided to have glimpse of important themes having significant spiritual and philosophical connotations in the Shiva Puran.

Amish Tripathi, in his Shiva trilogy, describes Lord Shiva in anthropomorphic terms, more as an extraordinary person who rose to become God: 'Shiva! The Mahadev. The God of Gods. Destroyer of Evil. Passionate lover. Fierce warrior. Consummate dancer. Charismatic leader. All powerful yet incorruptible. Quick wit, accompanied by equally quick and fearsome temper.'[7]

The Shiva Puran eulogizes the glory and greatness of Lord Shiva, describes the philosophical principles of Shiva Tattva, the greatness of his divinity, his attributes and symbols, apart from the rituals of his worship. For a plain reader, there are plenty of interesting stories with deep philosophical undertones and hints for a Bhakti Yoga to realize the Ultimate Truth. By directing the devotees to read the Shiva Puran, Guruji was motivating the devotees to start a philosophical journey through the easily understood Shiva Puran.

Interpretation of Dreams

These days, there are hundreds of satsangs being rendered by devotees every week. In several of these satsangs, using telepathy, Guruji interprets the personal dreams of a devotee for their doubts about materialistic attainments, decisions to be taken in real life and in rare cases, about spiritual pursuits. Some others are peddled as commandments of Guruji for the general sangat. This is a dangerous trend or phenomenon. When Guruji was physically present, he would directly or subtly corroborate such telepathy. Before the disciple or follower would mention the dream, Guruji would usually and invariably tell the contents of the dream and would direct the devotee to narrate the experience of his telepathy. Or Guruji would say, '*Dekha, Guruji nu yaad kita te Guruji tuhade kol kal rat nu aye si?* (See, you remembered Guruji yesterday night and I was compelled to go there).' But now, Guruji's physical corroboration and testimony will not be there, and under such circumstances, there is scope for mischief and misinformation. Elements inimical to Guruji's glory may exploit the gullible devotees with their sinister design to malign him, parading their own ideas as telepathy by Guruji. The other day, somebody told one satsang coordinator in east Asia that Guruji came in his dreams and told him that a particular devotee

[7]Tripathi, Amish, *The Secret of the Nagas*, Westland, 2011.

should not do satsang at the appointed time on the scheduled date and instead the gentleman would do the satsang.

Guruji Corroborating Telepathy

The couple, Bamby and Satty, are ardent followers of Guruji. It was Satty who was allowed to have Guruji's darshan at Empire Estate. Bamby was allowed to do sewa in the Bade Mandir during daytime. It was between the Guru and the disciple that this arrangement was going on for a considerable period. One day, Bamby had a dream in which Guruji said to her that Satty should take *theplas* (flavorful flatbreads) for the sangat to be served during langar. Bamby told Satty about the dream and Guruji's telepathy. But, Satty was of the view that such telepathies should not be taken seriously.

The day passed without any noteworthy event. Satty went to have Guruji's darshan, as usual, at the Empire Estate. Satty was also allowed by Guruji to do sewa during langar time. When he was in the kitchen, Chotto, Sudha Aunty's help came to him and said that Guruji was enquiring whether he had brought the theplas for the sangat. Satty got the shock of his life. He had to silently pray to Guruji to pardon him.

Guruji was there to confirm the telepathy for this case. In the absence of Guruji's physical presence, one cannot take all dreams involving Guruji as telepathy and act upon that.

Dreaming is a highly emotional process. Let us not parade those personalized details as having universal message for the sangat. Nor should we interpret the dreams as telepathy from the Divinity, our revered Guruji. Even if the dreams, according to our personal understanding, are telepathy from a higher authority, we should keep them to yourselves. That way, we pay greater respect to our revered Guruji.

Shloka 4 of the Mandukya Upanishad also describes the dream state and hence, the imperatives for interpretation. It states:

Svapna-stano'nta prajnah saptanga ekonavismati-mukhah.
Pravivikta-bhuk taijaso dvitiyah padah.

> The second quarter is Taijaso. Its field is the dream state. Its consciousness is inward-turned. It is seven limbed and nineteen-mouthed. It enjoys subtle objects.[8]

During a dream, the mind creates various kinds of objects out of impressions produced by experiences of the waking state. The mind reproduces the whole waking life in dream through the forces of avidya, kama and karma. The mind is the perceiver and it is also the perceived in the dream. The desires that are not satisfied during the waking state are gratified in the dream state. Dream is the state during which the atman is referred as *taijasa*. The dream state is the state in which the senses are at rest. Here, the object of experience is consciousness consisting of *vasanas* (affinities/desires), the impressions of subtle past experiences.

The dreamer creates a world of his own during this state. The mind alone works independently in this state. The senses are withdrawn into the mind, which also withdraws itself from the outside world and plays in the dream with vasanas and *samskaras*. It enjoys the objects made up of fine ideas, which are products of desire. The world of dream, being subtle, projects only in the mind.

'COMMANDMENTS' OF GURUJI?

It has been seen that some devotees of Guruji have reproduced the aphorisms of Guruji and termed them as 'commandments of Guruji'. However, the concept of 'commandments' is anathema to the great Indian spiritual tradition, as well as to other eastern traditions. Unlike the Indian spiritual tradition, the Abrahamic traditions of the West put greater value and emphasis on the authority of religious books and rules and commandments drawn directly from them. On the other hand, the eastern traditions (including the Indian traditions) do not frown upon rejection

---

[8]Krishnananda, Swami, *The Mandukya Upanishad*, The Divine Life Society, Rishikesh, 1996, https://bit.ly/3GT75hA.

of the books and the scriptures. These are considered as guides only. One is free to pick a way suitable to her/him there are no commandments, there are recommendations.

Guruji was neither known for sermonizing or preaching nor did he insist upon a particular way of life or spiritual practice. He abjured to prescribe rigid rituals or disciplines to be adopted by the spiritual seekers/devotees. His simplicity of spiritualism was Bhakti Yoga, and the freedom of the individual devotee to follow the path he thinks appropriate. Guruji would provide subtle hints, so the individual devotee or spiritual aspirant takes the right cue for themselves. The methodologies, the practices, the path so internalized are unique to that individual devotee. There was no standardized method/practice/path prescribed by Guruji to the devotees. There is no question of any commandments.

When Guruji did not prescribe a standard set of rules, principles, practices and disciplines, there is no need to create a narrative of ritualistic, cultist and dogmatic codes of conduct in the name of Guruji.

DRESS CODE AND FOOD HABITS

There are accounts by some sangat containing a rigid set of dresses (colour coded) to be worn and particular food items to be eaten on each day of the week. This has been presented in a tabular form for easy comprehension of the readers. It may be true that these sets of dresses or food to be taken were told by Guruji to that particular individual sangat. But Guruji would not have said that each and every disciple should follow these dress codes and food habits. Guruji is beyond such dogmatic, ritualistic rigidities that are contrary to his encouragement of the freedom of choice to the devotees in respect of worldly as well as spiritual matters. Hence, the food and dress codes are contrary to Guruji's spiritual and philosophical essence. He never preached a regimen of dress and food habits, not to speak of a diet chart for the week. If any devotee or sangat was prescribed a diet chart, it was specific to the requirement of the particular sangat. It is like he was prescribing distinct remedies for the cure of specific ailments suffered by the particular individual. In the spiritual context also, the paths or methods suggested to each aspirant were according to their spiritual moorings and attainment. The attempt to generalize and put up a standard to be followed by the sangat was beyond Guruji's spiritual call.

The sayings and practices of Guruji regarding food and langar could be better appreciated in the spiritual tradition of this great land. The Vedic and other spiritual texts, like the Bhagavad Gita, speak of the spiritual significance and importance of food and food intake.

The Indian spiritual tradition does not advocate for only vegetarian food. However, the principle of ahimsa (non-violence) enunciated in the Upanishads and the Bhagavad Gita does indirectly espouse vegetarianism.

Guruji never preached what was to be eaten. He never proscribed the intake of intoxicating drinks like whisky or wine to the devotees. But, as a true Guru or enlightened master, he would lead by example. He used to take a frugal meal of daal (lentil soup), a vegetable curry or preparation, and chutney. He used to take a glass of milk or fresh juice.

Guruji would not prohibit taking non-vegetarian food by any sangat. It is up to the individual devotee to adopt a particular dress code or food habit. Sometimes, some devotee would ask whether it is better to take vegetarian or non-vegetarian food. Guruji would not answer them directly. However, subtle hints would be there, in a course of conversations, as to what is preferred food for the particular sangat. For the non-vegetarians, he would say, '*Unnanu nahin patta ki oh kya kha rahe hain* (They do not know what they are eating).'

While Guruji was staying with the Ahujas in Panchkula, we used to go there for Guruji's darshan almost every day. Guruji would direct the sangat to accompany him to some social function or satsang organized by a particular sangat. On one occasion, we were told to accompany him to Patiala to the wedding function of one Mr Matkan's son. Our daughter, Jenny, of six years was also accompanying us. On the way, she suddenly told us that she feels Guruji is her heavenly father. We were surprised that these words were coming from the innocence of a six-year-old. We bowed our head to Guruji who was in the car just in front of ours.

After a couple of days while having her meal, our daughter stated, 'You people do not know what you eat. You are eating the flesh of the dead—fish, chicken and meat.' We were again stupefied. Guruji and God have given enough hints. Gradually, we, who are brought up with daily doses of non-vegetarian diet containing fish or meat, turned vegetarians. Guruji had never asked us to become a vegetarian!

CLEANLINESS OF BODY, MIND, CLOTHES, KITCHEN AND SURROUNDINGS

Guruji used to say, '*Man saf hona chahinda* (The mind should be pure).' The negative thought processes should be controlled by cultivating positive thinking and positive action. He also preached saying, '*Positive sochiya karo, positive kaam karo* (Think positive, and do positive).'

Guruji used to give a lot of importance to cleanliness of the kitchen in each household. The cleanliness extended beyond the physical cleanliness, it extended to the mental cleanliness of the person who cooks the food. He would have food in a house where the food is preferably cooked by the devotee themselves, or by the domestic helpers, with utmost devotion. In other places, he would politely decline to touch any food or beverages. The omniscient Guruji knew the standard of cleanliness of the kitchen in those houses.

What he was hinting in a subtle manner was that our kitchen should be clean and the preparation of the food should be done with the right mindset or shradha by the person cooking the food.

Similarly, he would love the devotees to wear clean and neat clothes and also have clean bodily habits. Beyond that, he had not prescribed any dress code or food habit. This resonates well with the spiritual essence of Guruji wherein he was espousing the concept and practice of positive thinking and positive activities. The cleanliness of the body and the environment, and the sattvic (pure) nature of food and food preparation with due regard to Anna Brahma (food that is Brahma) are the essentials for a clean mind and needs to be steadied for spiritual attainment.

RITUALS AND PILGRIMAGES

Guruji was not in favour of typical ritualistic religious practices. He was against the superstitions arising out of such practices. For example, he would discount the *beham* (apprehensions) of devotees about a cat crossing their path. He would say, just take the name of God and move ahead. He would discourage the practice of wearing stones to dispel evil. He would say that it is all superstition. '*Loki birth stones te khushali vaaste stones paa lende ne. Jeh ohi stone puttha asar kar raha hove taa kee? Nahin paane chahide.* (People wear birth stones and other stones for betterment of their lives. But, what about their negative influences? Better not to wear them).'

Similarly, he would beautifully dispel the misconceptions regarding giving alms to the beggars at traffic lights or whoever comes to your house. He was emphatic about the Sikh principle of sharing your income/wealth (acquired legitimately) with others. In that context, he would say: '*Gupt path aur Gupta daan kitta karo. Naal baithe nu na patta chale ki tussi path kar rahe ho* (People should engage in secret to give away a portion of their legitimate earnings as charity as well as being always engaged in silent prayers. Prayers or connectivity with the Lord should be such silent that the person sitting next to you would have no inclination that you are in deep meditative prayer and connected to God).'

As regards to the beggars, he would say: '*Je vikhari nu kutch nahin dena kadi dutkaro na, hath jodh ditta karo.. Kee patta kaun kide bhesh vich aa jave* (If you feel that you should not be encouraging begging, just raise your palms and do a Namaste begging excuse that you are not giving any alms. You may never know who has come to you in the guise of the beggar).'

This is because begging dissolves your ego, and in yogic tradition, this is one of the methods of annihilating the individual ego.

As far as religious practices and rituals are concerned, he was advocating primarily for a Bhakti Yoga. In Bhakti Yoga, starting from the Vedas, Upanishads, Bhagavad Gita, to Puranic literature and the several bhakti exponents of this land, there is no need of rigid ritualistic practices like the daily puja, offering to deities, and undertaking ritualistic and periodical pilgrimages to tirthas. He would not say so definitely, nor frown upon a devotee conducting these daily practices. What he was emphasizing on was the cleaning of the mind (*mann saaf hona chahinda*) and practising bhakti (through manan, kirtan and smaran). If this trinity is attained through your ritualistic puja and offering, then it is fair enough; there is no prohibition. But, if the superior goal of bhakti is forgotten and the devotee gets embroiled in these practices, then the rituals become an end in itself. Under such circumstances, nothing useful (spiritually) is attained.

He would not directly discourage pilgrimages. But he would say that there is no need for undertaking pilgrimages, as all the essence of the tirthas is present in the Guru. Moreover, he was hinting that the divine vibrations of twelve jyotirlingams are summated at Bade Mandir. He used to say: '*Is Mandir (Bade Mandir) vich 12 jyotirlingam-thirthasthan ka dham hai* (The Mandir contains the spiritual essence of the twelve jyotirlingams).'

Does it not resonate with the great Indian tradition of realizing God at each and every place and in each and every person? That realization is much more important than undertaking pilgrimages and adopting ritualistic practices.

Of late, there are several ritualistic practices being adopted by the sangat. Some of these are in imitation of the mauz or leela of Guruji when he was in the physical form. These days, the sangat adopt the practice of offering jal prasad, chai prasad, sabads and langar prasad, including Kaddah or sweet prasad while conducting satsangs. Each of these, in Guruji's divine presence, had significance. But, these should not be construed as the gold standard of satsangs. A couple of devotees, gathering together (virtually or physically) doing satsang without the accompaniments of jal, chai, langar, kaddah prasad and sabads, will also qualify for higher standards of the satsang. If it is possible and it creates the right ambience, then there is nothing wrong in such practises. But do not insist that, without these, there would no satsang, or in their absence, the satsang will lose its significance. Otherwise, we fall into the trap of ritualism—which is against the professed spiritual essence of our revered Guruji.

We again come back to the sayings of Guruji. If something has been told to somebody in private (nowadays, a lot of telepathies are reported), those are contextual, not universal. Those are for the individual sangat concerned. He never preached, never set standards, rituals or disciplines. The ritualistic regimen now followed is an invention of the sangat. If anything was done that time, that was for his mauz and leela—not a rigid prescription. For example, Guruji told Ms Bambi Singh not to practise the Mahamrityunjay Mantra in a ritualistic manner. It is for Bambi only. It is not for the general sangat. Many may be followers of Sikhism, Christianity, Muslims, Jews etc., apart from Hindus, and their *ishta devatas* (cherished divinity) may not necessarily be Lord Shiva.

If somebody, especially from the Hindu community, finds the Mahamrityunjay Mantra Jap useful, he connects with Lord Shiva with the right pronunciation (mantras help establish the right spiritual connection if pronounced and uttered in the right manner). The sabad or the vibration generated from singular or group chanting has its own spiritual connection. But it is for the individual follower to adopt and get the right training to practise this mantra. As Guruji used to say, there are other methods and paths of Bhakti Yoga for God-realization too.

Guruji's essence is spreading positivity—positive psyche, positive karma (action), empathy and kindness to others, sharing your wealth and income with others, and more importantly, the smaran, manana, kirtan of the Lord, Lord Shiva or Guruji after complete surrender and devotion with sincerity of purpose for spiritual attainment. There are many paths; the individual is free to adopt them as per his choice, spiritual level and spiritual goal.

THE PRACTICE OF AARTI AND MANTRA JAP

We have highlighted the non-rigid but broad cosmopolitan spiritual path(s), with individual freedom to choose the right path, as hinted by Guruji. But there are, willingly or unwittingly, attempts to create a rigid system and peddle it as if prescribed by Guruji. We will highlight two practices: one is offering *aarti* at the end of sabads and the other is doing the *mantra jap*.

The practice of aarti was adopted a couple of times at Bade Mandir and Empire Estate during Guruji's physical days. But it was not advised, directed or prescribed by Guruji. Some devotees, on their own volition, offered aarti as the concluding part of the sabad kirtan on special occasions. Guruji used to say no to any such suggestions by his beloved sangat. When he was going for satsang to a devotee's house or a social function at a devotee's invitation, or during the usual sangat and satsang at Empire Estate, no such practices were followed. Hence, aarti, a practice confined to a few religious communities, should not be construed as a defined and definite practice to be followed by the devotees during each satsang. It is up to the sangat or devotee to adopt the practice. Others are not bound to follow such practices and their freedom of choice should not be frowned upon.

The practice of mantra jap was a practice adopted by the devotees after Guruji left this world. Guruji's Jalandhar Mandir and Bade Mandir have the insignia '*Om namah shivay*' prominently displayed inside the mandir. After Guruji left his physical body, the devotees thought it appropriate to invoke the blessings of Guruji, in addition to Lord Shiva. Hence, they invented the prayer '*Om Namah Shivay, Shivaji Sada Sahay. Om Namah Shivay, Guruji Sada Sahay.*'

It was a prayer, and gradually the devotees started giving it the name 'Mantra Jap' to invoke the blessings of Lord Shiva and Guruji. The practice of mantra jap is an invention by the devotees of Guruji.

BEYOND FAMILY, COMMUNITY AND GEOGRAPHY

Geography

These days, some enthusiastic devotees attempt to characterize Guruji as 'Dugriwale Guruji'. The attempt may be due to a narrow understanding of the universal nature of the Enlightened Master. Guruji was never known as Dugriwale Guruji during his physical days. Such a narrative as Dugriwale Guruji would relegate him to an ordinary saint or sant of Punjab. There are numerous deras in Punjab catering to various socio-religious groups. Though many of these deras cater to the psychosocial needs of a section of the society, they are not necessarily known as spiritual centres. The persons heading these deras are not known to have any spiritual power or attainment. Hence, when Guruji, the divine incarnate, is confined to a village (even though it may be his birthplace), we undermine the elevated spiritual attainment of Guruji, bringing him down to the level of an ordinary dera head of Punjab. During his lifetime, he was never called Dugriwale Guruji.

Dugri Mandir

The family home of Guruji's biological family in village Dugri was modified in 2004 to accommodate a larger number of family members, as well as the ever-increasing number of visitors and devotees to Guruji's parental house. It is clarified that the present house of the biological family of Guruji is not the birthplace of Guruji. His birthplace is at a distance of half a kilometre from this house and inside the congested areas of Dugri. That was one reason, apart from the small size, for shifting the family home to the periphery of the village, along the village *phirni*—the circular road around the main village. After Guruji left Dugri in 1976 for his wanderings, it is not known whether he visited his family home and Dugri till 1995. Even his sister's wedding in 1985 was solemnized at Jalandhar. Guruji left Greater Kailash, Delhi, and headed to Dugri after learning about the death of his elder brother, Bahadur Singh, on 3 July 1995. He stayed in Dugri till the bhog ceremony was over. He stayed for a longer period during the wedding of his niece, Jyoti, in 2006. He also stayed a couple of days during the bhog ceremony of Maataji. Guruji used the word 'pind' for any reference to visit his family home. He used to say to many a sangat, including myself and Urvashi, '*Jaa, pind ghumke aao* (Go and visit the pind—the village).'

Maataji used to stay at our place in Sector 22, Chandigarh. Guruji desired that Maataji should have a change of place for better health. With Guruji's orders, she was being treated for her ailments from a particular Ayurvedic doctor at Panchkula. She passed away in 2000 while she was with us in Chandigarh. During the time she spent with us, she had expressed her desire on what Guruji should do for her and for the people in the locality surrounding Dugri, his ancestral village. Her first wish was that Guruji should establish a charitable hospital for free treatment of the people, particularly the needy and the poor. Secondly, Guruji should facilitate for the large number of *shradhalus* (devotees) who were flocking and who would flock to the ancestral place of Guruji. She was hinting at some facility in Dugri where the devotees of Guruji could come, pay respect to Guruji and also connect with the Almighty. Guruji gathered these wishes and desires of Maataji from Urvashi. After Maataji's bhog ceremony, he initiated the establishment of the Mata Surjeet Kaur Hospital in Dugri and also ordered the renovation and modification of the ancestral house to accommodate and facilitate the large number of shradhalus coming to Dugri. But, to our knowledge, he neither termed the modified house as a temple nor 'Dugri Temple', unlike his utterances for Jalandhar Mandir, Bade Mandir or even the villa at Empire Estate.

NON-INHERITANCE OF GURUJI'S SPIRITUAL TRADITION

Guruji used to say, '*Pahle vi main, hun vi main, te vaad vich vi mein. Eithe koi gaddi nahin chaldi* (I was, I am and I will be the sole spiritual Guru. There will no tradition of Guru Gaddi for inheritance).'

Guruji left his family and family home in 1976. For years together, neither was he in touch with the family nor was the family in touch with him. Guruji has created a bigger family, the family of his followers or sangat. He used to say, '*Sangat tuhada parivar hai. Ye tera kam mein ayange* (Sangat is your family who would come to your rescue).' Of course, he was not prohibiting his biological family members to come to the places he used to stay. He treated them like any other sangat or devotee. He used to say, '*Mere vaste mera parivar v sangat hai* (For me, my family members are like any other sangat).'

There are numerous occasions when the family members used to stand in the queue to get the prasad and blessings from him, Maataji and Bapuji included.

After Guruji left this world, there were vain attempts by certain devotees and non-devotees to claim his spiritual inheritance. One charlatan from the Delhi-NCR claimed that he had inherited the miraculous powers of Guruji and started the practice of gathering gullible devotees and holding satsangs in the manner Guruji used to do during his lifetime. Another from Punjab claimed that she is Goddess Parvati wedded to Guruji who was Lord Shiva himself. A third group started the rumour that Guruji has taken birth at a devotee's house. A pretender started sprinkling rose-essence perfume on his body and clothing, giving the impression that he was emitting body fragrance like that of Guruji.

It is a different matter that all these attempts to create spiritual inheritance of Guruji came to naught. The discernible devotees of Guruji outright rejected such hallucinations, pretentious claims and rumours.

ABOVE THE NARROW CONFINES OF ANY PARTICULAR COMMUNITY

We have already discussed the spiritual essence of the sayings of Guruji, 'One should read the Shiva Puran.' Without the spiritual context, it would appear that Guruji was propagating a religious practice of a particular community. Similarly, making the ritualistic practice of aarti as a gold standard of satsangs and ascribing it to the practice mandated by Guruji would put him in narrow confines of a particular religious practice or ritualism. The puran guru does not belong to any caste, community or religion. He is a universal guru and his doors and his spiritual tenets are open to everybody, irrespective of caste, community, race and religion. The permission to individual devotees to perform some practices or rituals on odd occasions should not be interpreted as Guruji prescribing any standard practice or rituals. Hence, the practice of aarti, reading of the Shiva Puran, mantra jap, etc., have their contextual connotations—spiritually for the individual devotee or group of devotees. These are not the ritualistic practices advocated by Guruji. The conversion of odd happenings to rigid ritualism is the invention of some devotees, more so after he left his mortal body, contrary to his spiritual essence. Ordinarily, humans have the tendency of falling into ritualism under the delusion of connecting with the Supreme Soul, because it is so difficult to attain stilling of the mind and establish communion with God, without the paraphernalia of rituals. After some time, the rituals become the end in itself, bereft of the spiritual quotient.

The realized soul, the enlightened master is beyond the narrow confines of family, friends, community, village and geography. We may again delve into the Nirvana Shatakam of Adi Shankara, where the enlightened soul sings:

> Neither am I bound by Death and its Fear, nor by the rules of Caste and its Distinctions,
>
> Neither do I have Father and Mother, nor do I have Birth,
>
> Neither do I have Relations nor Friends, neither Spiritual Teacher nor Disciple,
>
> I am the Ever Pure Blissful Consciousness; I am the eternal Shiva, I am the eternal Shiva.

Glossary of Indian Terms

Aarti	A Hindu ritual employed in worship, often part of puja, in which light (usually from a flame) is offered to one or more deities
Aasan	Sitting throne or pedestal
Abhyagatas	Guest
Adiyogi	Manifestation of Lord Shiva as the first yogi
Amrit	A drink distributed by Guruji during Jalandhar and Greater Kailash days. It was prepared by dipping his Rudraksha Mala in drinking water and offering to sangat as prasad.
Anna Brahma	Creative energy in the food (annam) is Brahma, as per Hindu spiritual traditions.
Asthi	The leftover bone or some collected ashes after cremation of dead people
Atman	Soul
Ausadhis	Ayurvedic medicines
Avatar	A manifestation of Lord or his representative in human/living form
Bhakta	Devotee/follower
Bhakti Yoga	A spiritual path or spiritual practice within Hinduism focussed on loving devotion towards any personal deity
Bhakti	Love-driven devotion
Bhandara	Community kitchen
Bhangra	A type of traditional folk dance of Punjab

Bhog Ceremony	The ceremony after fourth or tenth day of the death of a person
Bhog	A term used in Hinduism and Sikhism. In Sikhism, it is used for observances that are fulfilled along with the reading of the concluding part of the Guru Granth Sahib.
Bhoo Samadhi	Last rites of saints
Biswarupa	The depiction of the cosmic universe of Lord Krishna to Arjun in Bhagvat Gita
Brahmasmi	The realization of the individual of unity of the atman (individual self or soul) with Brahman within himself.
Brahmgiani	A highly enlightened individual who is one with the Lord
Chola	Special robe
Darghas	A shrine or tomb built over the grave of a revered religious figure
Darshan	Paying a visit in person to a guru or deity and paying abeyance or respect
Dera	A camp, abode, tent, house, temple, sacred shrine or habitation. In Sikh literature, it has been used for camp and cantonment.
Dharamashalas	Modest guest houses
Divyachakshu	The intuition, wisdom and knowledge of a higher self
Divyanubhuti	God-realization, divine experience
Doha	A form common to Hindi verse that consists of rhyming couplets made up of twenty-four syllables each
Durashravana	Ability to hear from afar
Dwar	Outlet
Ghanis	Oil extracting system
Gunas	Characteristics or traits; Everything within Prakriti—the illusionary world—consists of three gunas.
Gupta Daan	A secret gift

Guru Tattva	The principles that define Guru
Gyan Samadhi	Blissful state
Hukamnama	A hymn from the Guru Granth Sahib; directive to Sikh sangat
Iccha-mrityu	Leaving this world at their own volition
Indriyani	Senses
Japa	Meditative recitation of name and glory of the Lord
Jiva	Living being
Jivatma	An individual soul
Jutis	A Punjabi word denoting footwear common in north India and adjoining Pakistan areas; made up of fine leather, embroidered with golden or silver coloured thread
Jyotirlingas	The Shiva Puran describes twelve sacred places where the Shiva Lingas have manifested self-generated Lingas called Jyortirlingas from earth or rocks.
Kaflas	Caravan of vehicles
Kaivalyam	Absolute liberation; the pinnacle of yogic attainment
Kanal	A unit of area used in parts of northern India and in Pakistan, equivalent to one-eighth of an acre.
Kikars	The traditional Indian Babul, a common tree in Punjab, Rajasthan and adjoining nothern states of India. A small tree with needle-shaped thorns.
Kirpan	A dagger or a knife carried by Sikhs, obligating them to the ideals of generosity, compassion and service to humanity
Kirtan	A Sanskrit word that means 'narrating, reciting, telling or describing' of an idea or story, specifically in Indian religions
Kriya Yoga	The path of right action
Kundalini	A form of divine energy (or Shakti) believed to be located at the base of the spine. Swami Sivananda

	decribed it as the cosmic power in individual bodies, not a material force like electricity, magnetism, centripetal or centrifugal force. It is a spiritual potential Shakti or cosmic power. In reality, it has no form.
Langar	Community kitchen and serving of food in a religious place like a gurudwara or similar religious places regardless of caste, community or religion based on equality
Leela	Play or sport, game, pastime, performance
Lokachar	Socially acceptable practice or ethos
Mahaprasad	The term used for the 56 food items offered to Lord Jagannath in the holy Temple of Puri
Mahapurush	A person who has attained the pinnacle of spiritual goals
Mahasamadhi	The state a yogi enters when they consciously make the decision to leave their body
Mahasiddha	A person who, by the practice of meditative disciplines, has attained siddha (miraculous powers)
Mahima	Glory
Mali	Gardener
Manan	Meditate, thinking
Manglik	A person born under the influence of Mars (Mangala) as per Hindu astrology
Mantra Jap	The meditative repetition of a mantra or a divine name
Margs	Paths
Mathas	A sort of monastery or seminary of the Hindus
Mauz	Pleasurable activity
Maya	Illusion
Mazar	A Muslim shrine or enshrined tomb
Megh Malhar	A Hindustani classical raga
Mishri	Sugar cast into flat pieces; candied sugar

Mukhda	The chorus, the first few lines, which keep repeating throughout the song
Mukti	The liberation of the atman from illusion, cycle of births and deaths
Nath	Tradition
Nirankar	God in Sikhism; 'The Formless One'
Nirgun	Unmanifest form of God
Nirjiva	Inanimate things
Nirodha	The cessation or renouncing of craving and desire
Nirvikalpa Samadhi	The ego and samskaras (mental or emotional impressions) dissolve, leaving behind only pure consciousness.
Nishkama Karma	Action without expectations
Nitya Siddha	Souls liberated from birth
Niyams	The Yoga Sutra describes five different niyamas, including saucha (cleanliness), santosha (contentment), tapas (self-discipline), svadhyaya (self-reflection) and ishvarapranidhana (surrender to a higher power)
Niyat Karma	The prescribed or ordained action that needs to be done
Param Brahma	The 'Supreme Self (Brahman)' that which is beyond all descriptions and conceptualizations
Paramatman	The Absolute Atman, or Supreme Self
Parmatma	God
Prakriti	Forces of nature
Prasad	A devotional offering made to God typically consisting of food later shared by devotees
Pratibha	Enlightenment from purity
Pravachan	A term for any exposition of a doctrine or treatise, or to the recitation of a scripture or text

Puran Guru	A satguru, a true, enlightened guru, sometimes equated with God
Purusha	The Absolute Being, referring to the cosmic Intelligence or Consciousness. In Sankhya philosophy, Purusha is the plural immobile cosmic principle, pure consciousness, unattached and unrelated to anything.
Ragis	Religious singers, particularly in Sikhism
Rajas	The guna of passion and manipulation, rajas represents itself by passion, action, energy and motion. Rajas is characterized by a feeling of attachment, a longing for satisfaction and desire.
Rasik Vairagi	A devotee detached of desires
Rishis	Sages
Rudraksha	Refers to a stonefruit, the dried stones of which are used as prayer beads by Hindus as well as by Buddhists, Sikhs and Muslims
Sabads	The sacred hymns of Guru Grantha Sahib set to various musical tones
Sachkhand Prasad	A typical prasad, mixture of mishri and suji, occasionally materialized by Guruji
Sadhak	Spiritual seeker
Sadhana	Spiritual practices like austerities, disciplines, meditations, contemplations, etc., of a seeker
Saguna	Manifest form of God
Sakshat Avatar	A manifestation of God
Sakshat Parabrahma	God incarnate
Samskara	Mental or emotional impressions
Samyama	The combined simultaneous practice of dhāraṇā (concentration), dhyāna (meditation) and samādhi (union)

Sangat The word sangat is in use since the times of Guru Nanak, the founder Guru of Sikhism. Sangat is an institution, where the devotees gather in the name of God, Akal, the Timeless Lord, to pray and sing Guru Nanak's hymns, and partake in Guru ka Langar, where all sit together without distinction of caste or status.

Sanyasi A Hindu religious mendicant

Satsang Satsang connotes 'association or being with the truth' or 'communion with the truth'. The ultimate truth is the Lord, the Supreme. Hence, the company, the association or fellowship of seekers of the ultimate truth is called satsang. In other words, it can be said that satsang refers to associating with good people or being in the company of truth and refers to the act of gathering with like-minded people on a spiritual path.

Sattva Sattva manifests itself as purity, knowledge and harmony. It is the quality of goodness, joy, satisfaction, nobility and contentment. It is free of fear, violence, wrath and malice. Sattvic quality is pure and forgiving.

Satyam True, truthful or authentic

Sewa Selfless service, particularly at religious places like gurudwars and the like

Sewadar A volunteer who offers his or her services to a gurudwar or other community place for religious reasons

Shakti Pithas Shrines and pilgrimage destinations in Shaktism, the goddess-centric denomination in Hinduism

Shishya Disciple

Shivohm A Shiva mantra

Shloka Shloka or śloka is a poetic form used in Sanskrit, the classical language of India. In its usual form it consists of four pādas or quarter-verses, of eight syllables each, or of two half-verses of 16 syllables each.

Shradha Shradha is a combination of acceptance of divinity, connection with divinity, surrender to divinity, sincerity of seeking divinity and absence of doubts in the rational mind (no ifs and buts), and a positive frame of mind.

Shradhalus Devotees

Shravana The mental activity that needs to take place in order for the yogi to know the truth about Brahman

Siddha Perfected masters who have achieved a high degree of physical as well as spiritual perfection or enlightenment

Siddhi Attainment (spiritual); the boons, supernatural powers and ability to perform miracles

Smaran Remembering or retention

Sthitaprajna A term that means 'contented', 'calm' and 'firm in judgement and wisdom'

Suji Wheat granulated but not pulverized

Swadharma Action that is in accordance with your nature

Swaroop The photograph or sculpture of a spiritual guru or deity

Tamas Darkness/Destruction: Tamas manifests itself as impurity, laziness and darkness. It is the consequence of ignorance and it prevents all beings from seeing reality.

Tantrik A Hindu and Buddhist philosophy which affirms all aspects of the material world as infused with divine feminine power

Thali Large plate, sometimes having compartments for different food items

Tirtha Refers to any place that is holy

Trikal Darshi Knower of past, present and future

Vaid Traditional doctors, vaid or ved is a sanskrit word used for a practitioner of Ayurveda medicine

Vairagya Non-attachment or dispassion

Vartas	Refers to the practice of austerity, particularly in matters related to foods and drinks
Vasanas	Tendencies of the senses
Vihara Yamas	Ethical practices—the don'ts
Yajna	Sacrifice

Bibliography

Adgadanand, Swami, *Srimad Bhagavad Gita: Yatharth Geeta*, Shri Paramhans Swami Adgadanandji Ashram Trust, Mumbai, 1994.

Aurobindo, Sri, *The Bhagavad Gita with Text, Translation and Commentary in the Words of Sri Aurobindo*, Sri Aurobindo Divine Life Trust, 2008.

Aurobindo, Sri, *The Bhagvat Gita (Translated by Sri Aurobindo)*, Suryatra Communications, New Delhi, 2008.

Besant, Annie, and Bhagavan Das, *The Bhagvad Gita*, Theosophical Publishing Society, 1905.

Capritto, Amanda, 'What Sleep Experts Say Dreams of Falling Really Mean (and Why We Have Them)', CNET, 16 December 2022, https://cnet.co/3IC1hub.

'Chapter 19: The Man of Divine Realisation', *Sayings by Sri Ramakrishna*, Madras, https://bit.ly/3CBhR9C.

Chinmayananda, Swami, *Isavasya Upanisad: God In and as Everything*, Central Chinmaya Mission Trust, 2018.

Commentary by Shri Brahmananda Sarasvati on Shri Adi Shankaracharya's *Carpata-Panjarika*; available at Gannon, Sharon, 'Satsang', Jivamukti Yoga, December 2012, https://bit.ly/3GYGsbb.

Dharwadker, Vinay, *Kabir: The Weaver's Songs*, Penguin India, 2003.

Dvivedi, Manilal Nabhubhai, *The Yoga-Sutra of Patanjali: Translation, With Introduction, Appendix, and Notes Based Upon Several Authentic Commentaries*, Tukárám Tátyá, Bombay, 1890, https://bit.ly/3QIiVyk.

Feuerstein, Georg, *Encyclopedic Dictionary of Yoga (1st Edition) (Paragon Living Traditions Series)*, Paragon House, 1990.

Fish, Stanley, *Self-Consuming Artifacts*, University of California Press, 1992.

Gambhirananda, Swami, *Eight Upanishads: With the Commentary of Sankaracharya*, Advaita Ashrama, 2010.

Gita Press Gorakhpur, *Sankshipta Shiva Puran*, Generic, 2018.

Hari, D.K., and D.K. Hema Hari, *Understanding Shiva*, Sri Sri Publications Trust, Bangalore, 2017.

Islam, Md Didarul, 'The Philosophy of Guru Nanak: A Critical Analysis', *Arts Faculty Journal*, June 2016, https://bit.ly/402dWN9.

Kaur, Hardeep, 'A Post Existential Philosopher: The Relevance of Non Generic Philosophy of Kabir in the Contemporary Age', *International Journal of English Language, Literature and Humanities,* Vol. 3, No. 6, August 2015.

Kochhar, Sabina, *My Conversation with Guruji Maharaj at Different Times of My life.* (private circulation)

Krishnananda, Swami, *The Mandukya Upanishad*, The Divine Life Society, Rishikesh, 1996, https://bit.ly/3GT75hA.

Kumar, Anita, *Turning the Page*, Om Books International, 2012.

Meheta, Jyotika, *My Spiritual Journey with Guruji.* (private circulation)

Mukundananda, Swami, *Bhagvat Gita-The Song of God*, Jagadguru Kripaluji Yog, 2013.

Narayanananda, Swami, *Sri Guru Gita*, Divine Society Publication, 2008.

'Nirvanashtakam', https://bit.ly/3CH2Raa.

Osho Talks available at https://bit.ly/3GV83tx.

Pant, Jitendra, *Light of Divinity*, 2007. (private circulation)

Prabhupada, A.C. Bhaktivedanta Swami, *Bhagavad-Gita As It Is*, Bhaktivedanta Book Trust, Mumbai, 1990.

Satguru, 'Shiva Puran is All-Encompassing', The Hans India, 9 August 2018. https://bit.ly/408g5qv.

Sanatana Dharma, The Managing Committee, Central Hindu College, Benares, 1916

Saraswati, Swami Sadananda, *Ishavasyopanishad with Shankar Bhasya:*

Swami Sadananda Sarswati, Shri Shardapeetha Prakasham, Gujarat, 2000.

Sastri, S. Sitaram, *Upanishads and Sri Sankara's Commentary (First Volume)*, Paperback Alpha Edition, 2020.

Shastri, J.L. (ed.), *The Siva-Purana: Part I to IV*, Motilal Banarsidass Publishers, Delhi, 2014.

Singh, Dr Gopal, *A History of the Sikh People*, Allied Publishers, Mumbai, 1979.

Singh, Khushwant, *A History of the Sikhs: Volume 1 (1469–1839)*, Oxford, 2004.

Singh, Ms Bambi, *Jai Guruji*. (private circulation)

Sivananda, Swami, *The Bhagavad Gita*, Divine Life Society, 2008.

Sri Guru Granth Sahib available at https://bit.ly/3iwOi2e; https://bit.ly/3CRTt3K.

Tagore, Rabindranath (trans.), *One Hundred Poems of Kabir*, Pan Macmillan India, Delhi, 2019.

Tagore, Rabindranath, *Songs of Kabir*, New York, The Macmillan Company, 1915.

Tharoor, Shashi, *Why I am a Hindu*, Aleph Book Company, New Delhi, 2018.

The dohas of Sant Kabir available at 'Hindivarta', https://bit.ly/3w0BEeN.

'The Essence of Sankhya', Sri Aurobindo Studies, 24 May 2013, https://bit.ly/3Gx9zAP.

Tirth, Swami Shivom, *Shri Guru Gita: The Divine Song of the Guru*, Swami Shivom Tirth Ashram Inc, 2006.

Vasu, Srisa Chandra, *Kena Upanishad (Madhva Commentary)*, 1909, https://bit.ly/3ZtYLMA.

Vivekananda, Swami, *Patanjali Yoga Sutras*, Shristi Publishers and Distributors, New Delhi, 2021.

Vivekananda, Swami, *The Complete Works of Swami Vivekananda*, Advaita Ashrama, 2018.

Vivekananda, Swami, *The Complete Works of Swami Vivekananda, Volume 1*, Discovery Publisher, New Delhi, 2018.

Yogananda, Paramhansa, *Autobiography of a Yogi*, Jaico Publishing House, Delhi, 2000.

Yogananda, Paramhansa, *Whispers from Eternity*, Crystal Clarity Publishers, 2008.